Innovations in Acceptance and Commitment Therapy (ACT) for Acquired Brain Injury

Acceptance and Commitment Therapy (ACT) allows people with acquired brain injury to develop psychological flexibility, in order to lead a vital life, despite all the difficult thoughts, feelings and brain injury symptoms that are present.

Innovations in Acceptance and Commitment Therapy (ACT) for Acquired Brain Injury brings together contributions from highly experienced clinicians, using innovative approaches in ACT for acquired brain injury, in the context of individuals, working with relatives, groups and multidisciplinary teams.

This book will be a valuable resource for clinical psychologists, clinical neuropsychologists, counselling psychologists, cognitive behaviour therapists, psychiatrists and counsellors working therapeutically with clients with acquired brain injury.

Richard Coates works as a Consultant Clinical Neuropsychologist in Independent Practice. He co-founded the Neuro-ACT Facebook group, which aims to connect clinicians and researchers worldwide using Acceptance and Commitment Therapy (ACT) with people with neurological conditions. Richard is engaged with ACT in many contexts: his work with clients, supervision, training, research, community and himself. Connection, creativity, learning and kindness matter to him.

Neuro-Disability & Psychotherapy: Specialist Topics

Originally the *Neuro-Disability & Psychotherapy* journal, this book series covers themed topics around psychotherapy for a range of neurological disorders.
Dr Giles N. Yeates (Series Editor)

Previous titles in the series:
Volume One

Eastern Influences on Neuropsychotherapy: Accepting, Soothing, and Stilling Cluttered and Critical Minds, 1st Edition
Edited by Giles Yeates and Gavin Farrell

Innovations in Acceptance and Commitment Therapy (ACT) for Acquired Brain Injury
Edited by Richard Coates

For further information about this series please visit:
https://www.routledge.com/psychology/series/KARNNDP

Innovations in Acceptance and Commitment Therapy (ACT) for Acquired Brain Injury

Edited by Richard Coates

Routledge
Taylor & Francis Group

LONDON AND NEW YORK

Designed cover image: peepo © Getty Images

First published 2025

by Routledge
4 Park Square, Milton Park, Abingdon, Oxon, OX14 4RN

and by Routledge
605 Third Avenue, New York, NY 10158

Routledge is an imprint of the Taylor & Francis Group, an informa business

British Library Cataloguing-in-Publication Data
A catalogue record for this book is available from the British Library

ISBN: 978-1-032-04547-4 (hbk)
ISBN: 978-1-032-04548-1 (pbk)
ISBN: 978-1-003-19372-2 (ebk)

DOI: 10.4324/9781003193722

Typeset in Times New Roman
by Deanta Global Publishing Services, Chennai, India

This book is dedicated to vitality.

Contents

Acknowledgement

I would like to acknowledge all the people with ABI and their families and all the people working alongside them.

Contributors

Editors

Richard Coates works as a Consultant Clinical Neuropsychologist in independent practice. He co-founded the Neuro-ACT Facebook group, which aims to connect clinicians and researchers worldwide using Acceptance and Commitment Therapy (ACT) with people with neurological conditions. Richard is engaged with ACT in many contexts: his work with clients, supervision, training, research, community and himself. Connection, creativity, learning and kindness matter to him.

Giles Yeates is a Consultant Clinical Neuropsychologist, Series Editor of the *Neuro-Disability & Psychotherapy: Specialist Topics* series (Routledge) and past Neuropsychoanalysis International Fellow. After working in NHS community brain injury and stroke services for 20 years, Giles now works in collaboration with third-sector brain injury organisations to support emotional and relationship needs of survivors and their significant others on national and international levels. He also has a private clinical practice and develops new innovations in psychological therapies for brain injury survivors in his academic role at the Centre for Movement, Occupational and Rehabilitation Sciences (MOReS) at Oxford Brookes University. Giles is the Chair of the Thames Valley Brain Injury Forum and is an author of several books, chapters and articles. More information about Dr Giles' work can be found at www.ripplingminds.com.

Contributors

Sérgio A. Carvalho is a Clinical and Health Psychologist, Post-doctoral Fellow and invited Assistant Professor at the University of Coimbra, with training in Contextual Behavioural approaches, particularly in ACT. His research focus is on the psychosocial risk and protective factors of mental health in chronic illness (e.g., chronic pain), eating disorders (e.g., binge eating) and in sexual and gender-diverse populations. He has developed and pilot-tested ACT and Compassion-based approaches in different populations and through different formats (e.g., group face-to-face, online platform, mobile app). He values social justice, learning and knowledge, kindness and integrity.

Paula Castilho is a Clinical Psychologist and Assistant Professor at the Faculty of Psychology and Educational Sciences, University of Coimbra, with consistent training in cognitive-behavioural therapy and in mindfulness-, acceptance- and compassion-based interventions. Her research focus is on the psychoemotional risk and protective mechanisms in chronic mental illness (e.g., bipolar disorder, psychosis), eating disorders and personality disorders in different developmental stages (especially with adolescents and adults). She has developed and pilot-tested Dialectical Behaviour Therapy (DBT), ACT and Compassion-based approaches in different clinical populations in both face-to-face (individual and group) and online formats. She values knowledge, wisdom, interdependence and cooperation, compassion and equanimity, in all domains of existence.

Frank Deane is an Honorary Senior Professor in the School of Psychology at the University of Wollongong and a research consultant for the Peregrine Centre, a social innovation studio that focuses on research and evaluation to support service design and effectiveness. Frank has been an investigator on multiple studies aimed at understanding various components of ACT, particularly the roles of values and action planning (including therapeutic homework) on mental health outcomes.

Jenn Galvin Yoga means Union. Union of mind, body, spirit. That's my philosophy on rehabilitation. I'm Jenn, a yogi and a facilitator at Headway, Ireland, and for this, I feel blessed. I work on the knowledge and understanding that we have four bodies: physical; mental; emotional; energetic/spiritual. I believe all aspects of a person, right to their soul, will be hurt on some level, consciously or unconsciously, after a trauma. Tuning in to the holistic body and mind has so many benefits for people who have experienced an acquired brain injury (ABI). Yoga is many elements – the physical postures, energetic movement/release as well as the mental peace and connection to the self and the spirit. Connection. Integration. Stimulation. Relaxation. Whatever the psyche needs at the moment in time, one can find it in a yoga practice and meet themselves where they are at. The centre. The soul space. Namaste – the spirit in me sees the spirit in you.

Ambra Mara Giovannetti works as a Consultant Clinical Psychologist and Researcher at the Multiple Sclerosis (MS) Centre of the Fondazione IRCCS Istituto Neurologico Carlo Besta in Milan, Italy and in private practice. She also collaborates with the Italian MS Association and the Greek MS Association. She coordinates the Italian READY for MS Study that aims to evaluate the efficacy of an ACT-based group intervention to promote resilience in people with MS. Curiosity, creativity, sharing and kindness guide her life.

Fergus Gracey is a Clinical Neuropsychologist and Clinical Associate Professor in the Department of Clinical Psychology and Psychological Therapies, University of East Anglia (UEA), Norwich, UK. He was formerly the lead Clinical Neuropsychologist first at the Oliver Zangwill Centre for Neuropsychological Rehabilitation, and then at the Cambridge Centre for Paediatric Neuropsychological Rehabilitation (where he maintains an honorary role as Director of Research). At UEA, Fergus co-leads the neuropsychology module of the clinical psychology doctoral training programme. Fergus' current research includes family adaptation to life post-traumatic brain injury, post-stroke emotionalism and social connection, identity and wellbeing following brain injury.

Sharon Houghton joined the doctoral programme in clinical psychology team at the University of Limerick in 2009 and is currently the Assistant Director. She has worked as a clinical child psychologist for almost 20 years in a number of settings, such as New Zealand and the US. Her range of work has included areas such as child sexual abuse, early and school-age disability services and child and adolescent mental health in both the state and private sector. Her research and clinical interests are in the area of child and adolescent mental Health and the clinical application of mindfulness as an approach. This has led to an interest in therapeutic landscapes and how elements of our physical space and our interaction with them impact mental health.

Jo Johnson is a Clinical Neuropsychologist in independent practice. Currently, she provides ACT-based training to Hampshire constabulary. Jo speaks and writes for several national neurology charities. Client and family-related publications include, *Talking to Your Kids about MS* and *My Parent Has a Brain Injury*. More recently, Jo has published two psychological suspense novels. *Surviving Her* is the most recent. Both are infused with ACT principles. The most important areas of life for Jo are her Christian faith and her family. Creativity, honesty, connection, curiosity and openness are important to her.

Mairéad Jones is a Clinical Psychologist with an interest in supporting people adjusting to significant life changes. Her doctoral research explored the experiences of attendees of a novel group intervention, integrating yoga and ACT to support adjustment post-acquired brain injury. This experience outlined the importance to her of the need for resources within neurorehabilitation to support and sustain the ongoing journey of the whole person, body, brain and mind. She values the use of somatic practice within psychological therapy and continued curiosity and learning in that field matter to her.

Karen Kinsella Hello beautiful humans, Karen here. I was a graphic designer before becoming a Clinical Psychologist. ACT was introduced to me over ten years ago by my mentor Marcia Ward. For me, ACT allows a gentle space for every helpful or unhelpful thought, feeling, sensation or choice, reflecting compassion and empathy. I aim to practice what I preach. As a Gen X individual, quoting a favourite childhood movie, *The Goonies*, I say, "Goonies always make mistakes." Like all humans, I don't always get it right; I make many mistakes and ACT provides a gentle compass to guide my choices, based on the qualities I aim to show in my behaviour. The aim pretty much involves applying a lifetime of tender and gentle returns to try again, just like everyone else. Over the years, I have been honoured to walk with brave, vulnerable, resilient and courageous humans on their journeys using ACT. It has been humbling and rewarding to see how ACT continues to help beautiful humans help themselves. That's what matters most to me and fills my soul with joy.

Lucy Martin A "normal," fun-loving housewife, mother, businesswoman and public speaking teacher; fiercely independent, I suffered a traumatic brain injury at the age of 51 and, following a stroke on the operating table and a 22-day induced coma, was "lucky to be alive." Disabled, dependent, bewildered, frightened, hopeless, now "in the system," I was alive but wanting to be left to die. The neurosurgeon saved my life, but it was Fiadhnait O' Keeffe and Marcia Ward, psychologists, who introduced me to ACT and gave me a reason and a pathway to a new type of "normal life." I wanted my story told to shine a light on the possibility of a pathway through darkness to a wonderful, fulfilled life.

Louise McHugh is a Professor of psychology at University College Dublin (UCD). She is a world-leading expert in Contextual Behavioural Science (CBS) and ACT. She has published over 100 papers and two books in the area, and her work has been funded by national and international funding bodies. Louise has been a Fellow of the Association for Contextual Behavioural Science since 2014. Prof. McHugh is the Director of the UCD CBS lab. Ongoing research projects in the CBS lab involve behavioural interventions for people experiencing homelessness, smoking cessation and interventions for patients with inflammatory bowel disease.

Dee Mullins is a Trainee Clinical Psychologist at University College Cork, an Associate Lecturer with The Open University, and Fellow of the Higher Education Academy. She worked for over three years with people who had suffered an acquired brain injury and saw first-hand the meaningful and life-long impact that ACT had for these clients, their families and the staff who worked with them. Justice, honesty, humour and contribution are values which are important to her.

Fiadhnait O'Keeffe is a Principal Clinical Neuropsychologist who has had the privilege of working clinically with people who have experienced a range of neurological conditions, including acquired brain injuries, multiple sclerosis and dementias. Her clinical therapeutic work has been very influenced by "third-wave" therapies, particularly ACT and Compassion Focused Therapy (CFT) approaches. Fiadhnait believes in the importance of bridging clinical and academic worlds, through sharing real-world clinical experience with building the clinical research evidence base. Fiadhnait also believes in the importance in sharing and empowering others, and her role as Senior Lecturer on the Doctorate in Clinical Psychology programme in University College Cork epitomises this. Fiadhnait values integrity and authenticity, kindness, connection, sharing, curiosity and learning.

Fiona O'Neill qualified as a Speech and Language Therapist in 2005, working in the National Health Service (NHS) across a wide range of populations until 2015, before undertaking postgraduate training in mindfulness-based Interventions at University College Dublin (2017), and completing an MSc focused on the role of self and psychological flexibility in practitioners at the University of Sheffield (2020). Currently, among other roles, she works as a group facilitator on Aphasia Recovery Connections' Virtual Connections global programme, helping to connect hundreds of individuals with aphasia and their loved ones around the world with free, online meetups centred around the life participation approach to aphasia. In this context, Fiona has a particular interest in the effective adaptation of ACT and similar process-based approaches to enhance psychosocial wellbeing of individuals with severe aphasia. Fiona values creativity, courage, compassion and the full and equal inclusion of individuals and populations whose voices and experiences have traditionally been unheard and marginalised in mainstream health, education and social care contexts.

Kenneth I. Pakenham is an Emeritus Professor in clinical and health psychology at the University of Queensland, Brisbane, Australia. He developed the first university ACT course in Australia. He has developed innovative ACT interventions that build resilience in people experiencing health adversities. His career-long commitment to "practice what you teach" and to authenticity is epitomised in his recently published memoir *The Trauma Banquet: Eating Pain – Feasting on Life*.

Ana Rita Silva is a Clinical Neuropsychologist, Post-doctoral Researcher and invited Assistant Professor at the Faculty of Psychology and Educational Sciences of the University of Coimbra. She has training in neuropsychological rehabilitation after brain injury. Her main research areas are cognitive rehabilitation post-stroke and post-traumatic brain injury, prevention of cognitive decline during the ageing process and development of ecologic outcome measures for neuropsychological rehabilitation effectiveness testing. She has developed several cognitive enhancement programmes for several clinical populations (e.g., mild cognitive impairment, Alzheimer's disease, stroke, small vessel disease) and she is currently testing a dementia risk-reduction programme encompassing ACT, mindfulness, goal management and cognitive training, and reminiscence practices. She pursues to promote accessibility of mental and brain health services, particularly to the frailer sectors of society, and she values dignity to all, social connection and compassion.

Grahame Simpson has 35 years' experience as a Social Worker Clinician and Researcher in the field of traumatic brain injury, working at the Liverpool Brain Injury Rehabilitation Unit, Sydney, Australia. His main research interest focuses on developing new interventions to enhance positive psychosocial outcomes after traumatic brain injury (TBI). He is Associate Professor, Faculty of Medicine and Health, University of Sydney.

Alison Stapleton, PhD, is a Chartered Psychologist of the Psychological Society of Ireland, Post-doctoral Fellow at Smithsfield Clinic and University College Dublin, and a Lecturer in psychology at Dublin Business School. Alison co-founded the Association for Contextual Behavioural Science (ACBS) neurodiversity-themed sprint group, serves on the Steering Committee for the ACBS relational frame theory special interest group, and currently works at ACT Now Purposeful Living, a leading provider of ACT training in Ireland. Alison regularly delivers national- and international-level trainings and has experience working in psychological services to identify, accommodate and support a range of neurotypes. Alison has published 13 scientific articles and two book chapters, most recently contributing to *The Oxford Handbook of ACT* and a systematic review of adults' experiences of being identified as autistic in adulthood (manuscript submitted for publication).

Marcia Ward Hi everyone, I am Marcia. I work as a Clinical Neuropsychologist in stroke services in Ireland. I was first introduced to ACT almost 20 years ago. Since then, both my personal life and my professional practice have been shaped by ACT. In a way, ACT is not a therapeutic modality, which I use in my professional practice; it is in essence how I try (and try and try again) to live my life. Working with people in neurorehabilitation has brought huge meaning to my life. Every day, I am surrounded by such courage, empathy, compassion, determination and good humour. I have been really heartened to see ACT being adapted and used to support people with various neurological conditions and with various cognitive differences pursue what matters to them in life. About five years ago, I made the decision to "try on a value of courage," so I started saying "yes" to things that my mind would have typically talked me out of. This has led to new opportunities, which have been occasionally uncomfortable and always worthwhile. This book is one of those opportunities and I am grateful to have been involved with it.

Diane Whiting is a Clinical Psychologist working therapeutically with clients and also in clinical research. She has a strong interest in understanding the mechanisms of change in ACT and how ACT can best be delivered to individuals with a TBI and cognitive impairments. Diane's research has involved completing one randomised controlled trial of ACT and is currently undertaking a second to address psychological distress after a moderate-to-severe TBI, ACT-Adjust, contributing to the evidence base of ACT and TBI. She is also exploring the construct of psychological flexibility in individuals with executive dysfunction, including cognitive flexibility.

Neuro-disabilty and psychotherapy: Specialist topics

Series editor foreword

Neuropsychotherapy is a necessarily evolving field, always falling short of its ultimate aim – to evolve principles of psychotherapy adaptation, so all can be included and access an emotionally and interpersonally supportive experience, regardless of their neuropsychological profile of strengths and needs. It always falls short because of the myriad of neuropsychological needs, combinations and permutations that are manifest within and across differing neuropsychological conditions. Nevertheless, we are constantly motivated as a field to strive to narrow this gap and work towards this goal of inclusion wherever possible.

The evolution within our field to narrow this gap requires a vibrant membership of differing psychotherapeutic orientations/models and the creativity of clinicians and researchers in adapting core therapy approaches to optimise inclusion. This diversity and creativity now reaps continual rewards for the neuropsychotherapeutic practitioner. Earlier naïve applications of traditional psychotherapy models such as cognitive behavioural therapy and psychoanalysis in unadapted forms not only were limited in efficacy, but iatrogenically created new trigger points of distress. Requirements of unsupported recall across sessions, processing and taking in information at speed and performing mental gymnastics to respond to change/restructuring/insight-enhancing techniques within the core phases of a therapy all would leave service users feeling like a failure in the eyes of the therapist, alongside others in their life. Hopelessness would recruit these new experiences in its expansion within the lives of people with neurological conditions.

Many strides have been taken in retaining those aspects of therapy models that can be accessed by people with cognitive impairment and discarding those elements that frequently exclude despite their theoretical aims. However, for certain dimensions of post-injury/onset changes, many people ultimately still experience a talking therapy as excluding. Those with aphasia and other challenges to communication are at the top of the list here.

In addition, the application of psychological therapies within neurological/neurorehabilitation services has long suffered from being situated within a medical model and a corresponding neglect of process issues between clients and therapists and importantly between therapists and other therapists/clinicians. Technical delivery, with depersonalised dosage-response expectations, can leave much in the shadows, with the self-care and humanity of clinicians and whole departments suffering as a result.

No one model can provide all of the above and when new approaches start to be sourced and adapted by clinicians working in neurological services, new tools, resources and conceptual lenses and practice maps reveal themselves. I remember around 15–20 years ago, my trainee clinical psychologists started to bring Acceptance and Commitment Therapy (ACT) to the neurorehabilitation table. There was an air of excitement and possibility: process-focused, revelling in visual imagery and metaphor and values-focused that changed the therapeutic encounter with clients. Creative, so creative! A wide range of therapy resources, the availability and accessibility of which was equally creative and generous in its provision by ACT founders. These characteristics meant that the task of creating an emotionally supportive encounter with someone with neurological conditions was now nourished by a plethora of resources and was more likely to be achieved across clients. It was the process of connecting and supporting rather than an arbitrary outcome that was key. ACT is often described by some as part of the third wave of cognitive-behavioural approaches, but I feel that ACT's characteristics and scope are too profound to be held within this categorisation.

Importantly too, ACT provided a new conceptual connection between a therapy process and a neuropsychological dimension of difference. ACT's concept of psychological flexibility (operationalised within the hexaflex model) talked to neuropsychology's cognitive flexibility construct. Impairments/changes characterised by cognitive inflexibility/rigidity could now be formulated as nodal/interacting elements within differing presentations/experiences of emotional distress.

It has been a privilege to be involved in previous journals and Routledge book titles that have published individual neuro-ACT papers and chapters, situated alongside other therapy models within the same volume. More recently, this has evolved to ACT-centric publications that represent a community of ACT clinicians together, including one brain-injury–focused book. It is now an honour to have supported Richard Coates in assembling this community of ACT-inspired clinicians, to share their inspiring and varied work – with differing conditions and working in differing practice spaces (directly with clients, in teams and reflective practice with colleagues). This group has used isomorphism between therapy and professional practice to centralise both creativity and a values-based approach in the generation and articulation of this work. It has been fascinating for me to witness the genesis and gestation of this approach to writing. The result, I believe, and I trust that you will agree as readers, is a truly neuropsychotherapeutic tradition that optimises inclusion for those with diverse and challenging neuropsychological needs and also the nurturing/care of those clinicians who offer this approach within their work. As such, it is a prominent latest addition to the *Neuro-Disability & Psychotherapy: Specialist Topics* series.

Giles Yeates, Series Editor.

Foreword

Joe Oliver

Our sense of self is undeniably one of the defining aspects of our humanity. It grants us agency through which we interface with our environment. It shapes our identity and narrative of who we are in relation to those people around us. And importantly, it establishes our place in the world.

It is no wonder that anything that undermines this sense of self could have profound consequences on our being. Acquired brain injuries, in particular, can disrupt a person's ability to remember, think, speak and control our bodies and movements, all of which are crucial to the ongoing behaviour of *selfing*.

Any alterations to these abilities can present a fundamental challenge to one's core identity, leaving individuals with a sense of their essential humanity slipping away. Activities that were once pleasurable become incredibly difficult, if not impossible. The emotional landscape is transformed, influenced by grief, trauma and heightened reactivity, particularly towards anger and frustration. As a result, individuals may perceive changes in their personality, which not only deeply unsettle their family and loved ones but also elicit different reactions from them.

These resulting circumstances of a brain injury cannot be argued with, rationalised or managed away. They require an acceptance that most of us seldom need to draw upon in our lives. It is an active acceptance – one that requires a turning towards the changes that are now present, allowing the person to remain open to their values.

The work involved in rebuilding a life of purpose in the face of acquired brain injuries is complex. It demands practitioners who can deliver skilled interventions and strategies to navigate this intricate landscape. These interventions must equip individuals to effectively respond to immense challenges while avoiding the depths of despair and hopelessness. They must aid in the reconstruction of an identity that acknowledges significant losses while bridging the gap between their past and present selves in terms of their values. It is within these challenging circumstances that practitioners strive to help individuals not simply exist, but build lives that are truly worth living. Lives that are rich, fulfilling and imbued with purpose.

These complexities call for practitioners to constantly hone their skills and utilise effective tools. These tools must be applicable in a wide range of situations, catering to the needs of individuals who have experienced a brain injury, their support networks and the practitioners involved in their recovery. They must be relevant to the human condition. Furthermore, they should be grounded in evidence-based approaches, ensuring their maximum effectiveness.

In this book, you will find a collection of profoundly innovative practices in acceptance and commitment therapy (ACT) for individuals with acquired brain injuries. The editors of this volume have gathered international experts in the field to share their insights, research and personal experiences in applying ACT. The innovations you will encounter are firmly rooted in the latest cutting-edge research on ACT. You will also discover how this research has been translated into practice across various settings, including inpatient care, community rehabilitation, family support and professional training for practitioners working with individuals with acquired brain injuries. The book will explore the creative adaptations made to the ACT model as well.

Perhaps most importantly, you will have the opportunity to hear directly from individuals who have experienced acquired brain injuries and have undergone ACT. Their expertise and first-hand accounts take centre stage in this volume, providing a rich and vivid portrayal of the immense benefits this model can bring to people's lives.

This book offers a wellspring of hope and optimism for those who have experienced brain injuries, as well as their loved ones who accompany them on their journey. It establishes a solid foundation of purpose and meaning, even in the face of experiences that raise weighty questions about what it truly means to be human. This book will guide you through these latest innovations to expand your toolkit, enabling you to assist your clients and their loved ones in weathering the storms that a brain injury can create. Together, you can emerge from the other side, moving forward with acceptance, compassion, equanimity and purpose.

I leave you in the hands of these deeply talented and experienced authors and trust you will find this a useful addition to your library.

Introduction

Richard Coates

We are thrilled to share with you this specialist topic, *Innovations in Acceptance and Commitment Therapy (ACT) for Acquired Brain Injury*. This topic showcases the wonderful applications of ACT and is written with humanity and heart by the contributors. The authors share the human experience with the people they are working with and what they are writing about really matters to them.

A ProSocial process (Atkins, Wilson & Hayes, 2019) has been guiding this book from the start. This book was born in the Neuro-ACT Facebook group, inviting contributors from around the world to suggest and write chapters on topics that really mattered to them. The ACT Matrix (Polk et al., 2016) was used to help authors notice what mattered to them about writing, the difficult thoughts, feelings and sensations that also show up for them about writing and to notice what it would look like if they were moving towards what mattered to them or moving away from the difficult stuff. ACT holds the premise that living as a human being is hard. We are all guaranteed painful experiences at some point in our lives. We have the double-edged sword of language. It can be a blessing, for example, sharing learning through a book like this, and it can also be a cage, making our lives smaller and smaller, when we are pushed around by unhelpful thoughts. All of us contributing to the writing of this book have experienced thoughts like, "I'm not good enough… I'm not a writer." Finally, the process of writing has been transparent, with all contributors able to see and read drafts of other contributors as we have gone along.

Now, imagine you have an acquired brain injury adding to that already-tricky experience of being human and living. Life changes dramatically. Your sense of self has been shattered. All those fragments of your life – your story of yourself as competent, independent, healthy and invulnerable; your relationships with the people you love; your work or education and your hobbies – all that changed either overnight, or with a relentless progression. Add losing the cultural features that we generally define as being human: not being able to walk upright, not being able to talk, having facial deformity from a piece of your skull being removed, a droop to your face on one side, or not having agency over what you do. How would you cope with this challenge?

DOI: 10.4324/9781003193722-1

Working with someone and their loved ones to help reconstruct those pieces of their life, or live with those changes, is hard too. We usually do this work because we care and with this caring is going to come the flip side: pain. We're going to feel the distress of others; we're going to feel our own inadequacy in helping the client and their family.

This common humanity of shared experience is at the heart of ACT. Finding out about and learning ACT has revolutionised my way of working with people with neurological conditions. It was like two peas in a pod. The Psychological Flexibility Model at the heart of ACT wasn't about symptom reduction, but about life enhancement, even in the face of significant challenge and emotional pain. ACT views that pain is inevitable in life; we will all experience it at some point. Suffering is optional though; suffering comes through struggling with that pain, trying every possible way to fight it, escape it or hide from it. ACT helps the clinician and the client notice and open up to our experience, step out of the cage of the mind and the limiting stories it tells and repeatedly take small steps in doing what matters – an ongoing process for all of us in life.

The Psychological Flexibility Model

ACT is a third-wave Cognitive Behavioural Therapy that is growing rapidly in its clinical use and evidence base. There are in excess of 1000 randomised clinical trials (RCTs) reporting its effectiveness in helping with helping anxiety, depression, pain and so on (Association for Contextual Behavioral Science, 2023). There are several RCTs of ACT with neurological conditions, including traumatic brain injury, stroke, multiple sclerosis and epilepsy (Asqari & Donyavi, 2017; Giovannetti et al., 2020; Lang et al., 2017; Lundgren et al., 2008; Majumdar & Morris, 2019; Motlagh et al., 2020; Pak et al., 2017; Proctor et al., 2018; Rauwenhoff et al., 2023a; Sander et al., 2020; Shakernegad et al., 2017; Whiting et al., 2020; Yazdanbakhsh et al., 2016). Rauwenhoff et al. (2023b) reported a feasibility study of BrainACT (ACT adapted for people with brain injury). They found that participants and therapists were very satisfied with the intervention and would recommend the intervention to other people with brain injuries and therapists.

The context for behaviour is at the core of ACT. It is not the content of our thoughts, emotions, memories or what sensations we experience, but rather the relationship we have to these experiences that matters. Naturally, we can find ourselves trapped by patterns of overprotection, the stories we hear and tell about ourselves, or avoiding threatening situations and associated emotions. Developing the processes of ACT allows us to loosen the rigid grip of overprotection and allows us to consciously take tiny, ongoing steps towards what matters to us and to keep coming back to this commitment each time we humanly fail.

The Psychological Flexibility Model or 'Hexaflex' was developed to help clinicians apply the underlying processes (Figure 0.1):

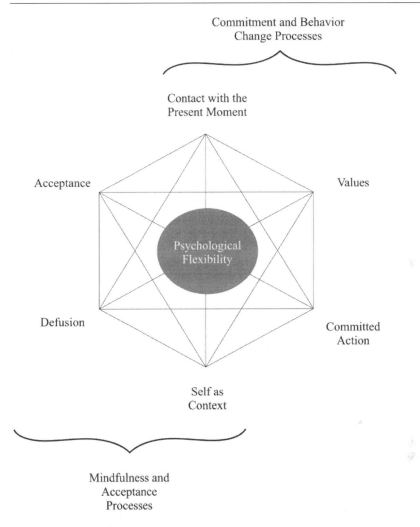

Figure 0.1 The Psychological Flexibility Model or 'Hexaflex' (Copyright Steven C. Hayes. Used by permission)

Defusion helps us to notice our experience for what it is, for example, thoughts as language that we have internalised and emotions that have an evolutionary role and are trying to help guide our movement. Defusion helps us free ourselves a bit from this sticky web of the human experience and have more freedom to choose our behaviour, rather than being forced around or trapped by it.

Acceptance or willingness helps usturn towards what we naturally want to run away from, or hide from. It allows opening to all the difficult human stuff that comes with living.

Contact with the present moment helps us flexibly move our attention to the here and now, rather than being stuck in the past or running ahead into the future. There is so much current reality to connect with that can enrich our perspectives and lives.

Values help us discover and connect with meaning and purpose in our life. They are unique to us and can guide us onwards, in an evolutionarily adaptive manner, as our context constantly changes.

Committed action helps us keep coming back to what matters to us and sustaining steps in those directions and all the rich, fulfilling life that emerges as a result.

Self as context helps us to see that we are not the content of our experience; we have an enduring quality that extends over changing contexts and multiple perspectives.

Psychological flexibility is the core process at the heart of all the other processes. LeJeune and Luoma (2020) describe it as "the capacity to respond adaptively to the challenges that life presents in ways that fit with our values." I find this is just what is needed when confronted with the challenges of acquired brain injury.

Our intention

Creativity, evolution and innovation are at the heart of the Psychological Flexibility Model. Developing ACT processes with acquired brain injury brings a fresh perspective and endless possibilities of moving forwards. We hope you will connect with the chapters in this special edition in so many ways and that you will be inspired in your own work, community and life, with your own unique style and context.

References

Asqari, S., & Donyavi, R. (2017). The effect of acceptance and commitment therapy on the life expectancy in patients with multiple sclerosis. *Journal of Nursing and Midwifery Sciences, 4*, 69–74. https://doi.org/10.4103/JNMS.JNMS_8_17

Association for Contextual Behavioral Science. (2023). *ACT randomized controlled trials (1986 to present).* https://contextualscience.org/act_randomized_controlled_trials_1986_to_present

Atkins, P., Wilson, D. S., & Hayes, S. (2019). *Prosocial: Using evolutionary science to build productive, equitable, and collaborative groups.* New Harbinger.

Giovannetti, A. M., Quintas, R., Tramacere, I., Giordano, A., Confalonieri, P., Uccelli, M. M., Solari, A., & Pakenhan, K. I. (2020). A resilience group training program for people with multiple sclerosis: Results of a pilot single-blind randomized controlled trial and nested qualitative study. *PLoS ONE, 15*(4), e0231380. https://doi.org/10.1371/journal.pone.0231380

Lang, A. J., Schnurr, P. P., Jain, S., He, F., Walser, R. D., Bolton, E., Benedek, D. M., Norman, S. B., Sylvers, P., Flashman, L., Strauss, J., Raman, R., & Chard, K. M. (2017). Randomized controlled trial of acceptance and commitment therapy for distress and impairment in OEF/OIF/OND veterans. *Psychological Trauma, 9*(1), 74–84. https://doi.org/10.1037/tra0000127

LeJeune, J., & Luoma, J. B. (2020). *Values in therapy*. New Harbinger.

Lundgren, T., Dahl, J., Yardi, N., & Melin, J. (2008). Acceptance and commitment therapy and yoga for drug refractory epilepsy: A randomized controlled trial. *Epilepsy and Behavior, 13,* 102–108. https://doi.org/10.1016/j.yebeh.2008.02.009

Majumdar, S., & Morris, R. (2019). Brief group-based acceptance and commitment therapy for stroke survivors. *British Journal of Clinical Psychology, 58,* 70–90. https://doi.org /10.1111/bjc.12198

Motlagh, L. V., Hosseini, S. M., Najafi, M., & Ghaleh Taki, G. Z. (2020). Effectiveness of acceptance and commitment group therapy on improving the quality of life and its components of drug refractory epileptic patients. *Komesh, 22*(3), 419–427. http://doi.org /10.29252/koomesh.22.3.419

Neuro-ACT Facebook group. https://www.facebook.com/groups/1070234856697739/

Pak, R., Abdi, R., & Chalbianloo, G. (2017). Effectiveness of Acceptance and Commitment Therapy (ACT) on disease acceptance and experiential avoidance in patients with multiple sclerosis (MS). *Contemporary Psychology, 12,* 63–72.

Polk, K. L., Schoendorff, B., Webster, M., & Olaz, F. O. (2016). *The essential guide to the ACT matrix: A step-by-step approach to using the ACT matrix model in clinical practice.* New Harbinger.

Proctor, B. J., Moghaddam, N. G., Evangelou, N., & das Nair, R. (2018). Telephone-supported acceptance and commitment bibliotherapy for people with multiple sclerosis and psychological distress: A pilot randomised controlled trial. *Journal of Contextual Behavioral Science, 9,* 103–109. https://doi.org/10.1016/j.jcbs.2018.07.006

Rauwenhoff, J., Bol, Y., Peeters, F., van den Hout, A., Geusgens, C., & van Heugten, C. (2023a). Acceptance and commitment therapy for individuals with depressive and anxiety symptoms following acquired brain injury: A non-concurrent multiple baseline design across four cases. *Neuropsychological Rehabilitation, 33*(6), 1018–1048. https:// doi.org/10.1080/09602011.2022.2053169

Rauwenhoff, J., Bol, Y., Peeters, F., & van Heugten, C. (2023b). Acceptance and Commitment Therapy is feasible for people with acquired brain injury: A process evaluation of the BrainACT treatment. *Clinical Rehabilitation,* 1–13. https://doi.org/10 .1177/02692155231218813

Sander, A. M., Clark, A. N., Arciniegas, D. B., Tran, K., Leon-Novelo, L., Ngan, E., Bogaards, J., Sherer, M., & Walser, R. (2020). A randomized controlled trial of acceptance and commitment therapy for psychological distress among persons with traumatic brain injury. *Neuropsychological Rehabilitation.* https://doi.org/10.1080 /09602011.2020.1762670

Shakernegad, S., Moazen, N., Hamidi, M., Hashemi, R., Bazzazzadeh, N., & Bodaghi M. (2017). Effectiveness of Acceptance and Commitment Therapy on psychological distress, marital satisfaction and quality of life in women with multiple sclerosis. *Journal of Health and Care, 19,* 7–17. http://doi.org/10.32598/ijpcp.28.2.3747.1

Whiting, D., Deane, F., McLeod, H., Ciarrochi, J., & Simpson, G. (2020). Can acceptance and commitment therapy facilitate psychological adjustment after a severe traumatic brain injury? A pilot randomized controlled trial. *Neuropsychological Rehabilitation, 30*(7), 1348–1371. http://doi.org/10.1080/09602011.2019.1583582

Yazdanbakhsh, K., Kaboudi, M., Roghanchi, M., Dehghan, F., & Nooripour, R. (2016). The effectiveness of acceptance and commitment therapy on psychological adaptation in women with MS. *Journal of Fundamental and Applied Sciences, 8,* 2767–2777.

Chapter 1

ACT resilience training in multiple sclerosis

Kenneth I. Pakenham and Ambra Mara Giovannetti

The READY (REsilience Activities for every DaY) for MS program was derived from its parent intervention referred to as READY. Therefore, we use the term 'READY' to refer to the parent program and the term 'READY for MS' to refer to the modified version of READY that is suitable for people living with multiple sclerosis (MS). We start with a brief description of the development of the parent READY program and then segue into the READY for MS story.

The initial standard READY program was developed by me (KIP) and my colleague, Dr Nicola Burton, from The University of Queensland, Australia. Prior to developing the program in 2006, I experienced a personal crisis with long-term ramifications. It triggered a vigorous personal search for resilience-building resources. In this context, I discovered Acceptance and Commitment Therapy (ACT), explored it and applied it to my personal challenges. I was energised and revitalised by the inner renewal and personal values-driven behaviour changes that I experienced through the personal application of ACT. The benefits I experienced from practising the ACT strategies prompted me to undertake professional training in ACT. As an eclectic clinical psychology practitioner with a bias towards Cognitive Behavioural Therapy (CBT), I slowly transitioned to a greater reliance on ACT in my clinical practice. I then included it in my teaching and established the first university-dedicated ACT course in Australia in 2009. Subsequent evaluations of the ACT course showed that students improved in self-care, distress, stress, clinical skills and the ACT processes (Pakenham, 2015; 2017). My journey into ACT and how I experienced it from the inside is described in my memoir *The Trauma Banquet* (Pakenham, 2020).

My personal practice of ACT and my reflection on such experiences were and are a source of personal and professional insights, motivation and energy that have informed, inspired and sustained my clinical practice and research, and in particular the development of the READY program. A theme throughout this chapter is the contagious energy that arises from the personal practice of the ACT strategies and how it incites curiosity and self-practice in others which, in turn, ignites the same energy in those they connect with, and so on – 'a pebble in the pond ripple effect.'

DOI: 10.4324/9781003193722-2

While I was exploring the personal, clinical and teaching applications of ACT, Dr Burton and I began developing READY. We created READY to promote resilience in adults; hence, it is identified as an adult resilience-training program. We used a contemporary conceptualisation of resilience to guide the creation of a READY resilience framework, which defines resilience as a psychological protective factor that enables a person to bounce back and sustain good mental health while dealing with adversity (Leppin et al., 2014). Resilience involves negotiating, managing and adapting to significant stressors or trauma by activating both internal (i.e., mindfulness, acceptance, cognitive flexibility and active coping) and external (i.e., social support, financial capital and community services) resources (Windle, 2011). It can be both a process and an outcome.

At the time (2007) of developing READY, there were few published resilience training interventions for adults, hence there was little intervention research to inform the development of READY. In view of the well-established empirical support for CBT, the growing evidence supporting positive psychology interventions and our prior clinical and research experience with these approaches, we used CBT and positive psychology to inform the development of READY. However, given that ACT is a modern variant of CBT and is closely aligned with positive psychology, we incorporated it into the intervention as a foundational unifying framework and approach. ACT therefore informed the core READY modules. Due to my growing expertise in practising ACT, I took responsibility for developing all but one of the ACT modules.

Psychological flexibility, the core overarching construct underpinning ACT, is the cornerstone of psychological health and is positively related to resiliency (Kashdan & Rottenberg, 2010). There are likely to be numerous pathways by which the ACT processes promote resilience (Hulbert-Williams, Storey, & Wilson, 2015). For example, in the context of MS, the psychological flexibility processes of mindfulness, acceptance and defusion may increase the following internal resources: tolerance for MS-related distress, decentring from unhelpful illness-related cognitions, emotional processing of MS-related stressors through contact with the present moment and flexibility in switching between different coping strategies in response to fluctuating MS symptoms. Greater flexibility in managing unwanted emotional and cognitive responses to illness is likely to free up resources to enable effective action in pursuit of revised and realistic values-informed goals, thereby improving resilience to MS and maximising quality-of-life outcomes. Indeed, psychological flexibility has been shown to mediate improvements in resilience and quality of life in READY for MS participants (Giovannetti, Solari, & Pakenham, 2021).

We designed READY to target five key resilience protective factors identified from the empirical literature: (1) positive emotions, (2) cognitive flexibility (e.g., acceptance), (3) life meaning, (4) social support and (5) active coping strategies (including physical activity) (Southwick et al., 2005). Although the intervention approach is largely based on ACT, it also includes CBT processes such as skills training in relaxation and building social support. One READY module promotes participation in purposive and incidental physical activity. Physical activity has previously been identified as a potential coping resource (Southwick et al., 2005) that can provide enduring resilience to stress (Salmon, 2001) and enhance well-being (Stathopoulou et al., 2006). Informed by the abovementioned theories and empirical research, we created a READY resilience model to provide an easy-to-understand visual map of the program structure and content. To this end, the READY resilience model is metaphorically described as a shield which is composed of five life domains (thinking, feeling, doing, relations and being). The shield is presented in Figure 1.1. Within each life domain, an empirically supported key resilience protective factor is highlighted and targeted by the intervention. These protective factors reflect one or more of the core ACT psychological flexibility processes. Although the shield contains seemingly separate facets for ease of presentation and understanding, the domains and protective factors are dynamic and overlapping. The ACT psychological flexibility processes impact multiple domains. In particular, mindfulness and self-as-context occupy central pivoting roles due to their diffuse and synergistic psychosocial effects. Qualitative feedback from people with MS who have participated in READY for MS suggests that the shield model of resilience is helpful and easy to understand (e.g., "I like the shield concept") and when asked which part of the program was of most value, some have identified the shield (e.g., "The idea of the shield of elements that work together").

Figure 1.1 The READY Resilience Shield (this figure is reprinted from Giovannetti, Pakenham et al. 2022)

The Standard READY Program

The original standard READY program has 11 modules as follows: (1) Introduction to the READY Resilience Model, (2) Physical Activity, (3) Mindfulness, (4) Defusion I, (5) Defusion II and Self-as-Context, (6) Acceptance, (7) Mid-Program Review, (8) Values, (9) Social Connectedness, (10) Relaxation and Pleasant Activities and (11) Review and Planning for the Future. The program structure is summarised in Table 1.1. Program strategies include psychoeducation, discussion, experiential exercises, self-reflection tasks, self-monitoring, in-session practice activities and home practice assignments. READY was developed for delivery in a group. The 11 modules are delivered weekly in 2.5-hour group sessions. Ideally, groups consist of 8–20 participants.

Participants receive a hard-copy workbook that has two components: (1) written module content and (2) the READY Personal Plan, which is comprised of in-session and home practice exercises. Participants record and make notes on their personal practice in the Personal Plan. The Personal Plan constitutes a personalised

Table 1.1 Intervention structure for the standard READY and READY for MS programs.

Standard READY		READY for MS	
Module Number	Topic	Module Number	Topic
1	Introduction to READY Resilience Model	1	Introduction to READY Resilience Model
2	Physical Activity	2	Mindfulness
3	Mindfulness	3	Acceptance
4	Defusion I	4	Defusion I
5	Defusion II and Self-as-Context	5	Defusion II and Self-as-Context
6	Acceptance	6	Values and Meaningful Action: Social Connectedness# and Self-Care* Values
7	Mid-Program Review	7	Review and Planning for the Future
8	Values and Meaningful Action	*Five-week gap*	
9	Social Connectedness#	8	Booster
10	Relaxation and Pleasant Activities*		
11	Review and Planning for the Future		

Note. # The READY Social Connectedness module topic is incorporated into the READY for MS Values module.
* The READY Relaxation and Pleasant Activities module topic is relabelled Self-Care and incorporated into the READY for MS Values module.

resource to help participants apply program information and strategies to their specific context and individual style.

Participants also receive an audio file which contains guided meditations and relaxation exercises. A facilitator manual provides program instructions and session content for group facilitators and is accompanied by PowerPoint slides for each session.

Applications of READY

The standard 11-module READY program was piloted in a single-arm study with pre- and post-intervention assessments in a workplace setting (Burton, Pakenham, & Brown, 2010). The program was delivered by Dr Burton and I. Participants improved on measures of mastery, self-acceptance, autonomy, personal growth, positive emotions, mindfulness, acceptance, stress, valued living and total cholesterol. Participants reported high levels of satisfaction with the program and materials.

READY is modulised so that specific modules can be selected and delivered and easily adapted for specific populations and contexts. The five modules focussing on the ACT strategies (Mindfulness, Defusion I, Defusion II/Self-as-Context, Acceptance and Values) were included in a telephone-delivered intervention targeting multiple health behaviour changes in 410 colorectal cancer survivors (Hawkes et al., 2009). The intervention was delivered by health coaches who had training in nursing and/or the social and behavioural sciences. The intervention was evaluated in a two-arm randomised controlled trial (RCT) with baseline and six- and 12-month assessments. Intervention effects on health behaviour (Hawkes et al., 2013) and psychosocial (Hawkes et al., 2014) outcomes were evaluated. At 12 months, there were significant improvements in physical activity, body mass index, energy from total fat and saturated fat and posttraumatic growth. At six months, there were significant improvements in vegetable intake, spirituality and acceptance. Quality of life significantly improved at both six and 12 months. Mediational analyses conducted on the psychosocial outcomes showed that the ACT processes, acceptance and mindfulness mediated the improvements in posttraumatic growth, spirituality and quality of life (Hawkes et al., 2014).

The standard READY group program was applied to 20 people with diabetes and evaluated in a single-arm pre- to post-intervention pilot study (Ryan, Pakenham, & Burton, 2020). The only change to the standard program was the omission of the mid-program review module. All sessions were delivered by a clinical psychology postgraduate student. There were significant improvements in resilience, psychological flexibility, positive affect, valued living, physical activity, sedentary behaviour, depression, and stress. Feasibility data showed high program engagement and satisfaction.

READY was modified for application to people with congenital heart disease while in hospital and after discharge at home (Steele, 2016). The intervention involved a two-hour group session in hospital followed by four individual telephone sessions after discharge. All sessions were delivered by a clinical psychology postgraduate student. Two modules (Introduction and Values) were delivered in the single group session and the mindfulness, defusion, acceptance and final review modules were delivered across the four individual telephone sessions, respectively. A mixed-method study evaluated the intervention. It consisted of a single-arm design with pre- and post-intervention and three-month follow-up assessments ($n=17$) and focus groups with all relevant stakeholders ($n=12$ patients, $n=3$ caregivers and $n=5$ clinicians). Results of analyses revealed statistically significant and clinically meaningful improvements on depression and quality of life. Patients indicated high satisfaction with the READY program. Caregivers and clinicians viewed the program as helpful and relevant to patients.

In addition to applying READY in a workplace setting and to people with cancer, diabetes and congenital heart disease, I modified the standard READY program and applied it to people with MS. As mentioned above, this version of the program is called READY for MS, and it is the focus of the remainder of this chapter.

READY for MS

I (KIP) began my research into the psychosocial aspects of MS in 1994 soon after I experienced significant neurological symptoms and received a diagnosis of 'suspected MS.' If I were to have MS, I wanted to understand the disease, so I researched the medical and psychosocial MS literature. I was astounded to find that with respect to the psychosocial research, the focus was on psychopathology correlates of MS while neglecting the coping capacities of people with MS to manage a complex and mostly degenerative neurological disorder with onset typically in young adulthood. This observation prompted me to conduct my own research into the coping potentials of people living with MS. I used stress and coping and positive psychology frameworks to investigate risk and protective factors that could explain variations in adjustment to MS. After 13 years of conducting this research, I encountered ACT, and I was eager to modify READY so that it could be used to foster resilience in people living with MS.

Development and Description

The original standard READY program was modified to reduce participation demands and burden given the high prevalence of fatigue and disability associated with MS. The 11 modules were reduced to seven by removing the mid-program review and physical activity modules and incorporating the social connectedness and relaxation and pleasant activities topics into the values and meaningful action module. With respect to the latter, the relaxation and pleasant activities module topic was relabelled self-care. The values and meaningful action module therefore focused on social connectedness and self-care values. Another modification was the addition of a booster session five weeks after the seventh module. The booster session reviewed content from modules 1 to 6. The modified READY for MS program therefore consisted of the introductory module (Introduction to the READY

Resilience Model), followed by the five ACT-based modules reflecting the six ACT processes (Mindfulness, Acceptance, Defusion, Self-as-Context, Values and Meaningful Action), the concluding review module (Review and Future Planning) and a booster session. The READY for MS program structure relative to the parent READY program is summarised in Table 1.1. READY for MS is delivered in eight group sessions of 2.5 hours each. Seven modules are delivered weekly, followed by the group booster module five weeks later.

The READY participant handbook was revised to reflect the abovementioned changes to the READY for MS program. Importantly, the READY for MS workbook retained the two components: (1) written module content and (2) the READY Personal Plan comprised of in-session and home practice exercises. Participants receive a hard copy of the workbook. The Personal Plan has been identified by many participants who have undertaken READY for MS as particularly helpful (e.g., "I liked having the Personal Plan to refer to. Completing the Personal Plan makes you analyse your thoughts, feelings, values, behaviours, relationships, and social interactions. There was something powerful about writing it down"). Participants also receive the READY audio file, which contains only guided meditations and excludes the guided relaxation exercises. The facilitator manual and accompanying PowerPoint slides for each session were also revised to reflect the abovementioned changes to the READY for MS program.

Evaluations of READY for MS

The READY for MS program was first evaluated in a single-arm pilot study in Australia (Pakenham, Mawdsley et al., 2018). This study ($n = 37$) used a pre-post group intervention design with three-month follow-up. The program was delivered by clinical psychology postgraduate students through a community-based organisation. Participants significantly improved in resilience, quality of life, depression, stress and three ACT processes: defusion, values and acceptance. Values and defusion emerged as mediators of quality of life and stress, respectively. Program feasibility was supported by positive participant feedback, good intervention fidelity and high rates of recruitment, attendance, retention and homework engagement.

It should be noted that this pilot study was not conducted with tight constraints regarding eligibility criteria for participation. Any person with MS who was 18 years or over with a self-reported diagnosis of MS, living in Southeast Queensland (Australia) and fluent in English could attend the program. Consequently, the 37 participants varied considerably regarding disability, MS symptoms (including cognitive impairment), illness duration, age and other socio-demographics. Several people with MS had to be accompanied by their informal carer who also attended the program.

The READY for MS program was later translated into Italian by Dr Ambra Mara Giovannetti (AMG), a psychologist and psychotherapist attached to the Italian MS Society and working at the Fondazione IRCCS Istituto Neurologico Carlo Besta, Milan. I (AMG) attended a two-day ACT and READY for MS workshop that

Emeritus Prof. Pakenham conducted in Milan for Italian psychologists working in the MS field in 2015. At the end of the workshop, I volunteered to assist him in a role-play in which he demonstrated the ACT and READY for MS strategies. The workshop experience and personal encounter with ACT motivated me to receive further training in ACT and READY for MS, so I visited him in Australia to undertake his ACT course and training in READY for MS, which included facilitating READY for MS groups under his supervision. During this period, I experienced immense personal and professional benefits from my reflective self-practice of the READY strategies. In fact, it marked my transition from a relational psychoanalytic-oriented practice to an ACT and more process-based approach. This encounter was enlightening as I was also dealing with the challenges of working on an innovative research project designed to develop a palliative care intervention for people with MS. In this context, I found being present, acceptance and connection to personal values to be key aspects in supporting people facing severe disability and possible death. These positive training experiences inspired me to enrol in a PhD and research the cross-cultural application of the READY for MS program, which led to the following research on the Italian version of the intervention.

The Italian program was first evaluated in a pilot RCT ($n = 39$) which had a nested qualitative study (Giovannetti et al., 2020). This study was conducted with tight methodological constraints with respect to eligibility and exclusion criteria regarding study participation. Participants completed three assessments at pre- and post-intervention and at a 24-week follow-up. READY for MS was compared to an active control group that received relaxation. Control group participants were offered the intervention after completing their final assessment. Interviews of intervention and control group participants were conducted within three months of finishing the READY for MS program. READY for MS was well accepted by people with MS with varied socio-demographic and clinical characteristics. Qualitative (but not quantitative) data provided evidence in favour of READY for MS. Interestingly, control group participants were able to report on the benefits and weaknesses of READY for MS relative to the relaxation intervention. Overall, these participants reported more positive impacts for the READY for MS program across a range of dimensions including intervention structure and materials, effects on various life domains and program-specific active elements. The superiority of READY for MS is illustrated by the following quote: "Different to relaxation, during the READY program I acquired new skills such as: mindfulness, defusion and acceptance. Learning new strategies has helped me feel the punches [of having MS] less strongly. This is really important."

The Italian READY for MS program was later evaluated in a single-arm longitudinal effectiveness study ($n = 237$) with pre- and post-intervention and three-month follow-up assessments (Giovannetti et al., 2021). This research also included a nested qualitative study. The intervention was delivered by psychologists who received training in the delivery of the program. Results showed that participants improved in resilience, anxiety, depression, stress, health-related quality of life and psychological flexibility and associated processes (acceptance, defusion and values). Improvements on most outcomes occurred at post-intervention and were maintained at the three-month follow-up. No demographic or illness variables predicted these improvements. Psychological flexibility mediated improvements in resilience, anxiety, depression, stress and health-related quality of life. Qualitative data confirmed the positive psychosocial impacts of the intervention. Consistent with the qualitative data from prior evaluations of READY for MS, participants reported marked positive effects of READY for MS on a variety of life domains including daily living, MS, work, relationships, personal growth and mental health ("I am no more on automatic pilot. I notice what is around me (sounds, smell, etc.). When my resilience is low, I stop, relax and breathe. Once per week, I cultivate my social relationships with family and friends. This program has changed my life, the way I connect with people, with myself and the disease"). Almost all participants stated that participating in READY for MS had positive impacts on their coping with MS in terms of adjustment, health and lifestyle. Consistent with the results of the Australian pilot, results from this study suggested that READY for MS can be effectively integrated into frontline services for people with MS without limitation in terms of participants' demographic and illness characteristics.

Findings from the two studies that evaluated the Italian READY for MS program have informed the development of a study protocol for a multi-centre cluster RCT comparing READY with a group relaxation program in 240 people with MS from eight centres in Italy (Giovannetti, Pakenham et al., 2022). This study addresses the limitations of the prior studies evaluating the READY for MS program and further tests its efficacy. This study is currently underway.

Digital and Online Video-Conferencing Applications

Demands for delivering the READY for MS program via modes other than an in-person group format arose from frontline MS services for several reasons. First, some organisations did not have the resources to train and employ healthcare practitioners to deliver the program. Second, because some organisations provided services to people with MS across large geographical areas, it was logistically difficult to provide an in-person group intervention to people with MS who resided in regional or remote areas. Third, for many people with MS, the emergence of the COVID-19 pandemic and associated strict public health social distancing measures, precluded participation in face-to-face interventions. Consequently, I (KIP) made modifications to the READY for MS program manual and workbook to make them suitable for digital delivery.

The manual content had to be modified because it had been initially written and formatted to accommodate group processes that necessitate some flexibility in delivery. Consequently, some content required written elaboration. In addition, excerpts of module content were made into voice recordings. All meditation scripts and most experiential exercises were voice recorded. Group discussion exercises were converted into self-reflective tasks. The review and booster modules each had a summary of program content in point form, which was converted into a narrative that provided a more in-depth and coherent summary of all modules. In the group delivery of the review and booster modules, facilitators relied heavily on group processes and the troubleshooting needs of participants to direct flow and more thorough discussion of particular content areas. In the absence of these interpersonal processes, for both modules, a more comprehensive summary of content was provided, and a voice-recorded guided meditation was included that offered experiential engagement with all strategies presented in the prior modules.

The group READY for MS participant handbook was revised to reflect the abovementioned changes to the digital program. Participants receive a digital or hard copy of the workbook. As with the original READY workbook, it consists of two components: (1) module content and (2) the READY Personal Plan.

At present, three digital versions of the READY for MS program have been or are being developed. All digital programs are designed to be delivered online. One digital program was disseminated nationally in Australia in 2022 via a pilot RCT through an organisation that provides support services to people with MS. Data analyses for this study are underway. The second digital program was distributed in the UK in 2022 via a UK MS Society-funded pilot RCT (Wicks, Horton et al., 2022; Wicks, Pakenham et al., 2022). The focus of this project is on evaluating the effectiveness of READY for MS to help people with MS stay in employment. A third digital version is currently being developed by a German team, with the intention of evaluating the program via an RCT. All three digital programs are based on the READY for MS manual and workbook developed for digitisation. The only differences among the programs are language and IT technology.

In addition to these projects investigating the digital delivery of READY for MS, a Greek team of psychologists is evaluating the delivery of the group program via a real-time video-conference platform (Theodorou et al., 2022). This project involves a single intervention condition with pre- and post-intervention and three-month follow-up assessments. I (AMG) trained the Greek psychologists to facilitate READY for MS groups during the COVID-19 pandemic. Capitalising on the experience of training Italian psychologists in the READY for MS program (Giovannetti, Messmer Uccelli et al., 2022), I invited the Greek team to participate in a READY for MS group as 'clients' and to subsequently facilitate READY for MS groups via video conferencing in their community. I provided supervision on a needs basis. The training was conducted via video conferencing.

Preliminary qualitative data collected from the Australian, UK and Greek projects show that most participants are highly satisfied with the delivery of the digital and video-conferencing versions of the program. For example, 90% of the first 22 participants in the Greek project reported satisfaction with the online group program and 100% said they would recommend the program to other people with MS (Theodorou et al., 2022). The preliminary qualitative data from these projects reflect the themes that have emerged from published analyses of qualitative data collected from studies that have evaluated the in-person group delivery of READY for MS (e.g., "Everything is part of life and is simply here for millions of years. READY for MS helped me to broaden my view in life and cope with MS in a flexible way"; "A unique experience for me, I really enjoyed it! In every session I was learning and trying something new for my personal development").

The preliminary data on the digital READY for MS programs are promising given our initial concern that the potency of the intervention might be diluted in the absence of the guidance and enthusiasm of the facilitators who have personally experienced the benefits of the READY strategies.

Impacts of READY for MS on Healthcare Professionals

Underpinning our training of qualified and student healthcare professionals in the group READY for MS program is the self-practice and self-reflective approach mentioned earlier in the chapter. Trainees are invited to apply the READY strategies to their daily living, which for most trainees inevitably produces personal and professional growth. Our observations and data suggest that this growth in the trainees ignites a positive contagious energy which 'infects' their READY for MS participants and colleagues.

The positive impacts on healthcare professionals who have received training in the delivery of the standard READY program and other applications of READY, including the READY for MS program, have been evident through anecdotal reports and qualitative and quantitative data. Anecdotally, we (KIP and AMG) have received overwhelming positive reports from many clinical psychology students, health coaches and qualified psychologists about the training they have received in delivering READY for MS. The positive impacts described have been both personal and professional.

We have conducted two formal evaluations of READY for MS training for healthcare professionals. The first study ($n = 34$) evaluated a two-day ACT and READY for MS workshop that I (KIP) conducted for psychologists in Italy working in the MS field (Pakenham, Scott, & Messmer Uccelli, 2018). Data were collected via online questionnaires before and after the workshop, and at six-month follow-up. Results showed that most participants (94%) mentioned the potential beneficial effects of the workshop on their work. Almost all participants reported their intention to apply ACT clinically. More than 90% of participants indicated that the workshop was efficacious. All participants scored higher than 75% on a knowledge examination. Mindfulness increased from after the workshop to the follow-up; however, there were no statistically significant changes in well-being, negative affect, positive affect and job satisfaction. Results suggested that ACT training is personally and professionally helpful for psychologists in the MS field.

The second study ($n = 47$) evaluated a READY for MS training program for healthcare professionals that I (AMG) conducted for psychologists in Italy working in the MS field and that was preparatory for the abovementioned multi-centre RCT (Giovannetti, Pakenham et al., 2022). The training had three phases: (1) training workshop; (2) participation in the READY for MS program as 'client'; (3) delivery of the READY for MS program to people with MS under my supervision. Self-report data were collected immediately before the workshop, before and after participation in the READY for MS program as a 'client,' and at three- and 15-month follow-ups. Forty psychologists successfully completed the training. The training was effective in fostering the acquisition of knowledge and skills for the effective delivery of READY for MS to people with MS. Participants improved over the course of training in resilience, positive affect, well-being, psychological flexibility and associated processes. These improvements peaked during the participation in READY for MS phase and continued to accrue at a slower rate three months later. Psychological flexibility mediated the improvements in resilience, positive affect, and well-being. Qualitative data confirmed the personal benefits of the training (e.g., "This experience affected me deeply, particularly in committed actions related to my family, health, and well-being. I have booked a trip, accepted the support of my husband and, unexpectedly, he is more present in our daily life."). Participants also reported many professional benefits from the training such as learning new strategies to enhance client work (e.g., "This training provided me a new method to unlock impasses in my patients, particularly when they were stuck in the fight. I can speed up their process of awareness and improve their way to manage their suffering.").

The nested qualitative study also provided information on trainees' views of the READY for MS program when delivered to people with MS. This data supported the feasibility of delivering READY for MS to people with MS by highlighting several strengths, including the program's solid theoretical framework, comprehensiveness and efficacy. In addition, trainees reported that READY for MS positively impacted a wide range of life domains in people with MS and attributed such gains to the enhancement of resilience protective factors (e.g., the ACT processes). These results are in line with the views of people with MS about the program reported in previous studies (Giovannetti et al., 2020; Giovannetti et al., 2021; Pakenham, Mawdsley et al., 2018). A few trainees suggested expanding the program duration by increasing the number of sessions, adding booster sessions or increasing the interval between sessions. These suggested changes are consistent with those reported by people with MS in the Italian pilot study that evaluated READY for MS (Giovannetti et al., 2020).

The Greek team of psychologists (mentioned above) who delivered READY for MS via video conferencing undertook a similar training program to the one delivered to the Italian psychologists. The main difference was that the training for the Greek team was delivered via video conferencing. After the training, the psychologists reported on the importance of both participating in the program as a 'client' and in facilitating a READY for MS group for people with MS. Their feedback shows the deep personal and professional growth that can be experienced by healthcare professionals who experience READY for MS as both a 'client' and facilitator (e.g., "During my clinical practice with people with MS, I was looking for a concrete, evidence-based and brief psychological intervention, which would provide them with all the essentials to build their resilience and, subsequently, participate more actively in their treatment and rehabilitation. The online facilitation of READY for MS was the program that helped me work with large groups of people with MS and feel more confident that I could meet their personal needs to achieve a good quality of life. More than that, READY training had a deep positive impact on myself, as I had hands-on experience of learning and practicing the ACT principles in my everyday life. Both participating and facilitating READY for MS online offered me a valuable experience that I believe shaped me as a better person and healthcare professional too.").

Community Impacts of READY for MS

The qualitative data from the longitudinal study that evaluated the training program for healthcare professionals (Giovannetti, Messmer Uccelli et al., 2022) showed that the training had positive impacts on the community of psychologists working in the MS field in Italy. The training facilitated stronger professional connections. The qualitative data also showed that the training improved interpersonal connections within the psychologist network by nurturing a sense of shared work-related values and meaning (e.g., "This experience increased closeness and solidarity between each other." "Now we share common values!" "Sharing this training experience… strengthened a sense of belonging. We feel that we are walking the same path. We share common meaning and principles in our job"). These closer social connections among members of the psychologist network fostered new research collaborations. For example, following the training, six participants developed and implemented projects that involved delivering READY for MS to healthcare professionals, to people with fibromyalgia, to caregivers of people with MS or other neurological conditions and to adolescents with MS.

The training also facilitated new connections between the different MS centres (e.g., "This experience allowed psychologists working on the periphery [like me] to have precious and enriching exchanges with other colleagues working in a more structured reality"). The training also consolidated the integration of READY for MS into a frontline MS service. To date, more than 50 READY for MS groups have been conducted in Italy for people with MS.

Results from all three studies evaluating READY for MS (Giovannetti et al., 2020; Giovannetti, Solari, & Pakenham, 2021; Pakenham, Mawdsley et al., 2018) and the two studies evaluating the training (Pakenham, Scott et al., 2018; Giovannetti, Messmer Uccelli et al., 2022) suggest that the program can be easily implemented in frontline MS services. Across all studies, participants with MS were highly satisfied with the program format. One Italian service has signed a copyright agreement to ensure the ongoing delivery of READY for MS in its centres. This integration of READY for MS into frontline services stands in contrast to the often-cited lack of uptake of validated psychosocial interventions in routine practice (McHugh & Barlow, 2010).

Conclusions

To our knowledge, READY for MS is the first published resilience training intervention for adults living with MS. Anecdotal, quantitative and qualitative data systematically collected from evaluations of the program converge on the positive impacts of the intervention across a wide range of psychosocial outcomes for people with MS and healthcare professionals who engage with the program. The fact that both people with MS and healthcare professionals have benefited from the program underscores the trans-diagnostic processes underpinning the intervention. Frontline services that have hosted delivery of the program have expressed enthusiasm about the kudos they experience from offering an innovative intervention that enhances service satisfaction among their members and makes observable differences in the lives of program participants. Evidence to date suggests the program can be flexibly applied across a range of contexts. The group program is adaptable to delivery in different settings including workplaces, hospital clinics and community locations. The READY for MS program can also be delivered by a range of healthcare professionals. For example, it has been effectively delivered by clinical psychology students and qualified psychologists from a range of theoretical orientations and specialties, and the original parent READY program has been delivered by health coaches. The program also has cross-cultural applications. Preliminary data suggests that the program is adaptable to a variety of delivery modes including group face-to-face, group online video conferencing and digital. Flexibility in modes of delivery has meant that accessing the program has not been hindered by COVID-19 public health social isolation measures. Results of mediation analyses have supported the theoretical integrity of the intervention by demonstrating that the framework underpinning the READY for MS program, psychological flexibility and its sub-processes mediate the intervention-related improvements in mental health, quality of life and other psychosocial outcomes reported by participants.

References

Burton, N. W., Pakenham, K. I., & Brown, W. J. (2009). Evaluating the effectiveness of psychosocial resilience training for heart health and the added value of promoting physical activity: A cluster randomized trial of the READY program. *BMC Public Health, 9*, 427. https://doi.org/10.1186/1471-2458-9-427

Burton, N. W., Pakenham, K. I., & Brown, W. J. (2010). Feasibility and effectiveness of psychosocial resilience training: A pilot study of the READY program. *Psychology, Health and Medicine, 15*, 266–277.

Giovannetti, A. M., Pakenham, K. I., Presti, G., Quartuccio, M. E., Confalonieri, P., Bergamaschi, R., Grobberio, M., Di Filippo, M., Micheli, M., Brichetto, G., Patti, F., Copetti, M., Kruger, P., & Solari, A. (2022). A group resilience training program for people with multiple sclerosis: Study protocol of a multi-centre cluster-randomized controlled trial (Multi-READY for MS). *PLoS ONE, 17*(5), e0267245. https://doi.org/10.1371/journal

Giovannetti, A. M., Quintas, R., Tramacere, I., Giordano, A., Confalonieri, P., Uccelli, M., Solari, A., & Pakenham, K. I. (2020). A resilience group training program for people with MS: Results of a pilot single-blind randomized controlled trial and nested qualitative study. *PLoS ONE, 15*(4), e0231380. https://doi.org/10.1371/journal.pone.0231380

Giovannetti, A. M., Solari, A., & Pakenham, K. I. (2021). Effectiveness of a group resilience intervention for people with multiple sclerosis delivered via frontline services. *Disability and Rehabilitation, 44*(22), 6582–6592. https://doi.org/10.1080/09638288.2021.1960441

Giovannetti, A. M., Uccelli, M., Solari, A., & Pakenham, K. I. (2022). Evaluation of a program for training psychologists in an acceptance and commitment therapy resilience intervention for people with multiple sclerosis: A single-arm longitudinal design with a nested qualitative study. *Disability and Rehabilitation, 4*(22), 6926–6938. https://doi.org/10.1080/09638288.2022.2025926

Hawkes, A. L., Chambers, S. K., Pakenham, K. I., Patrao, T. A., Baade, P., Lynch, B., Aitken, J., Meng, X., & Courneya, K. S. (2013). Effects of a telephone-delivered multiple health behavior change intervention for colorectal cancer survivors ('CanChange') on quality of life, fatigue and health behaviors: A randomized controlled trial. *Journal of Clinical Oncology, 31*(18), 2313–2321.

Hawkes, A. L., Pakenham, K. I., Chambers, S. K., Patrao, T. A., & Courneya, K. S. (2014). Effects of a multiple health behavior change intervention for colorectal cancer survivors on psychosocial outcomes and quality of life: A randomised controlled trial. *Annals of Behavioral Medicine, 48,* 359–370.

Hawkes, A. L., Pakenham, K. I., Courneya, K., Gollschewski, S., Baade, P., Gordon, L., Lynch, B. M., Aitken, J., & Chambers, S. (2009). A randomised controlled trial of a lifestyle intervention for colorectal cancer survivors (CanChange): Study protocol. *BMC Cancer, 9,* 286. https://doi.org/10.1186/1471-2407-9-286

Hulbert-Williams, N. J., Storey, L., & Wilson, K. G. (2015). Psychological interventions for patients with cancer: Psychological flexibility and the potential utility of Acceptance and Commitment Therapy. *European Journal of Cancer Care, 24,* 15–27. http://dx.doi.org/10.1111/ecc.12223

Kashdan, T. B., & Rottenberg, J. (2010). Psychological flexibility as a fundamental aspect of health. *Clinical Psychology Review, 30,* 865–878. http://dx.doi.org/10.1016/j.cpr.2010.03.001

Leppin, A. L., Bora, P. R., Tilburt, J. C., Gionfriddo, M. R., Zeballos-Palacios, C., Dulohery, M. M., . . . Montori, V. M. (2014). The efficacy of resiliency training programs: A systematic review and meta-analysis of randomized trials. *PLoS ONE, 9,* e111420. http://dx.doi.org/10.1371/journal.pone.0111420

McHugh, R. K., & Barlow, D. H. (2010). The dissemination and implementation of evidence-based psychological treatments. A review of current efforts. *The American Psychologist, 65*(2), 73–84. https://doi.org/10.1037/a0018121

Pakenham, K. I. (2015). Effects of Acceptance and Commitment Therapy (ACT) Training on clinical psychology trainee stress, therapist skills and attributes, and ACT processes. *Clinical Psychology & Psychotherapy, 22,* 647–655.

Pakenham, K. I. (2017). Training in Acceptance and Commitment Therapy fosters self-care in clinical psychology trainees. *Clinical Psychologist, 21,* 186–194.

Pakenham, K. I. (2020). *The trauma banquet: Eat pain, feasting on life.* MoshPit Publishing.

Pakenham, K. I., Mawdsley, M., Brown, F., & Burton, N. W. (2018). Pilot evaluation of a resilience training program for people with multiple sclerosis. *Rehabilitation Psychology, 63*(1), 29–42.

Pakenham, K. I., Scott, T., & Uccelli, M. (2018). Evaluation of Acceptance and Commitment Therapy (ACT) Training for psychologists working with people living with multiple sclerosis. *International Journal of MS Care, 20,* 44–48.

Ryan, A., Pakenham, K. I., & Burton, N. (2020). A pilot evaluation of a group Acceptance and Commitment Therapy (ACT)-informed resilience training program for people with diabetes. *Australian Psychologist, 55*, 196–207.

Salmon, P. (2001). Effects of physical exercise on anxiety, depression, and sensitivity to stress: A unifying theory. *Clinical Psychology Review, 21*(1), 33–61.

Southwick, S., Vythilingam, M., & Charney, D. (2005). The psychobiology of depression and resilience to stress: Implications for prevention and treatment. *Annual Review of Clinical Psychology, 1*, 255–291.

Stathopoulou, G., Powers, M., Berry, A., Smits, J., & Otto, M. (2006). Exercise interventions for mental health: A quantitative and qualitative review. *Clinical Psychology-Science and Practice, 13*(2), 179–193.

Steele, B. (2016). Evaluation of an acceptance and commitment therapy-based resilience training program for adults with congenital heart disease. Unpublished thesis Doctor of Psychology (Clinical Psychology), University of Queensland.

Theodorou, S. Goutseli, E., Kechayas, P., Kroupi, C., Giovannetti, A., & Pakenham, K. I. (2022). A resilience group online training program for people with MS: READY for MS Greece. Poster presentation European MS Platform Annual Conference.

van Gool, C., Kempen, G., Bosma, H., van Boxtel, M., Jolles, J., & Van Eijk, J. (2007). Associations between lifestyle and depressed mood: Longitudinal results from the Maastricht Aging Study. *American Journal of Public Health, 97*(5), 887–815.

Wicks, C. R., Horton, M., Pakenham,K. I., Pavitt, S., Thompson, L., Brownlee, W., Pepper, G., Tallanyre, E., Leary,S., & Ford, H. L. (2022). Co-production and pilot trial of a digital resilience-training programme to improve job retention in MS: Summary of baseline outcome measures. Poster presentation MS Frontiers Annual Conference.

Wicks, C. R., Pakenham, K. I., Pavitt, S., Thompson, L., Horton, M., Brownlee, W., Pepper, G., Tallantyre, E., Leary, S., & Ford, H. L. (2022). A digital resilience-training programme to improve job retention in MS: A multicentre pilot trial. *Journal of Neurology, Neurosurgery and Psychiatry, 93*.

Windle, G. (2011). What is resilience? A review and concept analysis. *Reviews in Clinical Gerontology, 21*, 152–169 https://doi.org/10.1017/S0959259810000420

Chapter 2

"Rather than be in a cage, be in a cocoon": A pilot yoga-Acceptance and Commitment Therapy group for people with Acquired Brain Injury

Mairéad Jones, Jenn Galvin and Marcia Ward

In my work as a clinical neuropsychologist, I have spent over 11 years support-ing people adjusting to living with Acquired Brain Injury (ABI) primarily through the paradigm of Acceptance and Commitment Therapy (ACT). We humans often struggle with the "doing" parts of therapy, the behaviour-change piece, the com-mitted action in the service of our values. This holds true in my own life and has been mirrored in my practice, where people struggle to move towards what matters to them in a form that is perhaps different from their pre-injury lives and in a body that may be different too. My clients often report a mind/body disconnection; bod-ies that don't respond to intention in the way they once did, limbs that look or func-tion differently, some that may not function at all. Survivors can report the body as a source of frustration, resulting from this changed sense of personal control over the body, physical ability and stamina.

Rehabilitation is organised around a cyclical continuous process of goal setting and goal attain ment. Typically, the mind or the brain is seen as the remit of clinical neuropsychology and the body as the domain of physiotherapy and/or occupational therapy. This splitting can be reinforced by the manner in which services are organised and delivered; different spaces both physically and interpersonally to work on rehabilitation goals. Added to this, I have found limited access to therapies, or time-limited access to therapies, adds an extra layer of stress, an extra struggle on top of what is often described by my clients as their "new job": rehabilitation. This additional pressure can manifest in people pushing themselves beyond what is comfortable or helpful in the drive to get maximum benefit from their limited sessions. "I have to, I must, this is my only chance" – I hear this a lot. This drive to perform can come at a cost, both physically and psychologically, and often against the background of exacerbated fatigue.

Attending to the body in therapy/embodiment of distress

The role of the body in both communicating/holding and managing emotional dis-tress has become more prominent in clinical practice in recent years, particularly in the field of trauma (Van der Kolk, 2014). The body provides cues which the mind interprets to guide behaviour. So, somatic expressions of emotions are increasingly

DOI: 10.4324/9781003193722-3

coming into focus within various therapeutic methodologies including ACT. Grounding sensory techniques are utilised to anchor an individual when dysregulated, and mindfulness uses the body as a tool to regulate physical and emotional responses by connecting with the present moment. A therapeutic approach characterised by unity of body and mind may offer a way of processing and integrating experiences of disconnection and subsequent distress in the lived experience of ABI (Levack, Kayes & Fadyl, 2010).

Emerging evidence has identified the practice of yoga, an ancient Indian Vedic system of physical movement with a focus on mindful breathing and relaxation, as offering a way for survivors of a brain injury to access a non-judgemental way of relating to the self and the body. The Sanskrit root of yoga, "yog," means to unite, and the practice relates to both the physical body and mind in unison. In a review of controlled trials of yoga interventions, initial evidence is reported as promising for the benefit of yoga in recovery from acquired neurological conditions (Silveira & Smart, 2020). Yoga is said to have originated in what is now known as India during the fourth, fifth and sixth centuries BC. At that time the traditional hierarchies of parts of the Indian subcontinent were being transformed, with the village structure being challenged by the growth of cities, hubs of social and economic importance. It is reported that the philosophies of the ancient Vedic system began to be questioned by figures described as *strivers*,with those renouncing the traditional hierarchies of priests and castes. An examination of the meaning of life and what it is to be human was undertaken by those *strivers* who asserted that self-realisation could be achieved not by external religious ritual but rather by internal investigation of the body and mind (Cope, 2006). The central treatises of the tradition are recorded in the *Yoga-Sutra* within a framework known as Eight-Limb Yoga by a philosopher-practitioner thought to be known as Patanjali. These components are *yama*:external disciplines and ethical practice; *niyama*:internal discipline; *asana*:posture for meditation; *pranayama*:breath regulation; *pratyahara*:withdrawal of the senses; *dharana*: concentration; *dhyana*: meditative absorption; and *samadhi*:oneness (Cope, 2006).

The embodied nature of yoga is cited as a particular strength for use with survivors of a brain injury. The practice offers an accessible way of addressing both physical and psychological concerns and acts as an alternative to wholly physical interventions which do not focus on the emotional impact of an ABI and talking therapies that require sustained attention, energy, the use of language and cognition (Yeates, Murphy, Baldwin, Wilkes & Mahadevan, 2015). A "LoveYourBrain" yoga programme was delivered to 1563 people with traumatic brain injury and caregivers across 18 US states and three Canadian provinces with reported significant improvements in quality of life, resilience, positive affect and cognition. It is reported that participants experienced an increased sense of mastery, with this translating to motivation to engage in activities in the community. Participants in the programme describe making a distinction between recovering and rebuilding through the course of the programme and how this lessened the pressure to wholly return to their pre-injury selves and rather encouraged them to develop acceptance of the making of a new life (Donnelly et al., 2021). An examination of the mechanisms of change in a yoga intervention with women with post-traumatic stress disorder (PTSD) suggests that yoga may reduce expressive suppression and may improve PTSD symptoms by increasing psychological flexibility (Dick et al., 2014). This mirrors the overarching goal of ACT, which is to increase psychological flexibility.

Yoga adopts a philosophy of accepting the body and mind for how it is presenting in the current moment and relating to the body and mind with gratitude and kindness. Similarly, ACT does not focus on pursuing the reduction of distressing thoughts or feelings but, in accepting things as they are in the here and now, focuses on supporting individuals to live alongside the uncontrollable and commit to living life according to one's values (Tooze et al., 2014). This overlap in theoretical foundations with ACT suggests that an integration of yoga and ACT may be of utility to those with an ABI.

ACT and yoga group

We designed a nine-week pilot combined yoga and ACT group in a community neurorehabilitation setting. There were nine participants in the group: seven males and two females. Participants' ages ranged from 38 to 57 years, with a mean age of 44 years. All participants had a physical or sensory disability secondary to acquiring a brain injury. The mean length of time post-ABI was five years and five months. Each group session lasted 1 hour 45 minutes and was co-facilitated by a yoga instructor experienced in working with people with ABI and a senior clinical neuropsychologist working with Headway Ireland. The group took place in a yoga studio; there was a 50-minute group session followed by a 50-minute yoga practice based on/complementing the content of the ACT group session, e.g., a session on defusion followed by a yoga practice featuring integration/reinforcement of noticing painful thoughts, feelings and sensations when they arise, any attempt to control, avoid or suppress them in the body or mind and letting the content pass in and out of the mind as the practice progressed. The content of each session covering the core ACT processes and the accompanying yoga practice was planned in advance. Seven participants chose to participate in a qualitative piece of research exploring their experience of participating in the group. The data generated were analysed using Interpretative Phenomenological Analysis (Smith, Flowers & Larkin, 2009).

Learning from the group

Participants' experience of the yoga-ACT group may be best represented within a dynamic cycle. This is represented within a continual circle with internal and external components to illustrate the oscillation described by participants between experiences both within the group and external application to their daily lives (see Figure 2.1).

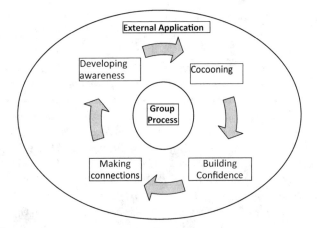

Figure 2.1 Process of participant experiences of yoga-ACT group.

The first facet of experience, entitled "Developing Awareness," describes experiences of a growing recognition of emotional processes, thoughts and behaviours. This facet of experience is comprised of "Information and Explanations" and "Recognition."

The second component of participant experience, entitled "Cocooning," explores participants' experiences in relation to growing self-compassion and accepting parts of the self in the moment. This part of participant experience is comprised of "Safety" and "Rest."

The third part of participant experience, labelled "Building Confidence," describes participants' reports of what it was like to develop a belief in the self in the aftermath of an event which for many destroyed self-esteem, confidence and predictions for how life would be. Themes of "Reflection" and "Repetition" permeated participant narratives at this time and will be discussed as part of this superordinate theme.

The fourth and final theme describing participant experience, entitled "Making Connections," examines participants' interpretation of the impact of the yoga-ACT group in linking the content and process of the group with managing environmental triggers and internal processes. These are described by participants as "Bridging the Gap" and "Continued Learning" and these will be discussed in relation to participants' descriptions of the extent to which attending the group has impacted daily life.

Developing awareness

A common thread throughout participants' experience of the intervention was the importance of accessible and accurate information regarding both their brain injury and understanding why it was challenging to cope with emotions and thoughts with an impacted brain. Many participants reflected on previous experiences of trying to ascertain what was happening for them in the aftermath of the brain injury and how difficult this was.

Jessica: I was back in the hospital seeing my orthopaedic surgeon and he was asking me how was I, and I mean I was green. I couldn't do anything. Just, I had, you know, found it difficult to form a sentence, memory and concentration issues, motion sickness, what else, emm, difficulty making decisions, finding it hard to control my feelings, all those types of things and so he asked me how I was, and I said, "God not great." So I was listing out the things, and I didn't know what they were at the time. So he said to me then that, "Sorry now I'm going to stop you there. I'm only interested in the physical injuries." "Oh, right," I said. "I thought you were asking me how I was!"

Gemma: I suppose initially because of my background in sport I would've known a lot of people who have had concussions and bounced back and you initially, I was like, "Sure this will be grand. I'll be grand in a week." And then it was, "I'll be grand in a month," and then, "I'll be grand in three months." So it took a long time, I suppose, for it… it took actually until I came to Headway for it to be actually identified that I actually had a brain injury.

Helen: I suppose understanding that I had a brain injury was a big thing, and it wasn't until actually that my husband came to Headway to a spouses group meeting, em, that it all kind of came together for us as to why I was feeling the way I was feeling and the symptoms that I was having and stuff, so that was, ah, the first step in acknowledging that there was something wrong there, I suppose.

Participants described how attending the yoga-ACT group facilitated a learning about how the brain works and that this offered some relief.

Mary: Before I started, I was literally all over the place. I just couldn't make head nor arse nor tail of it, and just with the work that the psychologist was doing, basically giving strategies and how to, you know… making me re-evaluate things and think about things. If I didn't have that, I think I would have gone off the rails over the last two weeks with the stuff that's going on at home. So that's really, really, really after helping.

The experience of accruing more information and knowledge about how the brain works appeared to be useful in developing compassion for the self and current experience.

Scott: I always felt good after the group anyway. You were kinda understanding more about the brain, like, and sympathy for yourself. That was weird. It felt good.

John spoke about how the practice of engaging with his body alerted him that he was holding on to something. While John did not label what that was, it appeared to be helpful for him to attend to movement within the yoga poses, and a release then took place.

John: When we was in the group and you could connect, consciously connect with your body, and you have to try and let go and doing the poses helped with that to just breathe, like, and let go.

Similarly, Jessica described a difficulty with knowing what was happening for her emotionally and that becoming more aware of emotions was a freeing process, and she described an ownership of her feelings.

Jessica: Before, I always looked outward in my jobs and in my, just in the way that I was. I never looked into myself, ever, so I think I was a bit of an emotional, I think I was a bit restricted emotionally actually, whereas now I'm more aware, and that helps things. I suppose it was kind of liberating in a way, you know, to say, "I have these feelings and yeah it's ok to feel that way," and really embrace them and stay with them and breathe. The breath of course has really resonated hugely with me, because it's helping me.

The process of developing awareness can, however, be experienced as somewhat aversive, as described by Helen.

Helen: I'm not great for listening to my body, my feelings, my emotions. I'm not great with that side of things. I'd be a great person for lifting up the carpet and putting all the problems under the carpet, you know. Emm, and maybe that's what I'm trying to say about not being able to express my feelings and stuff. I probably try and forget that something has happened and continue. Emm, it's hard to forget that this has happened, unfortunately.

Helen described becoming aware of how trying to forget about her brain injury wasn't working for her and that alternative strategies were necessary in order to cope, as well as feeling reassured when given information about the brain injury.

Helen: I think it was the one where she introduced dropping anchor, emm, towards the start of the sessions. Emm, and I just remember being able to relate to that, to drop the anchor, I took from that and learnt that that was where I needed to slow down and start dropping anchor a bit more often. I just understood things from the way that she (psychologist) explained them, which obviously helped me to think, "Ok, you're not going crazy. This is what's wrong with you and this is what you need to do."

The narrative of the yoga-ACT group as providing a sense of direction was shared by Maeve.

Maeve: I go to the monthly adjustment group, which is great too, but what was so good about this was I felt relaxed coming out of it after a rest at home, able to do a few things or plan for tomorrow, and that's huge for me.

Cocooning

Cocooning explores participants' experiences in relation to a growing sense of safety in their changed life experiences and self-appraisals and building a place of rest. This part of participants' narratives entailed a growing development of working towards a balanced view of the self and granting the self permission to rest while continuing to work towards achieving rehabilitation goals.

Jessica: Yeah and the nest, you know the cocoon, like, I thought that was a lovely thing because that really suits me down to the ground... So for her (yoga teacher) to say, like, you know, make a cocoon for yourself, and if you feel a certain way to actually say it's ok to feel that way and rather than being in a cage, be in a cocoon and feel it, and I suppose I was always running away from... like, since my brain injury, I haven't been able to access my feelings because I wasn't that way before it and this probably compounds it or something.

Jessica described experiencing the yoga-ACT group as a space in her life whereby she was not just permitted to engage with her emotions but encouraged to. The challenges Jessica described in accessing her feelings are shared by Scott, albeit in a different way.

Scott: Well before the brain injury I didn't have emotion. Now it's shit really. I'm having to feel things all the time. Just the bad emotions. It's exhausting. A couple weeks after I started (the group) I could sleep better. And that's lasted, like, it's gone back a little less now because I didn't have the yoga this week. I used to fall asleep at half nine when the yoga was on, but it's getting later now again. I used to be wrecked tired when half nine came, I'd be asleep by ten and sleep through the night.

Scott's narrative describes the exhausting experience of feeling his distressing emotions all the time and not having strategies to manage them. He also notes how tiring this process is and how he experienced the yoga group as helping him to sleep in order to have energy to manage those emotions. The need for rest and a place for healing was described as important by participants, with fatigue impacting significantly on daily life.

Mary: That was the only space for my healing. Other than that, I've done a lot of the talking, counselling and you know that helps, yeah, you get some accept-ance, but it leads to a lot of frustration, you don't really switch off, whereas with the yoga you get that chance to rest.

The importance of a space to rest and heal was described in stark contrast to other parts of the recovery journey.

Mary: Like, there was a couple of weeks where they would've said things like, "It's ok to just stop and feather your nest and go into your cocoon and actually heal and just stop pushing," and you know that's the opposite of what everyone else is telling you. Everyone else is telling you push, push, push, push, push, keep going, keep going, keep going, keep going and you know what, it was actually good to hear someone saying, "No just stop. *Just allow yourself a few weeks to just heal. And if you need to push you need to push, but sometimes you just need to ... heal. And you need to cocoon and you need to stop," and you know, you don't hear that from too many people. They're always saying you know try this, try this, do this, do that.*

John: I enjoyed the silence with myself. It just was different. I don't know I enjoyed the yoga, the lying down, the first bit lying down, and just relaxing and being in silence with yourself. I liked that and it's good to do it in the group. I don't get that chance often. I do a load of physiotherapy for my arm, and I really push myself.

Building confidence

Participants reflected how within the group, as yoga poses progressed, a sense of physical agency emerged.

Gemma: I could see as the weeks went on that yes, I did improve in physically able to do better poses or be more comfortable in the poses. Emm, so yeah, it was enjoyable. I don't often get that feeling of achieving something, whereas I used to a lot in sport, in work, but now it's pretty rare.

Participants reflected on what it is like to be different from their pre-injury selves and the impact this has for their sense of self. Jessica was an extremely busy professional with a full academic, social life and a passion for music prior to her injury.

Jessica: I was always busy busy. I was studying I had just finished the postgrad and was continuing to finish the master's, so I was always doing and always busy. And now I suppose it has changed, and I found that very hard. Emm, I found it hard to look at, to accept that I am different, I am changed.

Mary: Just as a teacher, you're kinda saying, "Why couldn't I do homework," ya know. But now, if I'm doing homework with them this year, I'm starting to do it with them, but I'm still not able to really. Stuff like maths, I just can't do it. I just go, "Pff, sorry, wait till Dad comes home." Or, one of them is falling behind in fractions, and that should be bread and butter to me. I'm a resource teacher; I should be up to it, and I just don't have the brain capacity it's as if my brain has so much energy for a week or a day, and once that's used up, it's used up.

Having the space to develop a new skill and repeating that skill over the course of the weeks was described as positive.

Maeve: I'll never be putting my leg behind my ears, but just seeing that I could do a tiny bit more over the weeks and maybe not needing the block or the bolster was great. I felt good about myself.

Jessica: You have that form of getting your heart rate up in a gentle way and you can do it with a mat on the floor of your house, so if you are house-bound you can do that. You don't actually have to go anywhere. It's gentle and you do it to your own level, and I think that's important as well, so you can say, "Yes I did it," and feel like a bit of an accomplishment of sorts.

The participants appeared to reflect on the group as a place where they could be an achiever again, particularly for those who perhaps experienced a great deal of accomplishment in life prior to the brain injury.

Making connections

The final theme describes participants connecting strategies from the group with situations in their life and applying those to manage those events.

John: Yeah. Like, in the group I didn't notice a whole pile of difference in me. But then my sister came back one week, and family can be a trigger for everyone, and I was calmer with her and I adjusted with her while getting my point across, like, she wants my bed, my car and half my dinner, so one day I says, "Come on, you want my bed, my car and my dinner. That's not on!" So I was calmer with her and still saying what I needed to say, like.

For other participants, integration took place within the group.

Gemma: The psychologist there who was, you know, always tying you back into your head and then with the yoga you had the connection with your body, so it was feeling a bit together when you were leaving the group.

Jessica spoke about how her emotions and body felt disconnected prior to beginning the group and then experiencing connection.

Jessica: Yeah, I couldn't bring them together, like, if I was doing one, I couldn't do the other. So I was going to the gym and I ... I couldn't... The emotion stuff was all funny then. You know, it was working against each other almost, because I was... You know what I was doing? I was tiring myself out so much that I couldn't emotionally invest in my emotions, you know. I feel the incorporating of the yoga with the psychology is brilliant because I had been going to the gym, but I think I nearly became obsessed with it because, I don't know, I just wasn't engaging with my emotions and I needed an injection of something, and this was perfect because it was linked to the emotion so it was all working together. So that was really powerful for me.

Mary spoke about how psychology and yoga combined allowed her to access the content of the group, and the process facilitated her connecting with the material and learning and applying discussed strategies throughout her week.

Mary: Even when the yoga teacher, she's still doing all of the psychology, kinda reinforcing everything again, so ya know, sometimes when you hear it once you mightn't take it in, but when you do it a few times, it's kinda like a kinaesthetic learner, you're moving and you're learning. So it was kind of like all the different types of intelligence were addressed in it, so no matter kind of, em, what your learning style was before the accident and your current learning style is, because they nearly hit every type of learning. You had the visuals, you had the sound, you had the movement, they had the music. You know, if you actually ticked off all the seven learning styles, each one was hit every week. I don't think I actually realised they were doing that, but it meant that you could take it in, you could process it, you could think about it, and during the week, then you could make the changes, you know.

Similarly, Jessica described a connection and a movement between knowing and doing.

Jessica: I'm beginning to change the knowing into the doing, you know, that bridge, that's a massive bridge. And I think that I am particularly slow at that personally. I find that transition is particularly difficult, because I find it difficult to make connections more now than I used to. Connections for me would be a difficulty and recognising could take me an hour. I'm kinda slower at making connections so I probably need it said more times or I need to think about it more times than I used to. And this kind of lets me do that without going mad at myself. Like, I still do a bit, but it's definitely less.

Contextualising the findings

The process of adjustment begins with developing awareness, before making sense of and coping with a changed life post-ABI can take place (Ownsworth, 2015). A brain injury is a physical trauma, however, it is also a psychological trauma, as the individual is left with the task of reconstructing the self. In the study, participants described a sense of loss of their pre-injury selves and how this acute awareness of the discrepancies of the present self was jarring and aversive and managed partly by avoidance of emotion. However, avoidance of emotion, while functional in some respects, is maladaptive in the long term, maintaining psychological distress and impairing engagement with rehabilitation (Shields et al., 2016).

Awareness of one's emotions, thoughts and behaviours must be facilitated in a tolerable manner, in order to promote useful self-reflection, continued engagement with an intervention and application of strategies in daily life. The intervention of concern in this study may provide a way of tolerating the confrontation of the participants' distress. Participants' narratives described the group as an enjoyable intervention, whereby psychoeducation was imparted in a space where emotion was co-regulated by both peers and the bodily practice of yoga. Co-regulation of emotion is key to developing the self-regulation ability to manage emotion post-ABI (Ownsworth, 2015). The intervention created a space where emotions were discussed and contained, and this process appeared to become somewhat internalised by participants for use when triggered in daily life. This is a significant addition to the participants' reservoirs.

A dual-process transactional model is proposed to conceptualise the continuous contradictory dynamic faced by survivors in striving for improved functional outcomes while also accepting loss (Brands et al., 2012). This is experienced as an exhausting process of oscillation between two very different spaces, and rest to process and manage this journey is necessary.

The focus of rehabilitation for survivors and their families is recovery, to retrieve previous functioning and recapture previous ways of being. However, as described by participants, this is not always possible and the continued attempts, though necessary, may be aversive and disheartening. Participants' narratives suggest that the yoga-ACT intervention offered a space, and perhaps most importantly, permission to rest and heal or "cocoon" and bolster resources for the challenges of recovery.

The act of managing different parts of the self, the "am, not, was" journey, significantly impairs self-esteem and confidence, which in turn inhibits motivation (Dewar & Gracey, 2007). Similarly, engaging in therapy, though the purpose is to support it, can be experienced as problem-focused, and attending to the past in a direct manner is an aversive experience to many. In comparison, participant narratives described the yoga-ACT group as a space where a focus on the presence of distress and strategies for managing emotion was balanced by a physical practice offering both energy and rest. The balance of that space appeared to facilitate growth in confidence and to offer a place where participants could experience mastery of a task. Survivors' experiences of adjustment in the later stages of recovery post-brain injury may be said to be characterised by disconnection, specifically disconnection between mind and body, pre-injury identity and current identity and disconnect from wider society (Levack, Kayes & Fadyl, 2010). The experience of having two distinct lives and being two different selves, pre- and post-brain injury, is reported by survivors. This process is perhaps best captured within a Y-shaped model, whereby the internal conflict between representations of past and current self is hypothesised as acting as the lynchpin of psychological distress (Gracey, Evans & Malley, 2009). The yoga-ACT group appeared to offer participants a space for connection with emotions, the body, identity and peers. It is the aim of therapy to support individuals in bridging the gap between knowing and doing in order to apply strategies, and participants' narratives suggested the successful application within the group of concepts to routines, with descriptions of increased ability to deal with challenging relationships, sleep and self-appraisals.

Strengths and limitations

These findings are solely representative of the experiences of this specific group of individuals within this specific intervention and should therefore be considered suggestive rather than conclusive in terms of their generalisability to other individuals with an ABI and how they may experience a similar group. The participants in the current study were unique in their individual characteristics, time since injury, type of injury, personality, socio-economic background and family support system. It was therefore challenging to construct a wholly coherent collective narrative among the sample. While all participants had experience of ABI and adjustment, it would be remiss to conceptualise these participants as indicative of a homogenous group. The possibility of retrospective biases throughout participant narratives is therefore a potential limitation. The researcher is also mindful that seven of nine participants agreed to interview and that the research is missing the voices of two participants' experiences.

Reflections of a clinical neuropsychologist

I was lucky enough to be introduced to ACT as a master's student. Since then, ACT has never represented a psychological therapy to be applied, but rather a chosen perspective in how I view the world. Yoga has served many functions in my life; it has helped me at times to pause, to come back into my body and connect with myself physically and psychologically with a sense of compassion and not criticism or judgement. Specifically, times when I have felt uncomfortable or uneasy in body either through inactivity, weight gain, pregnancy or post-partum, returning to yoga has been my first committed action, the first step in returning to a life guided by my values.

I remember one very vivid incident when I was walking toward the yoga studio, my mind had worked very hard reassuring me about how it was okay, probably even the best decision not to go in. I was uncomfortable, even in a battle of sorts with my body. How would focusing on it help? It would just magnify my distress – "Thanks, mind." As soon as I smelled the incense, my body relaxed; it was a physical, not a cognitive response. I spent the remainder of the night thinking about the clients I worked with, their relationships with their bodies post-injury and the expectations on them that they would just attend appointments, attend therapies, look at their faces, arms, legs in mirrors without enough consideration of the psychological impact of this. A number of consecutive "no shows" or "DNAs" results in termination of services, a punishment on top of pain. That was the genesis of the beginning of the idea of combining an ACT and yoga therapeutically in a group for people living with ABI. After some research, I came across Gordon, Borushok and Ferrell's wonderful workbook, *Mindful Yoga Based Acceptance and Commitment Therapy* (2019). This reassured regarding the synergy that exists between ACT and yoga and the clinical utility of combining both.

Jen, a superbly intuitive and compassionate yogi skilled in adapting yoga for people with differing abilities, joined me in creating this group. From the outset, we both wanted the studio to represent for our clients what the studio represented for us: a place of safety, a place to pause and a place of connection. Jen's call to "feather your nest" and "cocoon" allowed people to create a physical environment characterised by comfort and compassion. "Cocooning" in the pre-pandemic sense of the word relates to growing and transformative change. As a psychologist, I was able to work with the process in the room; the difficulties people encountered pausing and using adjustments such as chairs or blocks, etc., were often mirrored in the difficulties they experienced using adjustments or rehab techniques in their lives outside of the studio. Visuals were used in each group to support the participants' understanding and learning; many of these were ACT Auntie Louise Gardner's illustrations. The beginning of each group involved a visual overview of the previous session and questions/feedback regarding how clients found the practice or the ACT process in question. Each session closed with a repetition of that day's content. Clients were provided with copies of all materials; this was to support learning and memory. The group provided a safe, unified, therapeutic space to relate to what was happening, for people physically and psychologically "moving towards what matters," with a more whole, connected sense of self.

One of the group members, Jessica, despite attempting many times, had not played the piano since acquiring a brain injury. The end of the group was marked by a Kirtan yoga session, which involved Sanskrit chanting accompanied by the harmonium, an Indian instrument similar to an organ. The group, myself included, was moved to tears when Jessica asked the musician if she could play and she did. This move towards what matters for Jessica had not happened in her previous therapeutic engagement, either psychological or physical, as it had, she explained, represented homework of sorts, a challenge, a mountain to climb, and the fear of failing had led to avoidance, struggle and exacerbated distress. The group had refocused her on her values and playing the Kirtan in a safe space was a committed action towards what mattered to her. This group was undoubtedly my favourite part of my working week; it energised me personally and professionally. The vitality I felt made me aware of how much the group plugged me into my values of authenticity, acceptance, encouragement, flexibility and humour.

References

Brands, I. M., Wade, D. T., Stapert, S. Z., & van Heugten, C. M. (2012). The adaptation process following acute onset disability: An interactive two-dimensional approach applied to acquired brain injury. *Clinical Rehabilitation, 26*(9), 840–852. https://doi.org/10.1177/0269215511432018

Cope, S. (2006). *The wisdom of yoga: A seeker's guide to extraordinary living.* Bantam Books.

Dewar, B. K., & Gracey, F. (2007). "Am not was": Cognitive-behavioural therapy for adjustment and identity change following herpes simplex encephalitis. *Neuropsycholological Rehabilitation, 17*(4–5), 602–620. https://doi.org/10.1080/09602010601051610

Dick, A. M., Niles, B. L., Street, A. E., DiMartino, D. M., & Mitchell, K. S. (2014). Examining mechanisms of change in a yoga intervention for women: The influence of mindfulness, psychological flexibility, and emotion regulation on PTSD symptoms. *Journal of Clinical Psychology, 70*(12), 1170–1182. https://doi.org/10.1002/jclp.22104

Donnelly, K. Z., Baker, K., Pierce, R., St Ivany, A. R., Barr, P. J., & Bruce, M. L. (2021). A retrospective study on the acceptability, feasibility, and effectiveness of LoveYourBrain Yoga for people with traumatic brain injury and caregivers. *Disability Rehabilitation, 43*(12), 1764–1775. https://doi.org/10.1080/09638288.2019.1672109

Gordon, T., Borushok, J., & Ferrell, S. (2019). *Mindful yoga-based acceptance and commitment therapy: Simple postures and practices to help clients achieve emotional balance.* New Harbinger.

Gracey, F., Evans, J. J., & Malley, D. (2009). Capturing process and outcome in complex rehabilitation interventions: A "Y-shaped" model. *Neuropsychological Rehabilitation, 19*(6), 867–890. https://doi.org/10.1080/09602010903027763

Levack, W. M., Kayes, N. M., & Fadyl, J. K. (2010). Experience of recovery and outcome following traumatic brain injury: A metasynthesis of qualitative research. *Disabililty Rehabilitation, 32*(12), 986–999. https://doi.org/10.3109/09638281003775394

Lundgren, T., Dahl, J., Yardi, N., & Melin, L. (2008). Acceptance and commitment therapy and yoga for drug-refractory epilepsy: A randomized controlled trial. *Epilepsy & Behavior, 13*(1), 102–108. https://doi.org/10.1016/j.yebeh.2008.02.009

Ownsworth, T. (2015). To err is human; to self-regulate after brain injury, divine. *Brain Impairment, 16*(3), 236–242. https://doi.org/10.1017/BrImp.2015.26

Robinson, P. L., Russell, A., & Dysch, L. (2019). Third-wave therapies for long-term neurological conditions: A systematic review to evaluate the status and quality of evidence. *Brain Impairment, 20*(1), 58–80.

Shields, C., Ownsworth, T., O'Donovan, A., & Fleming, J. (2016). A transdiagnostic investigation of emotional distress after traumatic brain injury. *Neuropsychological Rehabilitation, 26*(3), 410–445. https://doi.org/10.1080/09602011.2015.1037772

Silveira, K., & Smart, C. M. (2020). Cognitive, physical, and psychological benefits of yoga for acquired brain injuries: A systematic review of recent findings. *Neuropsychological Rehabilitation, 30*(7), 1388–1407. https://doi.org/10.1080/09602011.2019.1583114

Smith, J., Flowers, P., & Larkin, M. (2009). *Interpretative phenomenological analysis: Theory, method and research* (Vol. 6). Sage.

Soo, C., Tate, R. L., & Lane-Brown, A. (2011). A systematic review of acceptance and commitment therapy (ACT) for managing anxiety: Applicability for people with acquired brain injury? *Brain Impairment, 12*(1), 54–70.

Tooze, O., Karl, A., Dysch, L., & McLaughlin, D. (2014). An exploration of Acceptance and Commitment Therapy for chronic pain in multiple sclerosis. *Neuro-Disability and Psychotherapy: A Forum for the Practice and Development of Psychological Therapies for Neurological Conditions, 2*, 1–18. https://doi.org/10.13140/2.1.3071.5524

Van der Kolk, B. (2014). *The body keeps the score: Brain, mind, and body in the healing of trauma*. Penguin.

Whiting, D., Deane, F., McLeod, H., Ciarrochi, J., & Simpson, G. (2019). Can Acceptance and Commitment Therapy facilitate psychological adjustment after a severe traumatic brain injury? A pilot randomised controlled trial. *Neuropsychological Rehabilitation*. https://doi.org/10.1080/09602011.2019.1583582

Whiting, D., Simpson, G., Ciarrochi, J., & McLeod, H. (2012). Assessing the feasibility of Acceptance and Commitment Therapy in promoting psychological adjustment after severe traumatic brain injury. *Psychological Assessment, 27*(2), 415–423. https://doi.org/10.1037/pas0000050

Yeates, G., Murphy, M., Baldwin, J., Wilkes, J., & Mahadevan, M. (2015). A pilot study of a yoga group for survivors of acquired brain injury in a community setting. *Clinical Psychology Forum, 267*, 46–51. https://doi.org/10.53841/bpscpf.2015.1.267.46

Chapter 3

ACT with older adults after stroke

Ana Rita Silva, Paula Castilho and Sérgio A. Carvalho

Using Acceptance and Commitment Therapy (ACT) with older adults on the onset of medical adverse events

The increasing demographic shifts in the world population (e.g., increase in average life expectancy) (e.g., Dattani et al., 2023) are expected to potentially result in a higher number of older adults seeking and/or needing mental health services. This has led to international joint efforts to duly provide mental health services for older adults (Age Barometer, 2020), which calls for the development of empirically supported therapies that are tailored to address the developmentally-specific mental health needs of older adults. Cognitive Behaviour Therapies (CBT) are amongst the most effective psychosocial approaches with older adults struggling with psychological distress. Also, interventions that focus on problem solving (an intrinsic element of CBT) have proved effective in reducing both depression and anxiety problems in older adults without cognitive impairment. However, these findings do not seem to hold for older adults with comorbidities, or those who are medically ill or significantly dependent. For example, with frail elderly groups, CBT showed suboptimal results in reducing anxiety and depression (e.g., Gellis & Bruce, 2010). This happens to be the case for post-stroke depressed older adults, for whom some studies suggest a standard CBT approach is no more effective than standard care (e.g., selective serotonin reuptake inhibitors; Lincoln & Flannaghan, 2003; Hackett et al., 2008).

In addition to the insufficient evidence supporting the wide use of standard CBT with older adults who have socially and psychologically impactful medical conditions (with the frequent co-occurrence of depression and anxiety as deleterious effects of their medical illness burden), the specific psychological and developmental characteristics of the ageing population suggest that a transdiagnostic approach would be a fitting and potentially more effective one for promoting mental health in this age group (>60 years old). Looking at the way Baltes (1997) describes determinants of successful ageing, one might put forward that the aims of well-living as we age are to accept declines that are permanent, as well as to identify goals that are still pursuable. As such, the ability to let go of unattainable goals and replace them with those more feasible is considered adaptive behaviour with beneficial effects on mental health. Additionally, accepting unsolvable problems, instead of simply struggling to eliminate them, is an important self-regulatory skill contributing

DOI: 10.4324/9781003193722-4

to older adults' well-being (Krause, 2004). Moreover, the fact that ageing is also a period of overall improved resilience, where individuals are more capable of dissociating from past feelings and current feelings (decreasing cognitive fusion) (Zautra et al., 2000), draws on the importance of a therapeutic approach that builds upon the individuals' strengths.

Acceptance and Commitment Therapy (Hayes, Strosahl & Wilson, 1999) appears as a particularly suitable approach for older individuals, considering both the intersection of the singularities of ageing psychological functioning patterns and the highest prevalence of co-occurring medical conditions posing the older individuals with more challenges to live according to their deep values and strengths (Wetherell et al., 2011).

Stroke and psychological distress in older adults: The suitability of ACT

Stroke has its highest incidence in individuals aged 65 years and older, with population-based studies describing approximately 70% of events of stroke occurring in individuals in this age group (Feignin et al., 2021), and is the third-leading cause of disability (Johnson et al., 2016). With associated physical and psychological sequelae, when stroke occurs in older individuals their frailty related to other organic ageing processes may increase significantly. In the process of recovery after stroke, older adults are at higher risk of functional dependence and institutionalization (Lui & Nguyen, 2018). Amongst the more impactful sequelae of stroke that can contribute to an increase in psychological distress and poorer mental health outcomes, chronic pain, depression, anxiety and fatigue are amongst the leading challenges for these individuals. Despite symptoms of post-stroke depression being increasingly recognised and considered relevant for physicians, older adults seem to be unaware of their mental health problems, presenting difficulties in recognizing their symptoms of depression or anxiety (Wetherell et al., 2011). Given that ACT's ultimate therapeutic goal is to promote skills that are conducive to a more meaningful life according to a person's deeply held values, rather than directly targeting symptomatology, one might conclude that ACT would resonate more with elderly clients and would likely result in higher engagement with the therapeutic process. As such, a core task of ACT with older adults is to clarify personally held values in the face of increasing dependence, frailty and loss of capacities (e.g., cognitive functioning), as well as promote commitment with meaningful valued actions. As a transdiagnostic proposal, irrespective of the level of impairment (e.g., functional, cognitive, emotional), severity or type of sequelae following stroke faced by an older individual, ACT is a flexible approach that should be adapted to the specific needs of these populations. Additionally, and related to this work of reconnecting the older adult with their values, at the heart of ACT with post-stroke older adults is the development of a more expanded sense of life *purpose*. Although purpose is an intrinsic element in values work, it needs to be addressed in a larger context when working with older adults struggling with post-stroke impairment (Pektus & Wetherell, 2013). For example, values work should contextualize and incorporate a perspective taking on end-of-life issues. Additionally, we suggest that the ACT therapist should be willing to address spirituality, as it might be a critical subject that could provide success for an ACT approach with older adults.

In addition to values work, a clear parallel and intersection pathway that should be acknowledged when using ACT with older adults is the fusion with a negatively conceptualized self (i.e., a "damaged" self) – whether resulting from the stroke sequelae of functional and chronic impairment, or from negative beliefs about ageing (self-ageism). Thus, another core goal of ACT with this population is to address clients' cognitive fusion with a negatively conceptualized self, and to encourage them to reconnect with their self-as-context, fostering a sense of self that goes beyond the limitations of the body, and that exists despite (or with, one should say) the chronic illness that resulted from stroke.

We will now describe several practical examples of exercises that address these issues, and that we suggest could be incorporated in ACT with post-stroke older individuals.

We will finish this chapter by addressing several adaptations that should be considered when implementing ACT with these patients when they have cognitive impairment (which accounts for about 35% of older adults' cases of stroke). We will also briefly comment on adaptations that might benefit an ACT intervention with patients who are homebound or institutionalized, taking these considerations upon our experience with older adults in psychotherapy and neuropsychology settings.

ACTing with purpose

Despite advances in modern medicine and medical technology, cerebrovascular accident (CVA), or stroke, encompasses a substantial mortality and morbidity risk to the individual with an increased economic burden to the society. Medical complications resulting from stroke impose on many patients a marked disruption in functioning, thus suggesting the need to promote not only a functional recovery but also a psychological and emotional one. Psychological suffering and the presence of mental disorders may contribute to a similar or higher impact on functioning, as well as on quality of life and satisfaction with life. Specifically, anxiety and depressive symptoms have a negative influence on patient rehabilitation, and increase symptom severity and the number of reported health and social problems such as fatigue, memory, physical complaints and less social connection (Aben et al., 2002; Nijsse et al., 2017; Schottke & Giabbiconi, 2015). As such, there is a need to develop an optimal stroke disease-management plan, incorporating a comprehensive stroke psychological program. ACT is an interesting approach for stroke patients who suffer from psychological distress (e.g., Graham et al., 2015; Majumdar & Morris, 2019; Siantiru, Keliat & Wardani, 2018). The emotional, cognitive and interpersonal impact of this clinical condition calls us to consider the role of psychological processes such as contact with the present moment, acceptance and commitment with valued actions on recovery, purposefulness and overall adjustment to stroke-related limitations. Instead of applying cognitive restructuring techniques as used in traditional CBT, ACT focusses on learning to accept both the negative and positive internal experiences (e.g., thoughts, feelings) related to circumstances that cannot be changed or controlled, to discover and carry out values-based behaviour while feeling distressed, to be present with both internal and external events and to experience the self as a perspective, a locus from which a person's experience unfolds – i.e., a sense of self that has no boundaries (Barnes-Holmes, Hayes, & Dymond, 2001). ACT may be considered a paradigm shift in behavioural therapy tradition in the sense that it postulates a change in the way a person relates to their psychopathological symptoms and maladaptive processes (e.g., anxiety, depression, apathy, shame and dysfunctional coping styles), from struggling to control it to willingly experiencing it, to increase functioning in contexts where avoiding or escaping anxiety, depression, rehabilitation or medical procedures and social interactions would lead to undesirable life outcomes (Hayes et al., 1999). Additionally, research suggests that changes towards more positive attitudes toward the self and others as a result of mindfulness and/or compassionate practices play an important role in improving mental and physical health (Germer & Siegel, 2012; Wilson, 2009).

In line with this, a deep acknowledgment and understanding that life abounds with suffering is the route towards resilience and acceptance of each life change, both good and bad, each moment at a time. This profound wisdom of the ever-changing nature of life opens the door to potentially transcending the physical, mental and emotional dimensions of suffering, and provides clarity to engage in actions that result in vital and meaningful lives. This awareness in each life trajectory and throughout the lifespan is free from impatience, judgment and categorizing (Tirch, Schoendorff, & Silberstein, 2014). Connecting to this place of nonjudgmental awareness, in all life circumstances, including when going through such an overwhelming experience as a stroke, means cultivating personal awareness and touching the unaffected stillness of who is the "I" who is experiencing it. The wisdom to develop a wise self necessarily involves self-reflecting practices that foster the ability to truly see ourselves as we are, as well as to wholly recognise the inevitable rise and fall of all forms of life. This wisdom also involves behavioural flexibility, curiosity and openness to the process of making choices in life in the face of pleasant or unpleasant experiences. Thus, wisdom also stands in recognition that the consequences will be present no matter the choices we make, which results in life being a dance in transient forms. If we look attentively to all there is around us, we realize that everything is in everlasting change: our cells die, the neurons in our brains deteriorate, our facial expressions are always changing according to our dispositions and our personality traits are in fact just a "mental stream". This wise understanding puts us before what we have – the present moment – thus rooting us in what really matters. One might argue that purpose is only truly found when we are willing to come into contact with our own ageing, bodily decadence and death (Chodron, 2000). Sitting with awareness of choice, its consequences and death may require being bold in life. This is flagrantly necessary when facing difficult challenges in life, such as when getting older and going through major negative health events such as a stroke. At the core of ACT's values work with post-stroke older adults is necessarily a reflection on what it means to be human, which inevitably drives a discussion on socially designed qualities that are phylogenetically engrained in our evolved makeup. We suggest that one key goal of ACT with post-stroke older adults is to foster a deep awareness that internal events rise and fall in a continuous stream of experience. In the context of therapy with post-stroke patients, moving into the space of conscious and connected well-being means facing life and its inherent chaos with flexibility – i.e., being able to respond, in the moment, in a way that is healthy and values-driven.

The impermanence and the uncertainty after stroke

Our contemporary existence did not prepare us for sudden illnesses and their limitations and sequelae, nor for social disconnection, loneliness, disappointment with a frail body and consequently with death. Most times we have to learn to cope with these difficult elements of life as we go along, when they actually occur and/or when recovering from them. Having this truism as a starting point helps us, as ACT therapists, to promote an understanding to those clients who are struggling with post-stroke impairment, by helping them cultivate a present-moment awareness, as well as get to know the nature of the mind and body. We tend to be forgetful that, everyday (even for those who have a meaningful life) illness, ageing, loneliness, detachment and death will inevitably come. It is mind-boggling that, considering all the infinite knowledge we accumulate, it does not include ways to effectively face illness, death and life's overall unpredictability. The loss of functioning and changes inherent to an acute stroke and the pain that might accompany it, as well as death itself, are natural and inescapable processes. In a certain way, the inevitability and uncertainty that go with the experience of having a stroke make worrying about its consequences a futile effort to control. It should be expected, understood and recognised as such. Understanding that life, just like health, is fragile is hence knowing it is precious. As an ACT therapist, one should help post-stroke older clients relearn how to cope with frailty, with irreversible changes, while simultaneously discovering a new sense of purpose and the beauty of life at each moment. Meditation about loss and death is the most straightforward way to convey this knowledge, as well as to help rediscover personal values. It is crucial for the ACT therapist to help the stroke patient learn the grammar of kindness, and to use it when navigating their daily experience. A few *mantras* might be incorporated in mindful meditations, with an open heart, such as, "*I am susceptible to ageing, to illness, to death*". The ACT therapist might also help cultivate a stance of acceptance and self-care, recognizing that one is suffering and responding to it with warmth and kindness, through a compassionate meditation (*metta*) practice directed at their illness and impairment. Helping clients cultivate compassion not only strengthens kindness and care towards personal suffering but also promotes practical and sustained determination in doing everything what is necessary and possible to alleviate one's suffering (Brach, 2003; Harris, 1997).

BOX 3.1 BRIEF COMPASSIONATE MEDITATION DIRECTED TO A SUFFERING AND VULNERABLE BEING

- Find a comfortable position, one that conveys presence and curiosity. Gently close your eyes. Take two or three deep breaths, exhaling calmly... letting go of any tension.
- Feel the weight of gravity on your body seated on the floor or on a chair. Imagine the physical sensations of your body as if they were roots connecting you to the earth, to its core. Let yourself feel the connection of your posture, firm, elegant, like a mountain.
- Bring to your mind someone that you like very much and is currently suffering – it may be an old friend who has suffered a stroke, or who is struggling with any other medical condition – one that needs compassion and kindness. It may even be yourself. Try to clearly visualize that person, or yourself.
- Feel the intention to be kind to that person (or towards yourself), as well as the quality of kindness. If you prefer, you can just gently smile, or you may let a word or image of kindness towards that person (or towards yourself) accompany your breathing.
- Try to connect with what that person (or yourself) needs to hear right now. What does that person or you need to hear? What does that person or you most want? What would that person or you want to receive from you?
- Just intentionally send that kindness to that person or towards yourself in each exhale. Just let this meditation be as easy as breathing itself.
- Now try to extend this stream of compassion in all directions, to all beings who currently struggle with physical, mental and emotional difficulties.
- Rest your mind in your present experience, and in your body.

Another important skill for coping with moment-to-moment changes is the ability to be in contact with present-moment experience with equanimity – which consists of a higher-level awareness of present-moment sensory, affective and cognitive experiences (Kabat-Zinn, 2005). This meta-cognitive awareness – "the element of the mind one continuously recollects while maintaining attention on a particular mental object" (Bodhi, 2005, p. 34) – leads to equanimity, which in turn leads to wisdom (Kabat-Zinn, 2013). The equanimity refers to a "neutral feeling", a mental experience that is neither pleasant nor unpleasant (Bodhi, 2005). Equanimity involves a level of impartiality that is not cold detachment but rather arises from a deep understanding of the transient, interdependent nature of reality (Goldstein, 2003). In a way, one might argue that equanimity is a different way of self-caring, based both on emotional intimacy and wise discernment.

Below, given that equanimity can be cultivated through self-directed language, we propose the combination of equanimity phrases with giving and receiving compassion – which is crucial in the midst of physical and emotional pain (Germer & Neff, 2019).

BOX 3.2 EQUANIMITY MEDITATION WITH A COMPASSIONATE ATTITUDE

- Please find a comfortable position and take a few deep breaths to settle into your body and into the present moment. Take a few moments to be aware of your body and breathing, giving yourself this moment to just be.
- Bring to mind someone who is in a similar situation as yourself – someone whom you care about, and who is suffering and has had a stroke. Visualize the situation and the person clearly in your mind and feel the struggle and the suffering of that person in your body.
- Now, please listen carefully to these words, letting them gently roll through your mind and heart:

Everyone is on their own life journey. (Pause 20 seconds.)
I am not the cause of this person's suffering, nor of my personal suffering, nor is it entirely within my power to make it go away, even though I wish I could. (Pause 20 seconds.)
Moments like these can be difficult to bear.
But still, I may try to help if I can.

- Be aware of the stress you are carrying in your body; inhale fully and deeply. Let yourself be soothed. Allow your mind to rest and to be soothed inwards in each inhale.
- As you exhale, send an inner smile, or just easily exhale towards that person, or towards yourself, who is suffering.
- Continue breathing. As you inhale, send to yourself something good and kind (a smile, a gentle word), and as you exhale, send something good and kind to the other person you imagined.
- You may say to yourself: *One for me, one for you.*
- Noticing how your body is caressed from the inside as you breathe. Let yourself float on an ocean of compassion – a limitless ocean that embraces all the suffering.
- Listen again to these words with an open heart, allowing each word to echo inside you.

- When you are prepared, you can let go of this practice, allowing yourself to be exactly as you are in this moment.
- Gently open your eyes.

Purpose and active engagement after stroke

Living with purpose takes effort. Establishing a connection with life purpose means clarifying what really matters, as well as being committed to acting in a way that builds that meaningful path. Engagement involves the ability to identify closely held personal values and create larger patterns of action that are consistent with those values. When the ACT therapist engages the post-stroke patient in discussing specific behaviours that might embody these values, they are helping the patient engage with the world on their own terms rather than under the influence of self-constraining rules, learned from the social world and their learning history. Awareness of the ageing process and of the experience of stroke moves the patient towards the importance of making choices in the service of meaningful-based action. Underlying the work on fostering purposefulness and active engagement in the midst of post-stroke impairment is the cultivation of wisdom regarding the ever-changing process of identity, i.e., the self.

According to ACT literature, there are three ways of looking at the self: self-as-content, self-as-process and self-as-context. Self-as-content includes one's personal verbal descriptions and evaluations, and it is the self that one evaluates, avoids, and is fused with (Hayes et al. 1999). Some descriptions of self are relatively permanent (e.g., ethnicity or racial identity) while others describe one's occupation or activities (e.g., retired, teacher), and others are evaluations that remain relatively stable over time or might change over the course of hours, days or years (e.g., old, different, best employee, best friend). During case conceptualization, the therapist should identify statements that demonstrate an attachment to the conceptualized self (for a deeper dive into ACT practice focused on the self, see McHugh & Stewart, 2012). Self-as-process is the ongoing self-awareness or the sense of self where one notices ongoing processes, such as thoughts, feelings, and bodily sensations (e.g., "Now I am feeling anxious"). Buddhist psychology suggests there is no such thing as a permanent, unchanging self (Olendzki, 2010), and mindfulness meditation is a way of deepening our understanding of the ever-changing nature of the self, thus promoting a detached relationship with the contents of the mind towards a broader sense of consciousness (Kabat-Zinn, 2005). Self-as-context is the sense of self in which one notices the one that is noticing ("pure consciousness") (Hayes et al., 1999). The work on self-as-context is experiential, with a focus on personal experience, as well as with the use of metaphors (e.g., the chessboard metaphor).

In order to increase vitality and active engagement, it is crucial for clinicians to help post-stroke patients to notice their attachment with their prior self-representation and former abilities (the "healthy self"). Thoughts such as "I am not the same person", "I feel limited and lonely", "My life is not the same and will never be", "My life is boring", "I want to go back to my old self, before the stroke" may occur. Part of the self-as-context work in ACT is about reaching the ultimate awareness by shedding over and again thoughts, desires, hopes and fantasies. In fact, promoting self-as-context is about gaining awareness of permanent change, decadence and death, thus promoting a shift in perspective. It is about fostering the wisdom that fear, hopelessness, sadness and pain, as well as their associated sensations, are waves rising and falling. Holding all concepts of the self lightly, stepping in and out of each in the service of meaningfulness and purposefulness, is what helps us find a values-based life. Learning to recognise that the sense of "I" is more than any conceptualization of the self results in a higher ability to choose freely and significantly.

Next, we propose an exercise that may help these patients increase their psychological flexibility, via training the self as observer (i.e., a safe space for observation where anything – emotions, thoughts, physical sensations – can happen exactly as they are). The importance of mindfulness exercises cannot be stressed enough, as they may play a crucial role in treating post-stroke patients who are especially entangled with verbal behaviour and/or require a greater sense of the present moment. Mindfulness exercises, such as noticing one's thoughts or counting one's breaths, can facilitate the process of noticing thoughts and sensations here/now as opposed to being caught up with private negative events. Simultaneously, other processes can be integrated into practice before the following exercise dedicated to the self-as-context – which also cultivates decentering ("I am not these thoughts", "I am not this pain, this body", "I am not this fear", "I am not this sadness", "I am not this stroke"). Decentering is similar to cognitive defusion (Hayes et al., 1999) in the sense that by strengthening the ability to mindfully observe the ongoing mental activity, there is usually a shift in the sense of self – which starts being experienced as a psychological construction, a transient and impermanent system of concepts, sensations and beliefs.

One practice that might help the patient be aware of cognitive fusion/defusion is the mental polarity exercise (Hayes et al., 1999). Also, acceptance-focused exercises that help the client embrace a certain event or situation, regardless of their evaluations, as well as help them let go of futile agendas of control are helpful and are based on the idea that attachment and non-acceptance should be presented as a trap or a loser's game (Hayes et al., 1999). Another interesting exercise is the Chinese finger trap and Asian monkey trap metaphor, which shows the futility of struggle (Hayes et al., 1999). For the less-willing patients, it is useful to use willingness-fostering techniques or cultivate a sense of creative hopelessness. So, the following exercise should be introduced after previously having practiced shorter exercises to develop the ability to (1) notice, (2) accept and (3) let go.

BOX 3.3 REFLEXIVE EXERCISE

- Sit in a quiet place and rest your attention for a while on your body and your breathing.
- Against the background of your medical condition (stroke), try to think about the part of yourself you least enjoy. The one who is perhaps afraid, possibly in despair or maybe intimidated by the constraining sequelae and the possibility of having another stroke. The one who is fragile, tired, diminished. Whatever may be the least favourable part of yourself, let this sense of you be present. Please, reflect on these characteristics and sense of you. Let yourself touch the emotions and thoughts wrapped up in this aspect of who you are, have been and will be again. Imagine that something has happened, and this sense of self is completely swept away. Notice if there is anything you would need to hold with you, anything you might particularly miss from you? It does not matter; it isn't you anyway. You are more than this sense of yourself. And what would it take to let go?
- Now, imagine your "best self". The one who has courage and stands strong. The one who is healthy, smart, fierce. The one who is young, who laughs and is full of fun, the one who did not have the stroke. Whatever the best part of yourself is, let this sense of you be present. Please, reflect on the qualities of that sense of you. Let yourself touch the emotions and thoughts wrapped up in this aspect of who you are, have been and will be again. Imagine that something has happened, and this sense of self is completely swept away. Notice if there is anything you would need to hold with you, anything you might particularly miss from you? It does not matter; this isn't you anyway. You are more than this sense of yourself. And what would it take to let go? Bear in mind that any conceptualization of the self limits your freedom, even a conceptualized self you enjoy.

Willingness and committed action

In ACT, willingness is about behaving with a values-guided purpose in the face of psychological and physical obstacles. One exercise that might be helpful in promoting willingness and awareness of barriers is to join the patient in the eye contact exercise (Hayes et al., 1999). In this exercise, the therapist sits in front of the patient, almost knee to knee, and explains: "For the next few minutes, let's make eye contact and be fully present with one another in silence". While beginning to make eye contact, the therapist points out how difficult this exercise is, while noticing and monitoring what the patient does to avoid being present. For example, perhaps the patient starts looking away, wringing their hands, laughing or suppressing a laugh or talking. The therapist may say, "Notice how difficult it is to be fully present with another human being. Are you willing to be present with me and with your discomfort?". The therapist goes on by saying "How incredible it is that you are present with another human being, and that another human being is present with you".

The purpose of this brief exercise is to show the patient that they can experience discomfort and nonetheless act purposefully while being present. The goal is not to desensitize the client to anxiety, worry, shame or depression, but rather to foster psychological flexibility and experiential willingness and openness, for the patient to learn "to *feel* better (i.e., become better at feeling) and not to feel *better*" (i.e., feel less anxiety, shameful) (Eifert & Forsyth, 2005, p. 82). In other words, ACT conceptualizes depression, anxiety and other psychological outputs associated with stroke in terms of contextually controlled avoidance repertoires. According to ACT, these experiential avoidance repertoires are maintained because they are verbally controlled (rule-governed), are successful in the short run and block contact with or create insensitivity to other contingencies (Hayes & Ju, 1998). Experiential acceptance exposure requires the ACT therapist to be fully aware of the post-stroke patient's body language, given their possible physical and/or cognitive sequelae. Being aware of the way the patient is able to communicate through their body will be an extremely important step towards helping them follow an acceptance-based stance. Working through body experiences and helping the patient connect with themselves and build awareness and connection is crucial.

Observing multiple body-language behaviours may help the therapist understand and connect with the patient's situation as a whole. Thus, it is important to assess the meaning of the patient's body language. Body-language behaviours are helpful because they provide valuable information regarding experiential avoidance – closing your body down (e.g., getting smaller, hunching) – and acceptance – opening your body up (e.g., putting your arms out, sitting up straight). In addition, the congruence between verbal and nonverbal behaviour is also a crucial element: Does the nonverbal expression of the patient communicate the same meaning as his verbal expression? Does their spoken word match the tone of their voice? Do their gestures ring true to a specific emotion? Does the patient breathe deeply, relax their posture, and maintain eye contact during willingness work, or do they gaze down and fold their arms immediately after agreeing to conduct willingness work? Noticing the patient's body language and detecting its patterns can help the therapist plan their session, as well as help the patient improve their psychological flexibility and well-being, thus buffering the impact of the illness impairment. Importantly, a therapeutic relationship that encompasses present-centered eye contact, soft and warm voice tone, emotional attunement and active engagement provides the context in which the post-stroke patient can experience feelings of safeness, openness and courage. Indeed, body-language awareness plays an important role in intra- and interpersonal processes.

There are several exercises that may serve the purpose of promoting acceptance-based communication through body language. Body-focused practices that intend to foster body awareness seem appropriate.

BOX 3.4 BODY SCAN – NOTICING HOW YOUR BODY IS DOING (BASED ON KABAT-ZINN, 2013)

- Find a time and a place where you won't be disturbed, and where you feel comfortable and secure. A time to nourish your health and well-being. Remember that mindfulness is about being with things as they are, moment to moment, as they unfold in the present. Give yourself the space to be as you are. There are no specific sensations you should or shouldn't feel; what is important is to realize what is present in each moment. Some of the sensations can be pleasant or unpleasant, or even intense and you may notice that in some areas of the body you don't feel anything.
- Begin by making yourself comfortable. Sit in a chair and allow your back to be straight, but not stiff, with your feet on the ground. You could also do this practice standing or if you prefer, you can lie down and have your head supported. Your hands could be resting gently in your lap or at your side. Allow your eyes to close, or to remain open with a soft gaze. Take several long, slow, deep breaths. Feel the weight of your body on the bed or chair. Notice the points of contact between that and your body. Each time you breathe out, allow yourself to sink a little deeper into the bed or chair. Now, bring your attention to your breath, to the sensations of your breath. Be aware, the best you can, of your breath wherever it feels most predominant and comfortable for you.
- When you're ready, move your awareness down to the left leg, past the knee and ankle and right down into the big toe of your left foot. Notice the sensations with a sense of curiosity. Is it warm or cold? If you can't feel any sensations, that's okay. Just be aware of the lack of sensation. As you breathe, imagine the breath going down your body and into your toes. As you breathe out, imagine the breath going back up your body and out of your nose. I invite you to use this strategy of breathing into and out of each part to which you are paying attention. Expand your awareness to the sole of your foot. Focus on the ball and heel of the foot. The weight of the heel. The ankle. Breathe into the whole of the left foot. Then, when you are ready, let go of the left foot.
- Repeat this process of gentle, kind, curious, accepting awareness with the lower part of the left leg, the knee and the upper part of the left leg. Gently shift your awareness around and down the right leg, to the toes in your right foot. Move your awareness up the right leg in the same way as before. Then let it go.
- Become, now, aware of your pelvis, hips, buttocks and all the delicate organs around here. Breathe into them and imagine you're filling them with oxygen. Move up to the lower torso, the lower abdomen and lower back. Notice the movement of the lower abdomen as you breathe in

and out. Notice any emotions you feel here. See if you can explore and accept your feelings as they are.

- Bring your attention to your chest and upper back. Feel your rib cage raising and falling as you breathe in and out. Be, as best as you can, mindful of your heart beating. Allow space for your sensations to express themselves.
- Now, go to both arms together, beginning with the fingertips and moving up the shoulders. Breathe into and out of each body part before you move to the next one, if that feels helpful. Focus on your neck. Then move your mindful attention to your jaw, noticing if it's clenched. Feel your lips, inside the mouth, your cheeks, your nose, your eyelids and eyes, your temples, your forehead, the back of your head and finally the top of your head.
- Stay mindful and open up to the physical sensations with curiosity and warmth.
- Imagine the top of your head and the soles of your feet. Imagine your breath sweeping up and down your body as you breathe in and out. Try to get a sense of each of the cells in your body being nourished with energy and oxygen.
- Now, get a sense of your whole body. Feel yourself as complete, just as you are. At peace just as you are. Remember this sense of being is always available to you when you need it. Rest in this stillness.
- Come out of this meditation gently and bring this mindful awareness to whatever activity you do next. Gently open your eyes.

BOX 3.5 THREE CHAIR-BASED MINDFUL MOVEMENT PRACTICES

- I invite you to take some time exploring each of the three simple movement practices below. Remember, present-moment awareness, in the midst of movement, is the single most important aspect of this practice. Don't worry so much about getting the movement "right". Be curious about your relationship with movement and stretching and bring a gentle and playful attitude to your experience.
- Begin sitting and lift your arms out to the side, palms up, until your arms are shoulder-level and parallel to the ground. Breathing in, touch your shoulders with your fingertips, keeping your upper arms horizontal. Breathing out, open your arms to the horizontal position, stretching your palms open.
- When the mind wanders off into thoughts, ideas, dreams or worries, gently label it and then guide the attention back to a sense of the body as a whole.

- Now, extend your arms in front of you and join your palms. Breathing in, raise your arms up and separate your hands so your arms can stretch over your head. Breathing out, continue the circle, arms circling back until your fingers point toward the ground. Breathing in, lift your arms back and reverse the circle. Breathe out as you bring the palms of your hands together, and your arms down in front of you.
- Lastly, breathe in and bring your arms up above your head, palms forward. Look up at the sky. Breathing out, bend over at your waist as you bring your arms down to touch the floor, your ankles or your shins. Release your neck. From this position, breathe in, and keep your back straight as you come all the way back up to reach your fingers up toward the sky.
- Take a few moments now to feel again the body as a whole, breathing freely and letting the attention flow naturally through all parts of the body. And during the next few moments, feel the whole body breathing. Notice the skin, and the sensations of the skin, which, like an envelope, unites the whole body into one.
- End this practice by congratulating yourself on having devoted your attention to your body and yourself during this time, in a form of self-care. And when you feel ready, you can gently open your eyes.

Wrapping it all up for living deeply

The first step when starting an ACT approach with a stroke patient is to be fully aware and to be present. Before anything else, be fully aware that the patient, as well as their struggle, share more similarities than differences with the therapist. The therapist should be in touch with the common human aspect of suffering that the patient is going through.

The decision of where, within the hexaflex, the therapy should start will depend on many variables. It is known that elderly post-stroke patients might lose their willingness to maintain or search for a genuine and meaningful purpose in life (Norlander et al., 2018). In addition to the limitations and sequelae from stroke, the ACT therapist should consider the values underlying the patient's motivation to change and should be focused on helping the patient identify their core values. By focussing on the hexaflex work, the therapist helps promote a set of psychological processes that will enable the patient to better give themselves what they need.

Research shows that engaging in values-based behaviour improves physical and mental health, quality of life and self-compassion (Lejeune & Luoma, 2019; Lundgren et al., 2009). Knowing our own needs and values sustains our ability to respond to challenging situations with compassion, wisdom and willingness, even in situations where one is struggling to survive (McGehee, Germer & Neff, 2017). So, core values – such as creativity, generosity, being present to loved ones – are inherently meaningful; thus, they are the compass that defines in a meaningful way who we are and guides us emotionally and behaviourally. Core values are usually related to the way we treat others (e.g., honesty, generosity, loyalty) and are deeply connected to our emotional needs (e.g., creativity, tranquility, peacefulness).

Starting with core values

When exploring core values, the therapist is looking for what the patient holds dearly, their hopes and dreams, or conversely what underlies their deepest fears and regrets. Values work lies in therapeutic conversations that are themselves energizing and conducive to a sense of vitality. These conversations around values are not intellectualized; i.e., the patient is not required to "figure out" why these are core values. The therapist pays close attention to the way in which the patients emotionally express themselves to accurately assess their core values. The therapist should uncover core values that have been motivating the patient throughout their life. When conducting values work, the therapist should bring into therapy the internal and external obstacles to valued living, as these will help promote awareness of the willing vulnerability. Values can indeed appear through painful moments in life. Helping the elder post-stroke patient attend to their suffering in an open and mindful way can teach both the patient and the therapist much about who they are and who they wish to be in the world.

Discovering the value underlying suffering through willing vulnerability

An intrinsic part of being alive is the inevitability of suffering. Learning to find one's core values in moments of pain and suffering is paramount when working with post-stroke patients. Often patients with stroke-related limitations, as well as their caretakers and family members, shut themselves off from self-care to avoid difficult internal experiences of vulnerability – which can be an understandable way of coping with stroke-related trauma and traumatic events. The therapeutic setting may reverse these avoidant processes by enduring a space where patients can open to vulnerability and be fragile, creating a willingness to contact with emotional and physical pain, as well as reconnecting with values that provide meaning, purpose and fulfillment in life (LeJeune & Luoma, 2019; Walser, 2019). The therapist may promote values clarification through willing vulnerability by asking questions such as, "What does this pain and limitation tell me about what really matters to me?" or "What does this pain tell me about what I need to learn?" This gentle questioning not only promotes values clarification but also helps the patients touch on their personal suffering as well as provides the opportunity to learn how to manage it more effectively. It is crucial for therapists to clarify that vulnerability and suffering are not an end, but rather a means through which the patient connects with and honours their values.

Fostering willing vulnerability to connect with values requires the therapist to help the patient slow down, explore and contact with painful feelings they normally avoid. Pain and suffering are thus transformed from something to be avoided, diminished or white-knuckled through into something that has value precisely because it is linked to something the patient cares about.

After acknowledging and validating the patient's struggle with the limitations of their body and sequelae, it may be helpful to clarify that living in line with personal values usually entails engaging in different types of health-related behaviours with flexibility, as well as making the necessary adjustments that one's body and physical condition require.

One exercise that may help promote willingness and values clarification is the "sweet spot". The therapist asks the client to recall a specific time when something painful occurred in relation to the domain they are focussing on, such as loss, hopelessness or emotional pain related to the stroke. From there, the therapist explores the scene as they would with a sweet-spot memory, looking for what the patient is doing or not doing, what the patient sees and feels in that moment. The therapist must ask the patient to indicate when they have been able to imagine themselves in the moment of the sweet spot. It is important for the therapist to explore the scene from the inside: "What do you see? What do you feel or hear or smell in this place?" More than just what they are doing, the therapist should help the client contact the qualities of their action and how they are behaving, through an observing stance: "How do you describe this person that is watching you?" The therapist may help the patient by asking, "Help me have a clear idea of what the sweet spot is like from behind your eyes?" As these memories might entail suffering, the therapist must help the patient connect with their values by asking, "As you are there in that scene, do you notice anything that matters to you? What do you notice yourself longing for in the midst of this pain?" From the same observer perspective, the therapist might ask, "As you are watching the you that is there in this painful situation, what do you want for them? In your ideal world, if you could have that person in that painful situation do or say anything, what might that be?" The therapist should try not to focus on getting the patient to name a value or come to any precise conclusion. The therapist should pay particular attention to elements of the scene that have more vitality or a sense of choice, or where willing vulnerability seems to show up. The underlying goal here is to use the pain of presence vs the pain of absence to guide values exploration.

Cultivating happiness

Our evolutionary need for survival has programmed and oriented us more towards problem solving than toward cherishing the enjoyable aspects of our lives. This innate negative bias (i.e., an overfocus on the negative) posits the challenge and the need to intentionally pay attention to our positive experiences to develop a truly balanced awareness. For example, helping patients recognise and enjoy pleasant experiences may constitute a useful therapeutic target when working with post-stroke patients. The simple pleasure of lingering with positive sensations and emotions can be a radical discovery for patients. An example could be to ask the patient to do things as a means to appreciate sensations from the experience. For example, the therapist may ask the patient to gently rub their hands together and notice the sensations and allow themselves to enjoy the sensation of rubbing the hands (choice to savour).

Gratitude

In addition to promoting instances of savouring, another way of cultivating happiness is through fostering gratitude. Gratitude means appreciating the good things that life gives us. Several studies show that gratitude practices enhance well-being (Wood, Froh & Geragthy, 2010). In the face of usually permanent stroke-related limitations, helping these patients cultivate gratitude entails increasing their wisdom and understanding of the complexity of their situation. When patients practice gratitude, they gain awareness of the multiple factors, large and small, that contribute to their lives, and increase their connection to life and to others (Germer & Neff, 2019). One way of fostering gratitude is by asking the patient to list ten small and insignificant things (i.e., things that the patient usually recognises in their daily life) that make them feel grateful. For example, a buttoned-up jacket, warm water or a genuine smile.

It is worth mentioning that although this practice has a positive effect in promoting happiness, some patients might feel worse because they judge themselves for not being happier or more grateful. The therapist can bring out the common humanity of those feelings and reactions and encourage a self-acceptance and self-compassionate response. The therapist should ask the patient to practice this exercise every day, right before going to bed, by taking notice of ten small things that happened during the day for which they are grateful. This experiential exercise was originally developed by David Dewulf and is based on empirical data suggesting that counting blessings (i.e., gratitude) can generate positive emotions (Tugade, Fredrickson & Barrett, 2004).

Self-appreciation

Therapists can also help patients experience happiness by promoting an appreciation for their good qualities. Being able to recognise our own positive qualities is the first step to developing our ability to enjoy them. Working on promoting the patient's appreciation for their good qualities is especially important when considering our tendency to criticize ourselves and focus on our inadequacies, taking our qualities for granted, and undervaluing them.

**BOX 3.6 BRIEF EXERCISE – APPRECIATING
THE GOOD QUALITIES**

- Please close your eyes and let your awareness go to your body.
- Take a moment to think about three or four things you appreciate about yourself. See if you can open to what you really, deep down, like about yourself.
- If you experience any sort of weirdness or awkwardness, please make some space for whatever you are feeling and let yourself just be as you are.
- As best as you can, now focus on one quality that you appreciate about yourself. See if there are any people who helped you develop this good quality (friends, parents, teachers or other people in your life). And as you think of each positive influence, send them some appreciation, honouring all those who helped nurture you. Let yourself savour, even if just for a moment, feeling good about yourself.

Radical acceptance

The medical, psychological and social complexity associated with post-stroke rehabilitation indicates that one of the most balanced and useful ways of increasing well-being (instead of the overfocus on symptom reduction) is through fostering radical acceptance. By helping the patient radically accept the things that are out of their control, the ACT therapist helps prevent the patient from becoming stuck in unhappiness, bitterness, anger, sadness, helplessness and hopelessness.

As Brach suggests, radical acceptance is "clearly recognizing what we are feeling in the present moment and regarding that experience with compassion" (Brach, 2004, p. 73). Radical acceptance is not vouching nor approving, but rather being completely and totally willing to experience one's mind and body, especially those experiences that we cannot currently change. Mindfulness practice increases the ability to be fully present and away from distressing rumination, as well as helps cultivate an observing stance towards distressing thoughts and feelings. This, in turn, promotes the development of a contextual self-identity, as well as fosters values-based action that creates a sense of purpose and renewed vitality. The ACT therapist might help the post-stroke patient imagine, through their mind's eye, what they would do if they accepted what is currently unaccepted. Then, the patients should identify body sensations that arise throughout the exercise. Therapists should create a space where the patient can experience disappointment, sadness or grief. Finally, the patient should recognise the pros and cons of resisting acceptance and of avoidance.

Adapting ACT to older adults in special conditions: A personal clinician account of working with older adults

Throughout our practice as psychologists working with older adults, both in institutional settings (nursing homes) and consultation for neuropsychological rehabilitation after stroke or traumatic brain injury, we have witnessed a shift in perspective regarding core issues in working with elder post-stroke patients. Next, we will briefly share some of our personal reflections on critical issues arising when working with this population.

A) *Implementing ACT with aged populations, multi- and severely impaired and preconceived notions of their frailty*

We were initially faced with the challenge of implementing acceptance-based strategies with a group of older adults with a minimum of three or four chronic conditions, and our initial concern was our own view of them (and on ageing itself) as "excessively frail" to be able to accept and let their feelings and thoughts about their condition flow. A more extensive contact with the holistic neuropsychological rehabilitation approach, and with the ACT paradigm, enabled us to surpass these a priori considerations that attached our expectations for the intervention to our own "views" about ageing (and ageism) with chronic illnesses.

B) *Personal setbacks when working collaboratively with nursing staff and family members*

Although a deeper knowledge of ACT and holistic rehab was essential to break some a priori views about these individuals, it is often the case that the systems where older people may live are ultimately full of these stereotyping "views". Whereas we may work towards developing effective goal setting, commitment with goals and work to maintain motivation, the nursing staff and the family members usually communicate with an a priori stance of "frailty" and "incapacity", not serving the goal-setting work we pursue. Thus, it is critical to engage with strategies that mitigate the impact of these stereotypes on the intervention's success. Introducing ACT-consistent psychoeducation moments with nursing home teams and with family members can be especially useful by focussing on promoting awareness without judgment and stereotypes built upon cultural and self-history reinforcement, and by promoting an observation of these thoughts as what they are.

C) *The importance of the delivery format*

Stroke-related research using ACT has pointed to the advantages of delivering ACT in groups to pursue a sense of belonging and safety – contrarily to the perceived isolation post-stroke patients live in. However, it must be taken into account, especially in institutional settings, the heterogeneity of older adults with a history of stroke. We suggest that a blended approach that comprises first individual sessions and then group ACT sessions would possibly be the best-fitted approach in these cases. This could be particularly relevant when interacting with older adults with cognitive deficits, which is expectedly the case for at least half of the older adults after stroke living in nursing homes.

D) *A note on exercises with cognitively impaired clients: educational, experiential, metaphorical, flexible!*

Older adults with cognitive deficits have already proved to benefit from ACT, mainly when sessions incorporate a good balance between didactical and experiential exercises, and when sessions are more time-limited and exercises are repeated across sessions. For example, session adaptations might include (a) eliciting the same experience across more than one session, (b) recording exercises or visual metaphors for practicing between sessions, (c) planning skills to take advantage of one experience in one session to benefit from the following session. However, we should point out that the practitioner should not hold clinical decisions according to a "preview" of these deficits beforehand. ACT-consistent sessions should be flexible enough to be client-led, and not prepared presupposing the older adult will forget or will not benefit from some exercise or another.

E) *ACT and standards-of-care compatibility*

A large set of pursued goals described by older adults in rehabilitation settings are related to participation, i.e., to be able to participate in several activities that, due to their illness-related limitations, they are unable to take part in. There are several small adaptations (e.g., technical aids that support connection with their peers; chair lifts for stairs) that may support valued goal setting and enable the individual to maintain their participation in personally valued activities. This aligns with the standards-of-care paradigm on successful ageing (selective with compensations – SOC), which is ACT-consistent. Nevertheless, one should not forget that incorporating these compensatory aids will require the therapist to work with the client in their acceptance of those as means to valued goal achievement and to maintaining a purposeful life (Alonzo-Fernandez et al., 2016).

Summary

We have expanded throughout this chapter on some of the issues and specificities of delivering ACT to post-stroke older patients, as well as hopefully provided some useful exercises and reflection points. We highlight the importance of integrating both chronic illness functioning as well as adjustment of personal views of ageing as therapeutic targets. Also, we suggest that health professionals working with older adults struggling with post-stroke limitations may benefit from engaging in self-reflection on their own fusion with ageist beliefs in order to provide effective ACT-consistent services.

References

Aben, I., Denollet, J., Lousberg, R., Verhey, F., Wojciechowski, F., & Honig, A. (2002). Personality and vulnerability to depression in stroke patients: A 1-year prospective follow-up study. *Stroke, 33*, 2391–2395.

Age Barometer. (2020). https://www.age-platform.eu/sites/default/files/AGE_BAROMETER_2020.pdf

Baltes, P. B. (1997). On the incomplete architecture of human ontogeny: Selection, optimization, and compensation as foundation of developmental theory. *American Psychologist, 52*(4), 366.

Barnes-Holmes, D., Hayes, S. C., & Dymond, S. (2001). Self and self-directed rules. In S. C. Hayes, D. Barnes-Holmes, & B. Roche (Eds.), *Relational frame theory: A post-Skinnerian account of human language and cognition* (pp. 119–139). Kluwer Academic/Plenum Publishers.

Bodhi, B. (2005). *In the Buddha's words: An anthology of discourses from the pali canon.* Wisdom.

Brach, T. (2003). *Radical acceptance: Awakening the love that heals fear and shame within us.* Random House.

Brach, T. (2004). *Radical acceptance: Embracing your life with the heart of a Buddha.* Random House Publishing Group; Reprint edition.

Chodron, P. (2000). *When things fall apart: Heart advice for difficult times.* Shambhala Publications.

Dattani, S., Rodés-Guirao, L., Ritchie, H., Ortiz-Ospina, E., & Roser, M. (2023). Life expectancy. https://ourworldindata.org/life-expectancy

Eifert, G. H., & Forsyth, J. P. (2005). *Acceptance and commitment therapy for anxiety disorders: A practitioner's treatment guide to using mindfulness, acceptance, and values-based behavior change strategies.* New Harbinger.

Gellis, Z. D., & Bruce, M. L. (2010). Problem solving therapy for subthreshold depression in home healthcare patients with cardiovascular disease. *The American Journal of Geriatric Psychiatry: Official Journal of the American Association for Geriatric Psychiatry, 18*(6), 464–474.

Germer, C., & Neff, K. (2019). *Teaching the mindful self-compassion program: A guide for professionals.* The Guilford Press.

Germer, C. K., & Siegel, R. D. (Eds.). (2012). *Wisdom and compassion in psychotherapy: Deepening mindfulness in clinical practice.* The Guilford Press.

Goldstein, J. (2003). *Insight meditation: A psychology of freedom.* Shambhala Publications.

Graham, C. D., Gillanders, D., Stuart, S., & Gouick, J. (2015). An Acceptance and Commitment Therapy (ACT)–based intervention for an adult experiencing post-stroke anxiety and medically unexplained symptoms. *Clinical Case Studies, 14*(2), 83–97.

Hackett, M. L., Anderson, C. S., House, A., & Xia, J. (2008). Interventions for treating depression after stroke. *The Cochrane Database of Systematic Reviews*, (4), CD003437. https://doi.org/10.1002/14651858.CD003437.pub3

Harris, E. J. (1997). *Detachment and compassion in early Buddhism.* Buddhist Publication Society.

Hayes, S. C., & Ju, W. (1998). The applied implications of rule-governed behavior. In W. T. O'Donohue (Ed.), *Learning and behavior therapy* (pp. 374–391). Allyn & Bacon.

Hayes, S. C., Strosahl, K. D., & Wilson, K. G. (1999). *Acceptance and commitment therapy: An experiential approach to behavior change.* The Guilford Press.

Johnson, W., Onuma, O., Owolabi, M., & Sachdev, S. (2016). Stroke: A global response is needed. *Bulletin of the World Health Organization, 94*(9), 634.

Kabat-Zinn, J. (2005). *Coming to our senses: Healing ourselves and the world through mindfulness.* Hachette UK.

Kabat-Zinn, J. (2013). *Full catastrophe living: Using the wisdom of your body and mind to face stress, pain, and illness.* Piatkus.

Krause, N. (2004). Stressors arising in highly valued roles, meaning in life, and the physical health status of older adults. *The Journals of Gerontology Series B: Psychological Sciences and Social Sciences, 59*(5), S287–S297.

Large, R., Samuel, V., & Morris, R. (2020). A changed reality: Experience of an Acceptance and Commitment Therapy (ACT) group after stroke. *Neuropsychological Rehabilitation, 30*(8), 1477–1496. https://doi.org/10.1080/09602011.2019.1589531

LeJeune, J., & Luoma, J. B. (2019). *Values in therapy: A clinician's guide to helping clients explore values, increase psychological flexibility and live a more meaningful life.* New Harbinger.

Lincoln, N. B., & Flannaghan, T. (2003). Cognitive behavioral psychotherapy for depression following stroke: A randomized controlled trial. *Stroke, 34*, 111–115.

Lui, S. K., & Nguyen, M. H. (2018). Elderly stroke rehabilitation: Overcoming the complications and its associated challenges. *Current Gerontology and Geriatrics Research, 218*, 9853837. https://doi.org/10.1155/2018/9853837

Lundgren, J., Lundgren, T., Plumb, J., & Stewart, I. (2009). *The art of science of valuing in psychotherapy: Helping clients to discover, explore and commit to valued action using acceptance and commitment therapy.* New Harbinger.

Majumdar, S., & Morris, R. (2019). Brief group-based acceptance and commitment therapy for stroke survivors. *British Journal of Clinical Psychology, 58*(1), 70–90.

McGehee, P., Germer, C., & Neff, K. (2017). Core values in mindful self-compassion. In L. M. Monteiro et al. (Eds.), *Practitioner's guide to ethics and mindfulness-based interventions* (pp. 279–293). Springer.

McHugh, L., & Stewart, I. (2012). *The self and perspective taking: Contributions and applications from modern behavioral science.* New Harbinger.

Nijsse, B., van Heugten, C. M., van Mierlo, M. L., Post, M. W., de Kort, P. L., & Visser-Meily, J. M. (2017). Psychological factors are associated with subjective cognitive complaints 2 months post stroke. *Neuropsychological Rehabilitation, 27*, 99–115. https://doi.org/10.1080/09602011.2015.1065280

Norlander, A., Iwarsson, S., Jönsson, A. C., Lindgren, A., & Månsson Lexell, E. (2018). Living and ageing with stroke: An exploration of conditions influencing participation in social and leisure activities over 15 years. *Brain injury, 32*(7), 858–866.

Olendzki, A. (2010). *Unlimiting mind: The radically experiential psychology of Buddhism.* Simon and Schuster.

Petkus, A. J., & Wetherell, J. L. (2013). Acceptance and Commitment Therapy with older adults: Rationale and considerations. *Cognitive and Behavioral Practice, 20*(1), 47–56. https://doi.org/10.1016/j.cbpra.2011.07.004

Schottke, H., & Giabbiconi, C. M. (2015). Post-stroke depression and post-stroke anxiety: prevalence and predictors. *International Psychogeriatrics, 27*(11), 1805–1812.

Sianturi, R., Keliat, B. A., & Wardani, I. Y. (2018). The effectiveness of acceptance and commitment therapy on anxiety in clients with stroke. *Enfermeria Clinica, 28*, 94–97.

Skolarus, L. E., Burke, J. F., Brown, D. L., & Freedman, V. A. (2014). Understanding stroke survivorship. *Stroke, 45*(1), 224–230. https://doi.org/10.1161/strokeaha.113.002874

Tirch, D., Schoendorff, B., & Silberstein, L. R. (2014). *The ACT practitioner's guide to the science of compassion: Tools for fostering psychological flexibility.* New Harbinger.

Tugade, M. M., Fredrickson, B. L., & Barrett, L. F. (2004). Psychological resilience and positive emotional granularity: Examining the benefits of positive emotions on coping and health. *Journal of Personality, 72*(6), 1161–1190. https://doi.org/10.1111/j.1467-6494.2004.00294.x

Walser, R. D. (2019). *The heart of ACT: Developing a flexible, process-based, and client-centered practice using acceptance and commitment therapy.* New Harbinger.

Wetherell, J. L., Afari, N., Ayers, C. R., Stoddard, J. A., Ruberg, J., Sorrell, J. T., Liu, L., Petkus, A. J., Thorp, S. R., Kraft, A., & Patterson, T. L. (2011). Acceptance and commitment therapy for generalized anxiety disorder in older adults: A preliminary report. *Behavior Therapy, 42*(1), 127–134.

Wilson, K. G. (2009). *Mindfulness for two: An acceptance and commitment therapy approach to mindfulness in psychotherapy.* New Harbinger.

Wood, A. M., Froh, J. J., & Geraghty, A. W. (2010). Gratitude and well-being: A review and theoretical integration. *Clinical Psychology Review, 30*(7), 890–905.

Zautra, A. J., Reich, J. W., Davis, M. C., Potter, P. T., & Nicolson, N. A. (2000). The role of stressful events in the relationship between positive and negative affects: Evidence from field and experimental studies. *Journal of Personality, 68*(5), 927–951.

Chapter 4

Relational approaches

ACT with female relatives of people with brain injury

Jo Johnson

Despite working with relatives over three decades, initial visits continue to trigger intense feelings of inadequacy and a loss of useful words. The sense of loss is overwhelming for them, but also for me.

Most people describe living regular lives expecting the next day to be much the same. Then, a phone call or doorstep visit informs of an injured loved one. In a few situations, the relative has also been involved in the incident, which adds further trauma and complexity.

From then on, a tsunami of thoughts and feelings overwhelms them, their imagined future is ripped away and their anchoring routines are obliterated.

For many years, my clinical practice was informed by traditional Cognitive Behavioural Therapy (CBT), narrative and systemic approaches. I did my best to listen and enable relatives to understand their inner experiences. When I stumbled across Acceptance and Commitment Therapy (ACT), I knew instantly this psychological model would be helpful to traumatised relatives. Using the model also enabled me to notice and relate differently to my own inner world.

An additional part of my working life is running ACT programmes for police officers. The bespoke programme I facilitate is broadly based on the *Acceptance and Commitment Training (ACT) For Workplace Settings*, Flaxman et al. (2019). My clinical practice with relatives is increasingly infused with the tools from this programme.

For reasons outside of the scope of this chapter, most of my referrals for relatives are women: mothers, partners or daughters of someone with a brain injury.

Starting reflections

I wonder if you might take a minute to complete an exercise for the purpose of this chapter. If so, please read to the end of this section and then create the two scenarios in your mind with reference to a person that makes sense to you.

Scenario 1

Would you be willing to think about someone who is very dear to you?

DOI: 10.4324/9781003193722-5

Choose someone you know extremely well or have known over many years. Perhaps choose a partner, a parent or an adult child, a close friend or a relative? Can you bring that person into your mind in this moment?

Can you take a few minutes to observe that person in your mind's eye? Where are they most likely to be right now as you ponder? Imagine their posture, the way they smile, laugh or frown. What colour or style will they be wearing? What jokes do they find funny? What annoys them? How are they as a passenger and as a driver in a car? Are they gadget-obsessed or techno-phobic? What's their favourite food? Do they care about where that food has come from or what it contains? If a situation is tense, do they take the lead or run away? Are they mostly indoors or do they take any excuse to go outside? Imagine this person with you. What are you doing together? Recall a sweet moment; a time when all was well. Think about their tone of voice and facial expressions in an argument. What means most to them?

Notice any thoughts and feelings as you reflect and remember. Take a few breaths and notice what it's like to feel connected to that beloved person.

Scenario 2

If you are willing, can you now imagine going to a social event, or activity that your chosen person might attend? Imagine going but not knowing they will be there.

As you walk in, you are surprised to see them and feel happy that they're there, excited at the thought of meeting in a different context.

Notice them from afar, across a crowded room, perhaps at the bar with their predictable drink or leaning against a wall with a few people you don't recognise. They haven't seen you yet.

Imagine they are laughing and chatting, but you are puzzled because something is amiss. The first thing you notice is that they are not drinking what they usually choose. Then you notice their clothes are a completely different style than usual. Perhaps brighter than usual, or less smart and their body language is the opposite to how it usually is. If they are usually quietly spoken, they are loud and moving a lot. If they are usually loud, they are quieter, shrunken, somehow.

Enhance the image in your mind. Be a curious observer, trying hard to make sense of the context that has changed your person's choices and made them look different to you but obviously not to anyone else. They have a different drink, an odd choice of clothes and their posture is awkward; it's just not the usual them. Perhaps you wonder if they're ill or if they are drunk.

Imagine as you get closer, they fleetingly meet your eyes over the heads of a small group, but they don't smile or properly acknowledge you. Instead, they look a bit puzzled, maybe anxious; you are not sure. You check yourself. Is it me? Am I imagining this change? There is something going on but you're not sure what.

Having watched them finish the last drops of a large glass of something alcoholic, you know they'll change now to a soft drink. Instead, they order two vodkas! Then, your person launches into a long story in a loud voice interspersed with several unsavoury jokes. You watch the listener's reaction, knowing the jokes are unkind, insensitive and unacceptable. Other people are now looking and elbowing each other to get a peek. This is not the person you love.

As you gently push into the group, imagine what you might be feeling. Embarrassed? Confused? Disgusted? Anxious? Then, as you greet them, you see a look in their eye that doesn't seem to be your person. It's almost like they've been taken over or invaded somehow. You can see that the person they are with has tears in their eyes, and you attempt to resolve the tension, expecting your loyal person to apologise and be grateful. Instead, they turn on you, muttering spiteful words about your controlling ways and walk off, leaving you alone, isolated and hurt.

Imagine the way you might feel, what you'd do next. Image the thoughts that might overwhelm your mind. Notice any thoughts and feelings as you try and reflect on the above scenario in a context that works for your situation.

Take a few breaths and notice what it's like to feel less connected to that beloved person.

Unacknowledged pain

In the above exercise, I wanted to create something of the confusion, fear, anger and helplessness that so many relatives talk about. Of course, for many, there'll be additional physical changes as well as cognitive, emotional and behavioural ones. But we know from the relevant research that it's the personality and psychological changes that relatives struggle with most of all.

When Marissa came into my office, she was already crying. As she steadied herself, using the filing cabinet, she explained, 'Derrick has used the toilet leaving the door open.'

She was distraught as she told me her husband had been such a private man, 'He preferred the cubicles, so he didn't have to use the urinals with a line of men.'

Derrick took some time to join us and by that time she'd composed herself. He was neatly dressed in a suit and tie. He shook my hand and introduced himself. If I'd met him elsewhere, I would not have spotted anything amiss. She told me, 'Everyone tells me how well he looks, how amazing it is that he's back to himself, that we didn't lose him.'

Katy was nine when I met her. She was unable to make eye contact; her head was supported by the wonky headrest of a large wheelchair, too big for her tiny frame. Above her seat was a photograph taken on a sunny day. A small girl holding her brother's hand. The two of them open-mouthed with anticipation, a few seconds before jumping into a clear blue pool. This was Katie a year before her accident, on a holiday with her grandparents. Later that day, she was injured in that same pool. She sustained a severe brain injury and won't ever walk or talk. Her mother can't look at that photograph.

I met Ian on his first day at a Headway day centre. As he narrowed his eyes to focus on what the instructor was telling him, he reached out to clutch his mother's hand. She returned his gesture with a reassuring squeeze. Ian is back home after many years travelling the world as a navy officer. Unfortunately, his wife was killed in the same accident in which he sustained a brain injury. He is now living with his parents who retired to the coast eighteen months ago.

In her seminal text, decades ago, Muriel Lezak (1995) described brain injury as a family affair. Yet, in my opinion, many services still don't formally acknowledge the emotional pain felt by those close to the injured person. The above scenarios are typical of the many ordinary lives shattered by a catastrophic life-lasting injury. Their relatives are frequently left alone to manage the painful inner experiences that threaten to overwhelm them.

Our anchoring relationships are so familiar, never perfect but, like comfy clothes, we know how the connection works. Much of the comfort and security comes from the predictability. Knowing their individual characteristics gives us a sense of control. Our relationships also give us a complementary role. A role that has consciously and unconsciously developed in the context of this relationship.

Have a think about your primary relationships. In which roles are you the more dominant person, the one who directs or chooses when you take a parent or adult role in that context? In which relationships do you have a more passive role? Which relationships are more equal?

How would the experience be for you if suddenly the roles were reversed or changed? Perhaps, you can think of a relationship when one person changed, and the consequential shift in roles made the relationship untenable or unsatisfactory.

Ian's mum told me, 'Ian was my sensitive son. He always knew what I was feeling and looked out for me in different situations. He was the one who carried my bag, hung back when I was too slow, knew when I was hurt or tired, and helped without being asked. Now he doesn't pick up those cues. The relationship has changed to me being the parent again. I miss him.'

Marissa said, 'Derrick was my anchor. I come from a volatile family and with him I felt safe for the first time; stable and secure. He did everything. Without him, I don't know who I am.'

Systemic thinking makes it clear that when one person changes – secondary to neurological injury – everyone's role shifts to accommodate the change. For each person, there'll be gains and losses. Each situation is different and often the changes are so subtle that most people are not aware of any change.

So many relatives tell me that friends and family comment on how well the injured person is looking or progressing.

Having worked with so many relatives, the central theme underlying much of the distress is 'unacknowledged emotional pain'; being in terrible emotional pain, having been through an awful trauma, but having their distress unacknowledged, unseen by everyone.

Prolonged grief disorder

In our society, we find it hard to acknowledge pain and distress and perhaps even harder to talk about death, loss, grief and endings. Many of the relatives I work with would match the criteria for prolonged grief disorder (PGD) apart from the fact their relative hasn't died. In PGD people experience separation distress, a yearning for the lost person, identity confusion, avoidance of reminders, bitterness or anger related to the loss, numbness, finding life meaningless and refusing to invest in hobbies and other relationships.

Relatives often express hurt in response to colleagues, friends and family talking or behaving as if they should move on and get over the loss. This often exacerbates their existing mind stories about 'I'm not coping well,' 'I should be over it by now.'

Perhaps, if we do nothing else as passing practitioners, we can explicitly acknowledge the hurt relatives feel when their beloved, well-known person is changed secondary to neurological injury.

Self-care

'It's not all about you,' is what my mind shouts whilst writing this section. My mind is also saying if this section stays in, it should go at the end. After all, this chapter is about distressed relatives who have a right to their distress. It shouldn't be about me as the psychologist or us as the practitioners, should it?

Two of my important values are self-care and self-compassion. Increasingly, the relevant research evidence shows how important these qualities are for psychological wellbeing. Relatives frequently don't care for their own wellbeing. Inappropriate guilt and feeling solely responsible commonly fuel self-sacrifice as an unworkable behaviour.

In my opinion, relatives benefit when we can model self-care and self-compassion. So, in the service of these values, I'd like to acknowledge something. For me, working with relatives is often more distressing than working with the injured person.

Perhaps, I find it too easy to put myself in their position. Hearing about their distress makes me wonder how I'd feel if my husband were changed, or if one of my adult children were injured. This arouses anxiety and sometimes guilt at my lack of gratitude for those close to me. It often reminds me of my shortcomings in my relationships.

When I don't acknowledge this distress, I don't practise what I preach. I work too hard to help, I take on too much and eat junk. Worst of all in this context, I'm lazy at home and unappreciative of those I love.

Discovering ACT radically changed the way I work with relatives after a brain injury, but it also changed the way I work with myself.

I am now more able to share with colleagues the personal impact of this work. I am more aware of the situations that trigger distress and anxiety in me; often situations that most closely match my own or when I experience their story as especially upsetting.

I acknowledge I've cried with relatives. Sometimes, that felt like the only reasonable response. Yet, my mind tells me this is unacceptable as a detached professional. I then feel guilty, ashamed and worried someone will find out that I too have feelings I can't contain!

So, if you are working with people in distress, I would encourage you to care first for yourself. We can't pour from an empty cup and a lack of self-care invalidates our advice to those we work with.

In order to empathise with those we support, we need to be open to our own pain, so it doesn't stay unacknowledged.

Normalising the starting position

If you are willing, please take a few minutes to reflect on a time when you have experienced loss or distress. What thoughts and feelings dominated? Were your thoughts mostly negative or positive? How much of your mind was consumed by the issue? What did you do in response to your distress?

Most of us feel upset in the face of suffering, our thinking becomes very negative; we cry, we feel anxious, sad, guilty or embarrassed. We shout, we eat junk, drink too much or blame others. We tend to do unhelpful things to make ourselves feel better.

Relatives are usually referred to me because they are expressing too much emotion; crying too much, feeling too low or too angry or too hopeless or too resentful of professional intrusion. Often, referrals imply the person is not doing what we as professionals consider helpful or positive. Often, they are not following our carefully written guidelines or constructive advice!

In our society, distress is frequently an unwelcome guest. Perhaps, accidents and injuries make us flawed humans aware of our own fragility. Perhaps, when there is no solution, we feel helpless, useless or not good enough.

A typical pattern of response from many, including us as health professionals, is to unwittingly imply the felt distress is disproportionate or abnormal. Here are some examples:

- Don't forget all the positive times
- It'll get better
- Calm down
- Don't upset yourself
- Don't worry
- It'll sort itself out
- It'll be ok
- Don't be sad

In the face of these responses, emotional pain stays unacknowledged, but even worse, these responses make people suppress their pain, feel guilty or ashamed about it or stay quiet.

One of the beautiful things about ACT is how it seeks to normalise emotional responses. As ACT practitioners, we need to make sure these key principles underpin services and team responses.

- We can't choose our thoughts and feelings
- It is normal to feel distressed after a loss or trauma – to not be upset is abnormal
- It is normal to have negative beliefs about the situation and the future

And thus, the aim of an ACT intervention with a relative can't be to

- Feel less bad
- Feel better or good
- Think positively or realistically
- To stop catastrophising
- To get people to do what is right or good in our eyes

These relatives have all experienced something terrible. If they weren't there for the incident, they were very soon after. They have seen things they'll never forget. Most probably at some point, their relative was at risk of death. Many have been verbally or physically abused by the person they love. Their imagined future has been taken, their familiar and enjoyed past has gone and they are potentially trapped in a situation they didn't choose. They have lost so much. Most of their pain will be unacknowledged by friends who don't understand and soon forget as the acute dramas subside. On top of that, relatives are expected to sit through meetings full of jargon and meet a constant array of new people.

Home visits make people feel judged for their home, their family dynamic and even their cooking and cleaning.

Perhaps your mind is saying, 'I would never judge'. But vulnerable people feel judged by professionals. Relatives are overwhelmed, exhausted and experiencing severe levels of emotional pain. Yet, they are sometimes confronted with neatly typed meeting agendas and goal plans from behind clipboards.

Our intention, of course, is to be friendly, accepting and helpful and get as much rehab as possible in those essential two years.

A relative's mind says, 'It's all up to me, I'm responsible, I'm the weak link,' and of course they feel 'not good enough.'

One of my favourite things about ACT is it encourages a climb down from our expert status, to recognise that we would think and feel as relatives commonly do. Having this conversation is so therapeutic for relatives. We can help them see how odd it would be in the face of such trauma to feel happy, content, hopeful, excited or optimistic.

It's often hard for the relative to recognise their understandable emotional pain and show self-compassion.

The cinema exercise

I frequently use this exercise in the early part of my work with relatives, often at the end of a first session. This exercise can strengthen awareness, give observer distance, help the person see the normality of their emotions, allow self-compassion and spot behaviours that are consistent or inconsistent with their values.

The pain and emotion can be connected to important values and how much love is evident. This hurts because this relationship was important, that future was chosen; these values are now under threat. You can ask what the person would need to stop caring about in order to stop the pain.

I might say, 'If we put this story into a film and played it at a local cinema, of you living your regular life, only for it to be shattered by that call, then those comments from friends…, that isolation…, that…' You can identify the emotionally relevant aspects for the individual.

Questions that seem helpful might include:

- How might the audience feel as they leave?
- What aspects might they find most upsetting or important?
- Who might the audience feel the most empathy for and when?
- What might they feel if it happened to them?
- Why might they feel that?
- What would it be unusual to feel?
- What might people suggest for each character going forward?
- What might each person need?

To end the exercise, I'll often ask about how everyone in the film is coping, how it's impacting others and what might happen if those coping strategies are continued.

To increase the impact, I often move our chairs towards a window or whiteboard to imagine watching the screen, and then discuss at this side-on-side angle. I'll frequently refer to the cinema audience as the work progresses.

Whilst ACT is a flexible approach, in my opinion, most interventions need to start with an attempt to normalise the tsunami of feelings that is being felt or avoided. The cinema exercise is frequently helpful as part of that process.

Moving further forward – the early work

On session one or two, I introduce PODD (pause and breathe, observe, drop back, do what is important; see Figure 4.1) as a brief starting and finishing exercise. I use this within my workplace training and have made this diagram into laminated cards as reminders. Many relatives find this useful in the early stages of treatment.

4 Step Pause: PODD

Pause and Breathe
Notice your belly

Watch how the sensations there change as you breathe in and out

Observe
What is going on for me right now?

Where am I? What thoughts? What emotions? How is my body from head to toe?

Drop back...
...into your body and the world

Stretch
Push my feet down
Five Senses

Do what is important
Refocus

Have a drink
Take a break...

Figure 4.1 Four step pause: PODD

Mind gears

I find the idea of 'two mind gears' from the workplace training programme a concept that is relatable for most relatives. Often, people express feelings of exhaustion, gaining no pleasure and not being able to switch off. I introduce the idea by asking what they know about gears on cars. Most people understand that driving a car on a motorway in a low gear would burn out the engine and using a high gear to drive out of a driveway might be dangerous. A colleague created the illustration in Figure 4.2 to communicate this idea to clients.

The key point is we need both gears; neither is objectively superior. But, to drive a car well, to get its best performance, we know low gears work better for slow and accurate driving but higher gears are for speed. Learning ACT skills helps people notice and name the gear they are in and choose whether to change.

The choice point (Harris, 2019)

Listening to a relative's story over one or two sessions means that the difficult thoughts and feelings, unworkable patterns and some important values become obvious.

I find a simplified version of Russ Harris' choice point (see Figure 4.3, with Marissa's context) a useful tool for consolidating these early conversations. Russ has produced an excellent video outlining this tool called *The Choice Point*. Much of the language I use here is taken from that video.

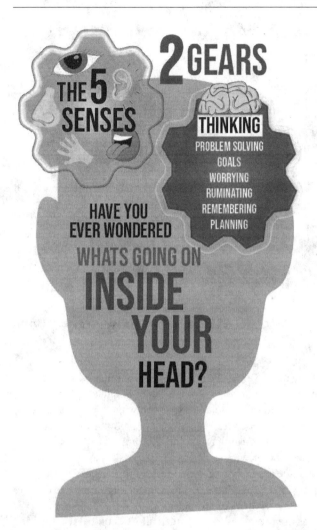

Figure 4.2 Two gears (Adapted from Flaxman et al. 2019)

This tool uses two arrows to divide internal and external behaviour into 'towards' and 'away' moves. Like Russ Harris, I generally use red to indicate 'away' moves and green to indicate 'towards'.

I draw this diagram in front of the person explaining 'towards' moves represent – the things they do or say to make life better for them and their other important people. For example, the behaviours they want to keep doing or do more of. I would often also include important values and people.

'Away' moves represent the things they do and say that are making life even worse, the things they'd like to stop or do less of. (NB: Russ Harris describes 'away'

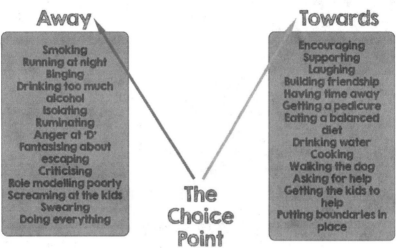

Figure 4.3 A simplified Choice Point (from ACT Made Simple, 2nd edition by Russ Harris) for Marissa

moves as moving away from one's values. Within the ACT community, some people use the term 'away' to refer to moving away from difficult thoughts and feelings.)

In my opinion, it's about being flexible and exploring what is most helpful for the client or context. Thus, I pay much less attention at this point to whether these are internal unseen behaviours like ruminating and plotting revenge, or external behaviours like shouting and swearing.

I find it helpful to gain a sense of whether these are new patterns of behaviour or exacerbations of old coping strategies. This also provides an opportunity to explore pre-injury relationship patterns in times of struggle.

Using this tool provides opportunities to strengthen all ACT processes. Looking at their personal choice point on paper promotes an observer position in the present moment. Writing it out offers at least minimal distance from thoughts and feelings. Individual inner experiences can be identified for further intervention. It's a good point to talk about what is important, values, whether they are the same or different from pre-/post-injury and which values are shared with the injured person. Often, values are very stable and shared.

Committed actions – facilitating early behavioural change

The choice point is a great way to identify small changes a person might be interested in making. I always remind people that the size of the action is unimportant. Katy's mum's first committed action was to 'text a friend once a week.'

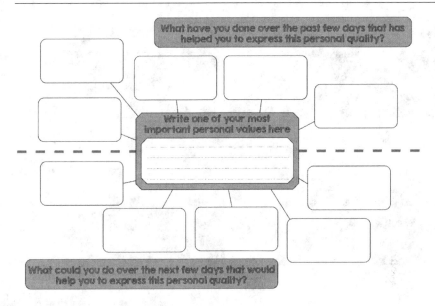

Figure 4.4 Octopus diagram

I use the 'octopus' diagram (Figure 4.4; from the workplace training programme) to work on committed action. This tool asks people to choose a value to place in the centre square. I give each of my clients a pack of value cards. There is an app called *Values Card Sort* which some people prefer.

Above the dotted lines is space to add a few specific committed actions towards moves that have been made the week before. Often, relatives feel disappointed with themselves when they can't think of many. This provides a nice opportunity to notice the 'harsh mind' and instead engage in self-compassion. Below the dotted line is space to add some 'planned towards moves.' Usually, I try to suggest only aiming for two above and two below the line.

Using the wellbeing or life lens

The ACT Matrix (see Figure 4.5) is a perspective-taking tool (see Polk et al., 2016) that facilitates psychological flexibility, the ultimate goal of ACT. I use a version of The Matrix with almost every client.

It can be used to plan overall goals, to focus on one area of life like health or self-compassion and to reflect and resolve relationship conflict. It also facilitates each of the three processes leading to psychological flexibility – aware, open, active.

I describe it to people as a four-part lens, a life lens or wellbeing lens. I utilise the four parts in a way that maps onto the choice point, so I can use the two tools together, the lens enhancing and adding further clarity to the early choice point assessment.

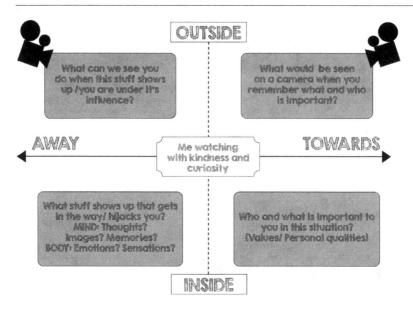

Figure 4.5 ACT Matrix

Marissa's husband Derrick was injured whilst on a business trip she had asked him not to attend. It clashed with their twenty-fifth wedding anniversary. They had compromised, he drove home in the afternoon of the second day so they could go out in the evening. Sadly, Derrick crashed his car. No one else was involved. Tiredness and a mild hangover were potentially contributory factors. He was admitted to a hospital far from their home which made early visits harder, and Marissa had to frequently leave her teenagers alone.

Guilt and anger were the feelings she talked extensively about in early sessions. Anger that her husband had gone to the conference and that he'd been careless in his driving. Guilt for making him come home, blaming him and neglecting the children. Soon after we met, he went back into full-time rehab. She was working full time, visiting him every day and doing everything at home even though her children were sixteen and eighteen.

Marissa's children were obviously suffering, but Derrick had been the strict parent. Marissa felt her parenting was terrible. She knew she did things that she told the kids not to do, like drinking too much and shouting and swearing. The kids did nothing to help, and whilst she resented that, she couldn't address it because she felt guilty for ruining their lives.

She was avoiding everyone she knew. She stopped walking in her local area for fear of crying if she bumped into friends or neighbours. She had withdrawn from all her exercise classes, book groups and she avoided college parents' evening. She was exhausted but couldn't sleep. She would get up at night to binge eat for energy, go for a night run until she collapsed and return for too many alcoholic drinks.

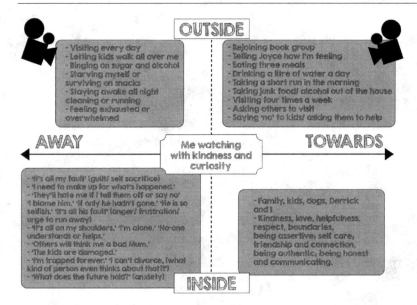

Figure 4.6 ACT Matrix for Marissa

She wanted to work on her parenting, improve her diet, reduce bad eating and drinking and feel able to see people.

So, we used a wellbeing lens to first better understand what was sabotaging her in each area (see Figure 4.6).

Together, we constructed the above and pondered together. Immediately Marissa was able to see why she felt so confused and overwhelmed with so much to manage. This gave another opportunity to pause for self-compassion – no wonder you feel this way; what would a friend say? How do you want to be to yourself in this?

She was then able to identify parenting as the priority and we completed a more specific wellbeing lens to clarify (see Figure 4.7).

Working with difficult thoughts

The life lens is a great way to clarify inner experiences that are sabotaging and allow the client to see that difficult thoughts and feelings only come in the face of important people or situations. For example, the fear of being a bad mum or damaging your children only arises when someone wants to be a good parent and help their children thrive.

Most relatives spend a lot of time with only their thoughts for company, from the early stages of sitting patiently by a hospital bed to the later stages when there is always a practical problem to solve. For many people, cognitive processes like worrying, problem-solving, ruminating and internal ranting become a soother for the difficult feelings they are currently unable to face.

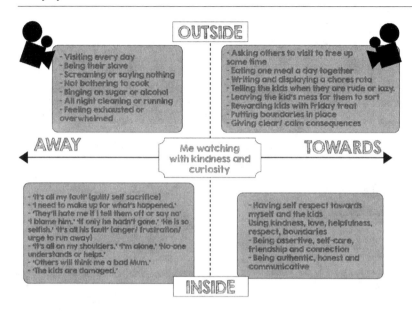

Figure 4.7 Updated ACT Matrix for Marissa

Common thought themes include:

- Idealisation of the past: Everything was perfect before the brain injury, we didn't argue, we discussed everything etc.
- Fear for the future: My relative is changed forever, how will I/they cope?
- Financial worries: What will I have to give up/start? (Jobs, friends, hobbies, driving, roles).
- The burden of responsibility: It's all up to me. I can't cope. My relative would've done it better or been a better parent.
- Relationship professionals: I'm not clever enough/what do they know? I'm being left out. They're in it for the money; I have no control; I have no privacy.
- Health-related: Will he ever be better? Will he be vulnerable to dementia? What if he's injured again?
- Parenting issues: He's harming them. The kids will be damaged. I'm a single parent.
- Intrusion from old self stories: I can't do this. I'm just like my mother. I'm not a coper. I don't understand.
- Relationship issues: He's become my child. Intimacy has gone or isn't good. I'm not happy. I'll never be able to leave. Will we divorce? We've become like my parents. We used to be equal partners.

Everyone has beliefs about feeling distressed, and frequently relatives hold unhelpful ideas about what it means to experience the emotional storms that threaten to overwhelm.

Common unhelpful beliefs include:

- This shows I'm not coping
- Others cope with worse
- I shouldn't be feeling this
- I can't stand it
- I'll have a breakdown
- I'm just like… (a friend or family member who is always down)
- I mustn't wallow
- I'm being weak, pathetic
- If the situation were reversed, he'd have coped
- The family mustn't see me upset
- It's stupid and unacceptable
- I should be over this by now
- This is not how I thought I'd be

As time progresses, these beliefs increase the struggle to get rid of difficult emotions.

For Marissa, her two most dominant thoughts were, 'It's all my fault' and 'It's all my responsibility.' We first identified a couple of situations in her past where these thoughts had dominated. She had been raised in a home where she was the unfavoured child who was frequently scapegoated.

We then completed some diffusion exercises. An exercise I use a lot is as follows:

1. Take a piece of A4 paper and turn it landscape. Write on the bottom-right corner the sticky thought. E.g., 'It's all my fault.' Take a moment to notice any thoughts and feelings.
2. Write on the same piece of paper before the previous words, 'I am having the thought that…' Take a moment to notice and chat. Most people notice the thought is a little less powerful.
3. Finally, add 'I notice that…' before the previous sentence. Thus, by the end of the exercise, the person has written, 'I notice that I am having the thought that…' Again, notice any thoughts and feelings.

When the person has sufficiently improved their awareness and is noticing more thoughts, I encourage them to ask these questions of any troubling thoughts.

- Is this a useful or helpful thought in this moment?
- Would a good mate say this?
- Is it an old story?
- How would I respond if I read it in a newspaper I don't believe?
- If I believe this as an absolute truth, how does that make me treat myself or others?

Another favourite diffusion technique to use with relatives is 'the mind story.' Often, after a traumatic event or injury, relatives' minds become understandably dominated by one cognitive theme. Examples might include all the 'what ifs' about the accident, one dominating fear or a decision about the future in terms of work or relationships. I suggest writing a mind story as follows:

- Use an A4 piece of paper and fold it in two like a book.
- Open and write in the middle all the thoughts, feelings, memories, urges and images associated with this topic.
- Fold it and write a title on the front. It seems to me it works best with a dramatic or memorable title.
- For ten minutes each day, allow yourself to open the book read all the elements. Notice and allow any associated feelings.
- Between the allotted time slots, notice if any of the contents come into awareness. On noticing, name the title and remind the mind it's in hand and return to the present using a PODD.

E.g., for Ian's mum

Title of mind story – 'My ruined son'

CONTENTS

- I'm going to kill the driver if I find him
- No one else sees the differences
- I miss his smile
- No one helps me
- Why wasn't it one of my other kids?
- I'm such a bad mother for thinking that
- My husband is in denial
- He's getting worse
- He might be injured again
- He should've died
- Guilt for thinking that
- Frustration, sadness, shame
- I hate his case manager
- Will he get put away when I die?
- I can't cope
- I should be enjoying retirement – anger/guilt, resentment
- The professional team makes money out of our distress
- It's so unfair

Working with difficult feelings

Most relatives have functioned perfectly well before their family member was injured. But like all of us, each relative has their own beliefs about what it means to be distressed and has developed patterns of responding.

Sadness and loss

By the time a relative is referred, they are usually traumatised and have lost a great deal. Consequently, their lives and sense of self are dramatically different from pre-injury and they are experiencing high levels of emotional distress.

In addition, most relatives have to deal with an enormous range of new demands. These might include visiting their relative, practical tasks, managing finances, lone parenting, meetings with health and social care professionals, case managers and legal professionals to name a few.

Loss is a massive theme in this work, leading to feelings of grief for the pre-injury often idealised past, for the imagined future and for the pre-injury relationship.

Guilt

Inappropriate or disproportionate guilt is a dominant feeling for relatives.

For example, guilt about:

- The 'what ifs', 'if onlys', 'should haves' – 'If only I'd not asked for a lift, left earlier, reminded him it was icy…''
- Relationship or blips in the past – 'I was a cow; I didn't appreciate him…'
- Survivor guilt – 'It should have been me; he would do better in this position…'
- Tasks/people being neglected – 'Parenting, work, friends, chores, exercise…'
- Not coping well enough, shouting at others.

Anger

Anger is also a dominant emotion. Often anger seems to be the 'security guard' for sadness and anxiety. Relatives frequently tell me anger is empowering and takes them away from difficult feelings, gets things done. Sadly, in healthcare settings there is usually something that could be done better, so there are plenty of justified reasons to shout.

Frequently people feel anger at the lack of understanding they get from friends, employers and even family. They feel others don't see the invisible disabilities or forget when the acute drama is finished. This can make relatives feel like there is something wrong with them.

Post-traumatic stress disorder (PTSD)

A lot of people will experience symptoms of PTSD. This might include flashbacks, intrusive thoughts, etc.

Many relatives report feeling numb, having no feelings, no pain or trauma, which of course is a common reaction after such intense and traumatic experiences.

In the face of distress, like all of us, relatives first manage the unwanted emotions using strategies they've always used. These might include exercise, extra alcohol or food, overworking, blaming others or mindless scrolling.

Whilst these strategies might bring short-term relief, they are insufficient for processing the overwhelming and complex emotions resulting from what has happened and the future consequences.

As we know, the struggle to get rid of distress increases the initial understandable distress.

Whilst we all have a favoured method to reduce or control our emotions, the extensive amount of liaison and problem-solving required by relatives provides plenty of opportunities to use thinking strategies, tasks and phone calls as distractions.

In my clinical experience, avoidance is another common strategy for many relatives. This might include avoidance of any reminders, internal or external, of the pre-injury situation, photographs, places and people.

Everyone is different but by the time of referral, relatives are often stuck in patterns of 'away' moves in response to trying to control and get rid of distress.

Relating differently to emotions

I would generally provide a small amount of psychoeducation as a starting point. This would include helping people understand these points about emotions:

- Emotional discomfort is part of the human experience
- It's abnormal not to have difficult emotions
- Emotions are important and useful
- Emotions help us survive
- Emotions are messengers; they communicate
- Emotions are transient and ever-changing

I would link emotional pain to important values. I often use the metaphor of a ticket. The front side of the ticket includes the values and the reverse side is the terms and conditions, which are the difficult thoughts and feelings, memories and emotional pain.

Below, you can see the worked example from a relative who gave permission to share. The pain comes because of what is cared about. You can ask, 'What do you have to stop caring about to lose this pain?'

The aim of my work is to help relatives relate differently to the emotions they are avoiding or trying to control. This can be broken down into five steps:

- Noticing the feeling because of improved awareness
- Naming the emotion – 'Here is anxiety'; 'I'm noticing guilt'; 'This is sadness'
- Watch the emotion – notice where it is in the body, how high, low, wide, etc.
- Choose an image that helps, e.g., a wave, a toddler, the weather or an express train
- Engage with the present using five senses
- Expect and manage the resurgence

Sometimes it's appropriate to teach this formally. With others, the learning happens implicitly, as part of processing the feelings in therapy.

For most people, together we create a personalised distressed script once they are familiar with the five stages.

Kate's example

Notice and name – 'Aha I'm feeling sad. This shows how much I miss my baby girl. It is ok, I can allow this feeling; I don't have to be afraid or try and get rid of it.'

Watch emotion – 'I can watch this, see what it does, where is it in my body? This is just a feeling. I am not my emotions; I am the observer. It's like a toddler; it'll tantrum but I can stand back and watch until it's run its course. It'll pass.'

Be present – 'I will turn my attention back to what's important in this moment – noticing what I can see/hear/touch/smell. I'll seek out the birds and make myself a milky drink.'

Deal with comebacks – 'I feel the emotion returning – that's ok, it's what toddlers do, I'll watch it again. This too will pass.'

Bringing a couple together

Having worked with a relative, if the person with a brain injury is willing and has sufficient cognitive ability to engage in a couple of sessions, I'll often see the couple jointly for at least a few sessions.

So often, a couple have never compared their individual stories. Couples who have had a close relationship pre-injury often report a shared relationship journey up to the accident. This might include where and how they met, marriage or moving in together, the ups and downs of the relationship, career decisions and parenting.

When one person is injured, both people experience trauma, grief and loss but in very different ways. For the relative, this starts with finding out about the accident, the touch-and-go/hospital experience, the early recovery when their partner might behave in a very strange and frightening way and then the new relationship when the injured person returns home.

For the injured person, they often don't recall much pre-injury or immediately after. They are then exposed to different professionals observing and intervening and a partner telling them they are different, but they don't know why or how to fix it.

Thus, both parties experience high levels of distress, but if not shared, they can become isolated, lonely and emotionally estranged.

Using the 'life lens' is a great way to start a conversation about what has happened and what is going on at the point of this intervention. The lens is accessible to a brain-injured person, even if they have moderate cognitive impairments to memory, attention and executive abilities. It provides a clear and lasting visual picture of the clashing perspectives. Usually, individuals instantly connect with why their partner is behaving how they are and how both people are under the influence of undiscussed inner experiences.

As you can see in the case example below, I encourage couples to do the right side of the life lens together, to identify their shared values and what that would look like on a camera.

Individually, but in the session, they work on the left side. Then, we compare and discuss. Couples can talk about the impact on each other when one person starts acting under the influence of their inner experiences and the circular nature of these patterns.

For example, in this situation, Peter was driving too fast and an accident occurred. Immediately post-injury, he was verbally aggressive, had severe memory deficits like forgetting he had children and did strange things like insisting the wardrobe was a tent on a campsite.

Peter couldn't recall any of it, but Sarah had to keep the children away from him, as he was inappropriate with them and she thought he would never be well. Peter made a very good recovery and returned to work. Despite some typical cognitive and emotional impairments, he was able to function as a good dad and partner.

Sarah has always experienced high levels of anxiety. She came from a fragmented family and in difficult times felt threatened by Peter's tight-knit one. She had promised herself that if he recovered, she would protect him and be responsible for his full recovery.

If Peter made a minor cognitive error or was impatient with the kids, Sarah would get hijacked by early memories and fear for the future. Additionally, old stories of being rejected and unwanted would come up. Under the influence of this, her control and furious problem-solving would increase. She would also create disharmony in Peter's family, suggesting they were trying to undermine and reject her.

In turn, her behaviour would make Peter feel rejected, more aware of his limitations and terrified she was planning to divorce him. In response to his fears and feelings of inadequacy, he'd do one of two things. Either he would rage at her in front of the kids or he'd run off and hide from his adult responsibilities at home. This would further exacerbate her nagging and fears, so the cycle would repeat.

Simply drawing out their life lenses, they could see these cycles and importantly acknowledge these patterns were not that different from pre-injury (see Figure 4.8 for Peter's matrix and Figure 4.9 for Sarah's matrix).

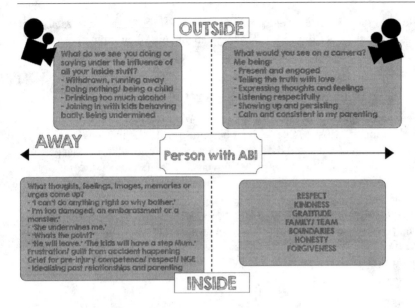

Figure 4.8 ACT Matrix for Peter

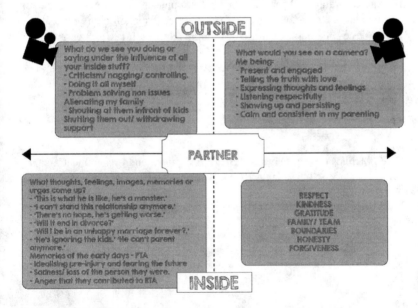

Figure 4.9 ACT Matrix for Sarah

Following this exercise, couples often find it helpful to share with each other what has happened since the accident so they can integrate their individual journeys into their couple history.

Working with relatives as part of a group

Five years ago, I set up an informal quarterly group for female relatives to meet for mutual support. Most people found it helpful to realise their thoughts and feelings are not unique, but instead a very normal response to what has happened. I understand this is called the principle of universality, realising you are not alone.

It is so powerful when a new member hears for the first time a truthful, 'I felt exactly the same.'

The group is facilitated at the house of one of the members, which is a particularly rural and peaceful setting. We don't have an agenda, but each time, I teach and we practise one ACT tool and discuss it. The host provides the ultimate intervention – tea and cake!

Summary

When someone has a brain injury, there will be people around them who have sustained a parallel trauma. Often these people are unseen. The key theme seems to be unacknowledged pain. As part of this complex psychological experience, it is normal to have a tsunami of difficult thoughts and feelings. Acceptance and Commitment Therapy has been recognised as an effective intervention for people after a brain injury. I have found it to be an ideal model for improving psychological flexibility and creating behaviour change in relatives, often resulting in further positive change within the family system.

References

Flaxman, P. E., McIntosh, R., & Oliver, J. (2019). Acceptance and Commitment Training (ACT) for workplace settings: Trainer manual. City, University of London (February 2019).

Harris, R. (2019).*ACT made simple: An easy-to-read primer on acceptance and commitment therapy* (2nd ed.). New Harbinger.

Lezak, M. D. (1995).*Neuropsychological assessment*(3rd ed.).Oxford University Press.

Polk, K. L., Schoendorff, B., Webster, M., & Olaz, F. O. (2016). *The essential guide to the ACT matrix: A step-by-step approach to using the ACT matrix model in clinical practice.* New Harbinger.

Chapter 5

ACTing through the stroke journey

Acute, inpatient and community neurorehabilitation from the perspective of a stroke survivor and two psychologists

Lucy Martin, Marcia Ward and Fiadhnait O'Keeffe

ACT in neurorehabilitation

Acceptance and Commitment Therapy (ACT; Hayes et al., 1999) offers an evidence-based therapeutic framework to work with people and their distress in neurorehabilitation settings (Curvis & Methley, 2022). ACT can be integrated into allied health therapies, and ideally can be embedded into a multidisciplinary team approach. The process-based structure of ACT can help develop a shared understanding and language within a team, which can be used to support the development and maintenance of hope and psychological flexibility for patients and staff in healthcare settings (Thompson et al., 2018; Teggart, Thompson & Rozwaha, 2022).

ACT and distress following stroke

Following stroke, distress is common, understandable and to be expected and should not be viewed as 'maladaptive' (Gregg, Callaghan, Hayes & Glenn-Lawson, 2007). ACT seeks to enable individuals to carry out valued behaviours while experiencing distress (Hayes et al., 2006). Mindfulness focuses attention on 'being present,' making contact with surroundings and being open to experiences beyond disability and distress. Key features of ACT explore 'core values' and facilitation of their use in values-based goals and committed action. This can provide more personally meaningful ways of approaching goal setting after stroke (Sugavanam et al., 2013; Plant et al., 2016).

Introducing Lucy

Many of you are familiar, I'm sure, with Lewis Carroll's story of Alice in Wonderland, who went down a rabbit hole one day: she shrank in size, doors were locked, she was without her family and could only see her home in reverse. Through the looking glass, she was shouted at, chased, threatened, sad and bewildered. She longed to be home safe and sound. This place was called Wonderland, which always puzzled me, as it seemed like a horrible scary movie. But like all

DOI: 10.4324/9781003193722-6

good stories, Alice and her family lived happily ever after; no need for physio after the fall or psychologists after the trauma. No lasting damage, as far as we know.

I was 51 when I went down a hole like Alice. I had two adult children. I had been working in the insurance industry for 33 years and was also a part-time speech and drama teacher, having tread the boards in pantomimes and plays. I had been suffering from bad headaches since my twenties, which was constantly diagnosed as vertigo. After a holiday in New York, I was quite poorly: the headaches were worse, I was unsteady on my feet and I began to drop things like cups, etc. I was advised to request an MRI when I returned home, which I did. I was diagnosed with a large brain tumour, which had wound its way around the part of my brain which manages my motor functions. Within a week, I was in hospital and after an operation which lasted 11 hours, my family were told that during the operation there was a bleed on my brain. I was put into an induced coma and while my family anxiously sat, prayed and watched the monitors, an infection raged in my brain, causing me to hallucinate, bringing me to my own 'wonderland / scary movie.'

I was seeing the most horrible things, trying to get out of a big cavern with straw on the floor, which sat under a big old farm building. I was carrying my daughter on my back, crawling over the rough ground, desperately seeking a door or light to guide me out; it was horrendous. I was so very hot and scared. I met evil people who did horrible things. I smelled and saw extremely hot oil being poured over young children, who were being set on fire as I tried to save them. The smell of burning skin and the screaming of the children was sickening.

While this was happening in my world, it was now day 16 of my induced coma, and my partner was approached with news that the infection in my brain was not abating and there were fears that the infection could not be controlled. My brain was continuing to damage itself. Thankfully, my partner rejected the suggestion that the machine be turned off, but I've been left with a lasting fear of coming so close to death.

When I eventually was brought out of the coma after 22 days, I was exhausted, bewildered and had no understanding of what had happened. Why did I now have a nappy? Why couldn't I move or get out of bed? I was a shell of the old Lucy: bald and skinny, some memory loss, lots of confusion, pure terror and utter sadness; it seemed to puzzle everyone that I cried a lot. The psychiatric team was called in, which added to my fear, terrified that they were going to lock me up. I was stuck: stuck in hospital, stuck in bed and stuck in my mind.

I underwent five further 'washouts' of my brain. I felt totally trapped again and there was no psychological help at this time, only a social worker who reported back to the team on my 'anxiety.' I was lost and suffering from PTSD (Post-Traumatic Stress Disorder) but neither I nor anyone else seemed to know that. I was labelled as 'anxious,' which would work against me; the pressure was on to free up the hospital bed and move me to the National Rehabilitation Hospital (NRH), but to achieve that, I had to make the grade physically, mentally and emotionally. This totally added to the pressure I was under; effectively, I couldn't cry in front of anyone and have it reported. Feeling like I couldn't escape out of the bed to hide and cry led to some of the darkest moments of my life; I wished I could have been allowed to die in peace.

My identity was gone. I felt sick and scared. My son was lifting me, sitting me on the toilet. My daughter was bathing me. I had become a child again. My children had become my parents. I was trapped in a bed, petrified of the nurses and the hospital. I wanted to go home but I couldn't even remember what my home looked like and felt like I couldn't let anyone see me cry or I'd never get out of there. My dream was that sometime in the future I might be able to get home, sit down and have a cup of tea at my own table. I was meant to feel lucky to be alive, but I didn't. I contemplated how I could die but wasn't able to do anything for myself, so the only way out was to get through it, like my partner's phrase: "We are all dealt a hand of cards in this life; learn to play them well."

Transfer from the acute hospital to neurorehabilitation – Lucy and Fiadhnait

The initial stages of post-acute rehabilitation were understandably difficult for Lucy. Lucy found herself having to relocate to Dublin for neurorehabilitation, far away from family and supports.

"I remember driving to Dublin to the NRH; I thought about opening the door and throwing myself out. I hadn't brought it as far as killing myself, but I knew it would stop me getting there. I was just so scared of everything. The only thing that stopped me was thinking I would be worse off or might injure the right side. I just knew it wasn't going to work out well."

Lucy described feeling like she was being watched or imprisoned, like she had been 'put away.'

"It seemed like there was fear everywhere."

"The morning after I arrived, I had a fall next to the bed. To me, all hell broke loose. Everyone who came said 'I heard you fell,' I was a 'Falls Risk.' I was in the bed next to the Nurses' Station so they could see me through the glass and I had to ask to get out of the bed. There were so many things that I was trying to explain that I'm a normal person."

Lucy's distress at this transition from the acute to post-acute neurorehabilitation and feeling 'like a prisoner' meant she spent a lot of time and energy focusing on how she could 'escape the prison': "How can I get to the railway station, from the bed, and then get back home?"

Lucy highlights the power of language, how words matter and how some phrases have stuck with her.

"I remember somebody telling me that that part of the brain was dead." "It always felt like there was bad news coming."

"I kept thinking, how did I end up like this? My son said, 'Mum you haven't ended up anywhere, this is only the start.'"

Referral to psychology in NRH

Lucy was referred to Psychology early in her admission to the NRH following reports from the team of significant anxiety, tearfulness and distress. I met with Lucy on the ward. We had individual weekly sessions and group sessions during her eight-week admission.

Lucy said she had always been a 'worrier' and she coped with anxiety and worry prior to her stroke by planning ahead for all eventualities, by walking, swimming and being out and about on the farm. Since her stroke and on admission to the NRH, Lucy was unable to engage in her previous coping strategies. Lucy was missing her family and friends enormously and the huge support they provided.

Through psychology sessions, it became clear that independence and control were hugely important for Lucy and, since her stroke, she felt that she had lost both her independence and control.

Lucy engaged extremely well in psychology sessions, reflecting on the areas she was finding challenging, trying out new coping strategies, and learning to live with her anxiety within the rehabilitation process as well.

Neuropsychological assessment

The multidisciplinary team requested a neuropsychological assessment for Lucy. Lucy subjectively reported noticing no changes in her cognitive abilities since her stroke. Lucy described finding it difficult and frustrating when she perceived family or staff to be talking to her "as if I had a memory problem." "They're speaking to me like I'm stupid. I know I've had a brain injury but I'm not stupid. It's just affected my hand. I found it patronising. I felt really vulnerable. I felt that I had moved from a person in the normal league to someone who people could say things to that I would never have put up with before."

Do what matters: Values-based approach to neuropsychological assessment

We collaboratively discussed the purpose of potentially engaging with a neuropsychological assessment with Lucy in terms of ruling out any subtle difficulties and highlighting Lucy's many strengths. For Lucy, returning to driving was really important, even though she had visual difficulties since her stroke.

Lucy found thinking about the assessment anxiety provoking, as she described "not wanting to hear any more bad news." Despite anticipatory anxiety, Lucy managed well within the context of assessment (**Doing What Matters**, **Opening Up**).

Overall, Lucy's assessment indicated significant cognitive strengths particularly within the verbal areas, including verbal comprehension, verbal speed of information processing, auditory immediate and delayed recall and working memory. All verbal abilities were maintained at premorbid levels in the 'average' to 'high average' range. Performance on visuoperceptual abilities, visual problem-solving and

visuoconstruction were poor across all visual tasks. The results of the neuropsychological assessment were fed back to Lucy who reported relief at their findings.
"If your mind was doubted, it made me all the more eager and determined to prove that my mind was good." "It's this thing about hope."

Supporting Lucy begin to make sense of her experiences

Lucy was finding the distress and fear she was experiencing upsetting. "My mind is telling me I'm a nutcase." Together, we gently normalised and validated her experience and began to develop a collaborative formulation. Through integrating the shared neuropsychological formulation (Figure 5.1 below), including assessment findings, Lucy's psychological distress and fear and identifying the visual field deficits, we took some steps towards helping make sense of Lucy's experience for herself and also for the wider team. This shared understanding and formulation helped make sense of some of Lucy's challenges engaging in neurorehabilitation programme in the NRH, far away from home.

Beginning Lucy's ACT journey

In our psychology sessions, we worked on **contacting the present moment** through supporting Lucy tonotice what is happening here and now, dropping anchor, breathing and introducing relaxation exercises to help sleep.
"I remember feeling safe in psychology sessions. You were calm, accepting the way I was. Nothing seemed to freak you out. You said you can understand why I'd

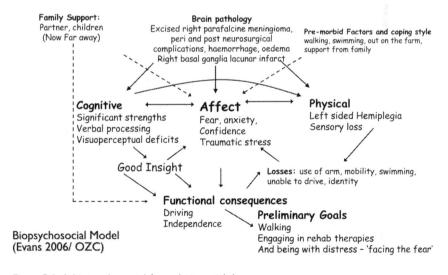

Figure 5.1 A biopsychosocial formulation with Lucy

be feeling this way given everything that I'd been through. Try this and try that. It became a safe place. You really respected me."

Once we had established some feelings of safety in our sessions, we began to identify fears and fused thoughts for Lucy. We began to work on **acceptance** of fears and distress through gentle **noticing** and **naming** emotions when they appeared and working towards **observing**, **breathing** and **allowing**. There was **normalising** Lucy's experience, including the unpleasant feelings and her experience in hospitals through listening and engagement, being with Lucy in her distress and listening to Lucy's story. We did **grounding** and **breathing** techniques together in sessions. We introduced the idea of dropping anchor (Harris, 2019).

From an ACT perspective, these early psychological therapy sessions were supporting Lucy psychologically to be with her distress during her inpatient neurorehabilitation (**Opening Up**);helping Lucy to begin to consider what's important to her (**Values**);becoming less fused with her thoughts and fears (**Defusion**);small steps forward (**Committed Action**).

"The psychology sessions were a safe place. I could talk to you. You were there with me, with my distress. You had acceptance, respect and hope for me. I started to believe there might be hope for me too."

Lucy also attended weekly psychology group sessions. She identified support from others, normalising distress and unpleasant emotions as an understandable part of the experience of having an acquired brain injury (ABI) and being in inpatient neurorehabilitation (**Opening Up**, **Acceptance**).

Lucy was very fused with thoughts around, "If I can't move my hand, then there's no point in anything. There's no point in being here"; "If I won't be able to get back to normal, then I don't want to be around"; "If I won't be able to drive, then I won't be able to go anywhere, I'll have no life."

Using the ACT framework, we slowly began identifying what was important for Lucy (**Values**), including independence, health, intelligence, determination, resilience and strength. All of these were challenged in the NRH because she was away from home, at her most vulnerable, away from her supports and facing difficult feedback on several occasions. Sessions included supporting her to be in the moment, taking small steps (**Committed Action**) and being in the here and now. Lucy was able to identify **Committed Action** –doing what it takes to get the most out of her rehabilitation, including attending groups, going shopping as part of her rehabilitation programme, engaging in neuropsychological assessment and coming back to the NRH after weekends home.

"My mind got stronger than my body, my mind was in a better place."

"Psychology gave me strength to try things, get up and try things. I can make decisions. If I fall, I can get up and all of the psychological help helps me take the next step. Instead of lying down and giving up."

An example of Lucy going to the patient canteen rather than eating on the ward showed Lucy's processes and support around managing these. Going to the canteen, Lucy felt anxious; it reminded her of where she was (in a hospital) and feeling disabled. Lucy had avoided facing her fears for several weeks by eating her meals on the ward. However, with support, she identified independence and determination as important for her (**Values**). Lucy decided to leave her wheelchair outside and walk into the canteen and felt this would help challenge the perception of being disabled and assert independence (**Facing Fears and Doing it Anyway**; **Doing What Matters**).

Overall, Lucy engaged extremely well in psychology sessions, reflecting on the areas she was finding challenging, trying out new ways of being with her distress and coping strategies and learning to live with her anxiety around the neurorehabilitation process as well.

Lucy was referred to community neurorehabilitation in Headway Services following discharge from the NRH. She was continuing to experience nightmares and flashbacks and was struggling with identity and loss. "I thought I would have made more progress." "I thought things would be solved." "Who am I?"

ACT in a community neurorehabilitation setting – Marcia and Lucy

The first time I met Lucy, she cried a lot and she frequently apologised for doing so. The focus of our initial work was on validating and normalising her distress. We discussed how the overwhelming sadness and fear she was feeling was normal given everything she had experienced. Lucy explained that up until she met Fiadhnait she had felt pathologised for her feelings; this resulted in her attempts to avoid her distress, exacerbating her deepest fear, that if she were to show others how she was really feeling, she would be considered 'mad' and 'locked up' or 'put away' in some sort of medical facility or residential home. In our very first session, while discussing the nature of distress and how minds work, I explained to Lucy that one day she would be able to tell her story without being hijacked by paralysing emotion, that she would be able to pursue what mattered to her without crying all the time, not by targeting crying for reduction but by building a meaningful life. Lucy later told me that while she agreed with me at the time, she didn't believe me. "I believed in you and trusted you, but not in that statement at all, it was so far-fetched at the time, you might as well have said I was going to the moon, there was so much blackness and darkness."

Delirium

"It felt like a horror film, or a play and I was the main character, but nobody told me the plot line, so I was completely bewildered. While I was in the coma, I was trying to communicate with the outside world all of the time. I knew I was in a really bad way and if people knew, if I could communicate this, they could help me. I am petrified of ever being put in a coma again."

Lucy had experienced delirium while in the intensive care unit. Delirium refers to the sudden onset of mental confusion caused by a physical condition. Someone experiencing delirium does not know where they are, what time it is or what's happening to them (Royal College of Psychiatrists, 2019). As a result, Lucy had no continuous, coherent memory of her acute, inpatient hospital stay. However, Lucy had vivid and terrifying memories of the nightmares she had experienced. Lucy believed that if she "could just make sense" of what had happened to her, the associated distress would resolve itself. This is a relatively common theme I have encountered when working therapeutically with people with memory loss, namely, that if they could just remember or 'fill the gaps' in their memory they would no longer experience psychological distress. For Lucy, while psychoeducation about the nature and consequences of delirium was important, it did not fully satisfy her stated need to "understand" or "make sense" of what had happened to her.

ACT offers a useful paradigm to work toward elevating psychological distress of people with memory loss because rather than focusing on the 'why,' in the past, we compassionately work toward building a meaningful life in the here and now guided by a person's values.

Psychological assessment and PTSD

Lucy and I co-constructed a psychological formulation over several sessions. We discussed the possibility that Lucy was experiencing Post-Traumatic Stress Disorder. Specifically, Lucy had intrusive images and vivid flashbacks of her hospital experiences, such as waking up in nappies, being unable to move, wash herself or go to the toilet, in addition to extremely disturbing nightmares and sensory experiences. She would become panicked and physically tremble at any mention of hospitals and/or residential/nursing homes, even in passing in the media.

While Lucy tried very hard to remember the details of what had happened to her, she simultaneously tried to avoid specific thoughts and feelings associated with it. Most notably, she avoided contacting her sadness at her multiple losses in addition to any feelings of vulnerability. She became extremely distressed in reaction to thoughts about growing older, becoming sick, more disabled or requiring any personal care support in the future. She tried instead "to focus on the positive." This message was being reinforced by others in her life, including healthcare professionals.

Lucy described herself as "jumpy." She had a strong reaction to loud or unexpected noises. She was hypersensitive to any indication from people in her life that she was somehow lesser, disabled or incompetent and moreover was hypervigilant to any suggestion that she would have to be readmitted to hospital "or put away." In response, Lucy wore 'a mask'; she used her acting skills to portray to others that nothing was wrong, she took on more tasks and responsibilities than she was likely able for, driven by her need to feel and be perceived as 'the old competent' Lucy, and significantly exacerbated her post-stroke fatigue.

As a result of her post-stroke experiences, Lucy had developed a number of trauma-related beliefs including that the world is a very unsafe place, you cannot trust medical professionals, nobody understands what I am going through, this is somehow my fault, a punishment from God for perceived previous transgressions and overwhelming feelings of being a burden to others.

The unexpected nature of Lucy's illness, the surgeries, the complicated and traumatising recovery and the fact that she came so close to dying left Lucy feeling completely "terrified of everything." She explained that her slower ability to respond to situations since her brain injury left her feeling vulnerable, particularly in novel or unknown situations.In terms of therapeutic process, I could feel her fear when we were together. Our co-constructed formulation that Lucy was experiencing PTSD was supported by her scores on psychometric measures of trauma, which fell in the extremely elevated ranges. *"That was the first time it made sense, I wasn't going mad, I had PTSD." "It felt like a vortex of horror, that I could be pulled back into at any moment, I have escaped and I am desperately holding onto it and that's why I am so on guard."*

ACT processes/therapy

Observing self and mindfulness

We designed personalised visual imagery scripts and we practised many self-as-context, mindfulness and compassion-based exercises. We opened and closed each session with some form of grounding exercise, in addition to more spontaneous in-session practices. *"I still find this hard; I can be pulled back into the past or worrying about the future. I used to really watch my granddaughter learning how to walk again; I used to watch her, where she put her feet and used it to teach myself how to walk again too. I am fully in the moment with my grandchildren and we spoke about how it's probably because I don't feel judged by them, or feel a burden to them; I am just me to them, pure acceptance again I suppose."*

Contact with the present moment and defusion

We used many standard ACT defusion techniques playfully. Sometimes, Lucy would close her eyes when speaking in session; this usually meant that she was fusing with content. We worked on helping Lucy become aware of when this was happening in the moment so she could open her eyes, anchor herself 'in the here and now' and describe her memories from a 'there and then' perspective, in the past. We learned that times of physical illness and/or falls were also significant triggers for Lucy, as they reminded her of past vulnerabilities. When Lucy became physically ill or had fallen, she was more likely to feel psychologically threatened and more likely to fuse with past content about being a burden and terrorise herself about the potential for her "to be put away." It was important that as with all aspects of therapy, Lucy's experience was validated. *"That is where you were so important, nobody else gets that, all the kindness of others, nobody else gets, yes, it gets better, but you still carry it with you and it unexpectedly opens on you. It makes me totally prickly about so many things still, friends talking about older relatives and their needs." "Words are like weapons; I had so many negative comments from healthcare professionals. I still hear (what an OT (Occupational Therapist) told me when I wanted to go back swimming), 'You will always look like a banana in the water.' I now go swimming four/five times a week, or, 'That part of your brain is dead' and I grieved even though I didn't understand that that is what I was doing. I try not to allow the thoughts and memories guide my behaviour just like we worked on. So the words of others are like weapons and they can also give hope."*

Values

Identifying and working with values was definitely the most challenging of all of the ACT processes for Lucy and me. Lucy initially identified emotional goals. "I just want to feel happier."

"I don't want to feel afraid anymore." This is both understandable and common. People often think they are coming to therapy 'to feel better.' Lucy and I spent time discussing what values are/are not. We used familiar ACT techniques (values lists, bullseye, 80th birthday party), in addition to a more fluid 'we hurt where it matters' approach woven into sessions to identify some of her values. Lucy later told me that from her perspective, I introduced values too soon, that she didn't really understand them or 'fully get' their relationship to goal setting and committed action. There is a lot of pain in value-based goal setting in neurorehabilitation. We ask people what matters to them most in their hearts and then problem-solve ways in which they can access them in forms often radically different from how they did before. It's crucial that this is done with compassion, all the while validating the person's losses, and whatever normal human reaction they are having to these losses.

"I didn't know what you meant, cause I never had these discussions before. I was too busy before my brain injury for values, but it was so helpful in the long run. In terms of acceptance, you accepted me just the way I was. I wasn't strange to you. "Yes that's fine, that's ok," I remember you saying it millions of times. I don't think I had that since I was a child. I could say anything to you, so it was the acceptance from you as well as well as the acceptance from me, as well as acceptance in ACT."

Exposure in ACT is not used to reduce negative emotions, but instead to develop a wider range of values-aligned actions. This enables the person to become more willing to experience pain, more able to recognise that their thoughts are temporary and may not always represent reality, and more able to be fully present instead of remembering the past or predicting the future (Lauwerier et al., 2012). Lucy and I worked on creating safety and we engaged in gradual compassionate exposure. I remember one session where Lucy arrived at the session exceptionally distressed; she was shaking, crying and unable to tell me what had happened. Again, I could tangibly feel the terror in the room. After some grounding exercises, she explained that she had gone to a shopping centre prior to our session and she had passed a vendor selling doughnuts; this triggered her distress and at the time she was not clear about why. We were able to work through her experience and learn that the smell of the hot oil to cook the doughnuts was the same smell she had experienced while in a coma, when she saw, smelled and heard the screams of children being burned alive. She remembered trying to crawl away from this horrific situation with her daughter on her back. Obviously, this was an extremely distressing experience for Lucy and one perhaps we may not have had the opportunity to process in such depth had it not been for her smelling the doughnut oil just before our session. By anchoring the exposure in her values, Lucy had reasons for continuing. Lucy's valuing compassion for others supported her to visit acquaintances in nursing homes and hospitals, settings which she could barely refer to in words at the beginning of therapy. "*Just the smell going into the hospital, it was like trying to put your toe into the terror. You don't ever want to face those things, you just want to go the other way.*" "And *being aware of how important being compassionate towards others is to me, I won't say it made it easier, it gave me a reason to do it.*"

Committed action

"*If you were to feel more self-confident, what would you be doing more of?*" "*I would tell my story so that others would not have to go through what I went through.*"

Lucy and I first spoke together about psychological adjustment to stroke at a conference (March 2019). Lucy and her story had such an impact on the audience that we subsequently received many invites to events and lectures. Lucy teaches and contributes to a number of third-level courses. She has written a chapter about herself in a book about stroke survivor stories. The willingness to co-author this present chapter is another of Lucy's courageous committed actions. Committed action is hard; ACTing when your feelings are pulling you elsewhere is really hard. "*I am often where I just need to put one foot in front of the other, there are times where you feel a little bit sorry for yourself and have a little cry. Then I draw on gratitude, the debit and credit on my life, my values.*"

Lucy has a number of messages advocating for others on an individual level and also on a systems level. "*I really feel like a survivor that didn't take them all out with me. Every bit of good I have I feel the absence of it more for people that don't have self-determination and I don't have the answers either, but I want to be an advocate for people who can't advocate for themselves in whatever way I can.*"

Hope in neurorehabilitation

"*When there is no hope, when there is an absence of hope, there is only darkness and you are on the edge, because you want peace, very close to taking your own life when you are hopeless. I wasn't looking for any false promises, just to be told that things will get better, it won't always be as hard as this, and it isn't, ever because nothing stays the same, time changes everything.*

"*I wondered, where are all the others that have gone before me? Where are they now? I just needed some hope. I needed a signpost that said hope.*"

Lucy's hopes were that she would become less fearful, that she would cry less, that she would regain some personal autonomy and be more self-assured and more secure about her role as a woman, as a mother and as a wife.

Hope is considered to play a key role in adapting to illness and disability (Soundy et al., 2014c; Amati et al., 2019). People "draw on hope as a natural response to the experience of having a stroke" (Soundy et al., 2014c, p. 210). Soundy et al. (2014b) describe a spectrum from 'no hope' to 'concrete hope' with 'hope in possibility' falling in between. Hope in possibility encapsulates an aspect of uncertainty. It is a 'useful' form of hope as it represents a willingness to accept that what is desired or hoped for might not happen. Hope in possibility is crucial for motivation. "Without hope in possibility, an individual's reason for continuing rehabilitation and engaging in life may be lost"(Soundy et al., 2014b, p. 258).

Hope in possibility may be mistakenly interpreted as false hope or denial (Soundy et al., 2014b). False hope has been described as "an illusion or the unrealistic expectation of the recovery process" (Amati et al., 2019, p. 6). A label such as 'false hope' represents a failure to understand the multi-dimensional nature of hope. Splitting hope into 'realistic' and 'false' hope can function to 'stereotype' or even invalidate a patient's experience (Soundy et al., 2014b).

How many times in neurorehabilitation settings do we find ourselves in conversations about 'patient motivation' or 'unrealistic goals?'

Healthcare professionals can play an important role at a vulnerable time by influencing patient hope (Soundy et al., 2014a; Bright et al., 2019). The ability to interact with patients, to manage their goals and hopes is an essential skill. An overemphasis on realistic or narrow goal setting can negatively impact a person's hopefulness (Soundy et al., 2014a).

"I don't need them to promote hope; please just don't take it away, don't steal last vestiges of hope, 'I won't waste time working on your arm.' I go to physio at least twice a week, I am not looking for someone to give me hope without doing the work, I know that no one wanted to work on my hand, but it is my body, I will continue to work on it. It's like my baby and I am not going to give up on it; I still treat my hand like a baby to this day."

Final word from Lucy

"Through psychology, I found the most important gift: hope. Hope that I could live again, laugh again, have my identity restored and live by the values in life that are important to me."

"The neurosurgeons saved my life, but it was the psychologists who showed me there was a life to live." "Like Alice, I can now live happily ever after, though it took a lot of hard work from me and my family. All the things I was told I would never do again – walk, drive, swim, look after myself – I now do with joy. Being able to shower myself is now a gift. Waking up every morning in my own bed, married to my partner, who wouldn't let go of my life; spending time with my children and grandchildren and attending to their needs; swimming with them: these

are moments of complete happiness. Life is precious. An acquired brain injury or stroke is no joke, but it is not the end, just the beginning of a new chapter."

References

Amati, M., Grignoli, N., Rubinelli, S., Amann, J., & Zanini, C. (2019). The role of hope for health professionals in rehabilitation: A qualitative study on unfavourable prognosis communication. *PLoS ONE*, *14*(10), e0224394. https://doi.org/10.1371/journal.pone.0224394

Bright, F. A., McCann, C. M., & Kayes, N. M. (2019). Recalibrating hope: A longitudinal study of the experiences of people with aphasia after stroke. *Scandinavian Journal of Caring Sciences*, *34*(2), 428–435. https://doi.org/10.1111/scs.12745

Curvis, W., & Methley, A. (Eds.). (2022). *Acceptance and Commitment Therapy and brain injury: A practical guide for clinicians* (1st ed.). Routledge. https://doi.org/10.4324/9781003024408

Evans, J. (2006). *Biopsychosocial model*. Oliver Zangwill Centre.

Gregg, J. A., Callaghan, G. M., Hayes, S. C., & Glenn-Lawson, J. L. (2007). Improving diabetes self-management through acceptance, mindfulness, and values: A randomized controlled trial. *Journal of Consulting and Clinical Psychology, 75*(2), 336–343. https://doi.org/10.1037/0022-006X.75.2.336

Harris, R. (2019). *ACT made simple: An easy-to-Read primer on acceptance and commitment therapy*. New Harbinger.

Hayes, S. C., Luoma, J. B., Bond, F. W., Masuda, A., & Lillis, J. (2006). Acceptance and commitment therapy: Model, processes and outcomes. *Behaviour Research and Therapy*, *44*(1), 1–25. https://doi.org/10.1016/j.brat.2005.06.006

Hayes, S. C., Strosahl, K. D., & Wilson, K. G. (1999). *Acceptance and commitment therapy: An experiential approach to behavior change*. Guilford Press.

Large, R., Samuel, V., & Morris, R. (2020). A changed reality: Experience of an Acceptance and Commitment therapy (ACT) group after stroke. *Neuropsychological Rehabilitation*, *30*(8), 1477–1496. https://doi.org/10.1080/09602011.2019.1589531

Lauwerier E., Van Damme, S., Goubert L., Paemeleire, K., Devulder, J., & Crombez, G. (2012). To control or not? A motivational perspective on coping with pain. *Acta Neurologica Belgica*, *112*(1), 3–7. https://doi.org/10.1007/s13760-012-0020-6

Plant, S.E., Tyson, S.F., Kirk, S., & Parsons, J. (2016). What are the barriers and facilitators to goal-setting during rehabilitation for stroke and other acquired brain injuries? A systematic review and meta-synthesis. *Clinical Rehabilitation, 30*(9), 921–930. https://doi.org/10.1177/0269215516655856

Royal College of Psychiatrists. (2019, October). *Delirium*. www.rcpsych.ac.uk. https://www.rcpsych.ac.uk/mental-health/problems-disorders/delirium

Soundy, A., Liles, C., Stubbs, B., & Roskell, C. (2014a). Identifying a framework for hope in order to establish the importance of generalised hopes for individuals who have suffered a stroke. *Advances in Medicine, 2014*, 1–8. https://doi.org/10.1155/2014/471874

Soundy, A., Sayers, J., Stubbs, B., & Roskell, C. (2014b). Don't take my hope away: Understanding the patient's hope in neurological rehabilitation. *International Journal of Therapy and Rehabilitation, 21*(6), 257–258. https://doi.org/10.12968/ijtr.2014.21.6.257

Soundy, A., Stubbs, B., Freeman, P., Coffee, P., & Roskell, C. (2014c). Factors influencing patients' hope in stroke and spinal cord injury: A narrative review. *International Journal of Therapy and Rehabilitation, 21*(5), 210–218. https://doi.org/10.12968/ijtr.2014.21.5.210

Sugavanam, T., Mead, G., Bulley, C., Donaghy, M., & van Wijck, F. (2013). The effects and experiences of goal setting in stroke rehabilitation - a systematic review. *Disability and Rehabilitation, 35*(3), 177–190.

Teggart, V., Thompson, C., & Rozwaha, T. (2022). Integrating acceptance and commitment therapy into holistic neuropsychological rehabilitation. In W. Curvis & A. Methley (Eds.), *Acceptance and Commitment Therapy and brain injury* (pp. 7–15). Routledge. https://doi.org/10.4324/9781003024408-3

Thompson, K., Bulls, H., Sibille, K., Bartley, E., Glover, T., Terry, E., Vaughn, I., Cardoso, J., Sotolongo, A., Staud, R., Hughes, L., Edberg, J., Redden, D., Bradley, L., Goodin, B., & Fillingim, R. (2018). Optimism and psychological resilience are beneficially associated with measures of clinical and experimental pain in adults with or at risk for knee osteoarthritis. *The Clinical Journal of Pain, 34*(12), 1164–1172. https://doi.org/10.1097/AJP.0000000000000642

Chapter 6

Creative interventions with ACT and severe brain injury

Richard Coates

I now work full time in independent practice with adults and their families who have mostly experienced a severe traumatic brain injury as a result of a road traffic accident.

I really value connection, caring deeply, helping, fun, learning and creativity. Working in this context and having worked with some great colleagues and services over the years have really helped me to put those values into action with my clients. It was when I discovered Acceptance and Commitment Therapy (ACT) that my value of creativity became clear and led to a greater vitality with my work. ACT itself facilitates creativity. It is a non-linear, process-based therapy, meaning that you can have fun with it, adapt it and evolve it, whilst still holding the underlying processes and the philosophical stance of functional contextualism. I have valued watching other colleagues share their creative work. I hope to inspire others to follow their values and heart in their work too.

Severe brain injury poses many challenges to clinicians. Dramatic life changes to work, independence, health, parenting, friendships and hobbies would be enough for anyone to navigate. Add to the experience significant problems with fatigue, stimulation from the environment, pain, concentrating on what you are doing, remembering your day-to-day experience, making and following through on plans, controlling your frustration and coping with anxiety and depression and not being aware of these difficulties and you have a complex challenge. There have been suggestions for how to adapt ACT for clients with cognitive impairment (Whiting et al., 2017). I find that creativity and playfulness add to this, in terms of engagement and remembering the intervention and equally, adaptations, such as making things more visual, feed back into the creativity and process of psychological flexibility.

For me, creativity particularly seems to come when I am faced with a complex challenge: a client not wanting to engage, significant cognitive difficulties getting in the way of change and feeling stuck with a client. Indeed, Iain McGilchrist (2021) highlights the need for an opposing force for something new to emerge.

I find learning about the work others have done with clients enlightening, helpful and sparking of further creativity. I share some examples of creative work with

DOI: 10.4324/9781003193722-7

clients here in the hope that it might open up possibilities for you, the reader and will lead to you coming up with further creative ways of working with your clients. The client examples are practical, so that you can see what I did and you can generate ways that you could do. There is no one way to do things, which is crucial to creativity. Variation is key. Follow your own creative path, even though there will be influences to your work. Be curious, try things, make mistakes, be kind with yourself if it doesn't work, see what works with particular clients and contexts and it if it works, keep going with it and evolve it further.

Client examples used have either given consent and details are still changed to maintain confidentiality, or their details have been changed so that the information is completely mixed up and does not represent the client details at all, just the approach used.

Client examples

The man who turned into a tiger – use of metaphor

Human language is brimming (case in point) with metaphors. ACT, along with other psychotherapies makes use of metaphor in eliciting behaviour change. Stoddard and Afari (2014) say that, "good psychotherapists are good storytellers. They know how to open clients up to what is truly new by using knowledge that is old. They know how to create experiences that inform and heal." "Metaphors and exercises are stories and experiences that link the richness of what you already know to domains in which you are unsure what to do."

I find that ACT in particular helps to bring precision to the use of metaphors, owing to Relational Frame Theory (RFT). Törneke (2017, 2020) describes how at the heart of a metaphor is a 'target' and a 'source.' For example, 'he' is a 'beast.' 'He' is the 'target' and 'beast' is the source. Without knowing anything about 'he,' you can quickly transfer the functions of the 'source' 'beast' to the target.

In this context, I had initially been working with a client, John, who had sustained a severe brain injury as a result of an accident. The client was married to Sarah, but was living separately from her and their daughter, as a result of frequent occasions of not being able to control his anger following his brain injury. This had resulted in him beating Sarah. Sarah was very scared of him. John was very sad that he wasn't living with Sarah and their daughter. John had received previous brain injury rehabilitation to help with his anger. This hadn't made any difference, although he believed that it had. Sarah was being pressured by his family to return to live with him. John and his family were telling her that he had received treatment and that he was better now and that he wouldn't get angry with her again.

Sarah had indicated that she was considering living with him again. I had been asked to provide some information independently to his family that would help her have an informed decision about what to do, as part of wider support from statutory services.

In preparing for meeting with Sarah, I was aware that she had previously received brain injury education from another professional, but that the information was hard for her to understand and was easily discountable by John's family, that he had had treatment and that he was better now. Sarah also felt incredibly guilty that she was not supporting her husband, "in sickness and in health."

I had the thought that further brain injury education wouldn't make any more difference. I also knew that I would want to get across certain points: John hasn't changed; he still gets angry; he isn't aware that he still gets angry; that this change in him can be difficult for people to see from the outside; and that he could cause harm to his wife and possibly his daughter.

Faced with this challenge, I went for a run. Whilst running, I had thoughts about the power of stories and metaphors to convey the points that I wanted to get across. A story about a man who had been turned into a tiger came to mind. John would be the target and the source would be the tiger. The source of the tiger would evoke danger and the function of keeping away from it. There were certain elements that I wanted to keep the same, i.e., potential danger of the client, whereas there were other elements that I wanted to change, i.e., the client isn't better, they still get angry and aren't aware of it. I developed the following metaphor:

> A man was travelling to work one day. On the way to work, he had an accident and on the inside he was turned into a tiger. On the outside, he still looked like a man. The man knew he had been in an accident, but didn't know that he had been turned into a tiger.
>
> The man went home to his family and started behaving like a tiger. His family didn't know why he was behaving differently. His family felt scared by how he was behaving and could not live with the man.
>
> The man went to a doctor, who tried their best, but the doctor couldn't change him back from a tiger to a man. The man thought that the doctor had changed him back to a man, but he was still a tiger. The man was sad without his family and didn't understand why his family wouldn't live with him anymore.

When I met with Sarah, I initially built rapport and heard her perspective about John in detail and asked her for the perspective of John and his and her family. I asked her what would be helpful for her from our visit. She told me that she would like to know whether he was better now. I then asked if it was ok if I told her a story. I read the metaphor to her. At the point where I said that the man had been turned into a tiger, Sarah became tearful. I knew that she had connected with the story at this point. At the end of the story, I asked Sarah what the story means about the situation with her husband. She said, "he is still a tiger," and cried. This then allowed us to open up about considering alternative behaviours to returning to live with her husband, based on her own values and not based on 'rules' about what she should do, according to other people or institutions.

Steve – grabbing the mic

Steve had a severe traumatic brain injury as a result of a road traffic accident. He had significant fatigue, attentional, memory and executive difficulties. In addition, he experienced worry, anxiety and high levels of self-criticism.

Prior to his accident, he was very competent at MCing (rapping). He had sustained some reduced fluency with his speech as a result of his brain injury. Improving his MCing ability was highlighted by him as a main goal. He worked with an excellent, creative Speech and Language Therapist (SLT) to improve his fluency. His goal was to post a recording of himself MCing on his Facebook stories for 24 hours. Despite good feedback from SLT and his family, he was very critical of his ability after his brain injury. Through defusion, Steve identified these thoughts as being like a critical 'judge.' The creative work of the SLT inspired me with my work with Steve.

Visual representation was very helpful for Steve, in terms of supporting his working memory and making the process 'fun' and 'engaging.' I created some PowerPoint slides to illustrate defusion and experiential acceptance to Steve. I used a background photo of a stage with spotlights and found additional photos of a judge. With permission, I also used a photo of Steve MCing before his brain injury. The first PowerPoint slide showed the 'judge' being centre stage on the microphone. There were five slides that gradually moved Steve closer to the centre of the stage and made his image bigger. This was like frames from a film. Changing them gave the perception of the images moving. The final slide had Steve centre stage MCing some lyrics that we had written together about his brain injury. I emphasised for defusion and experiential acceptance processes that the 'judge' would still be on stage, just more at the side of the stage.

Steve agreed to do a role play with me playing the 'judge' and him MCing to some instrumental music. The session was via Zoom, due to COVID-19 restrictions. I had previously felt stuck with helping Steve defuse from self-criticism. I had tried other techniques, such as "I'm having the thought that," which helped at the time, but didn't have a lasting effect, as it was quickly forgotten. I also got him to repeat a word he was fused with over and over again. This just highlighted how much slower he was with his verbal output, compared to me doing it. Out of this challenge, I had the idea of being creative with Zoom. I changed my background to an image of a judge's chair in court, I borrowed my child's dressing up cape and found a cleaning duster as a substitute for a wig. Steve did not know what I was going to do. He just got his music and microphone ready. He was willing to record this exercise. I was able to turn off my video, change into the 'judge' and then come back on. This made Steve smile. We started the music and I MCed Steve's self-critical thoughts: "This is shit…you sound drunk." Steve started moving to the beat of the music. He then thanked the 'judge' for his MCing and took over with his own pre-injury lyrics he knew well. He finished with a massive smile on his face.

Using the slides mentioned above, Steve said that he had moved two steps 'towards' the centre of the stage. He agreed to let me post the video in a closed

Facebook group for ACT professionals for feedback. He received lots of positive feedback about his rhythm, timing and clarity. This feedback then helped him move 'towards' another step. Dressing up as a judge myself modelled a willingness to Steve, to show vulnerability myself, even though my Mind was coming up with thoughts about what my peers would think. The experiential exercise was fun, memorable and effective for Steve. Steve has enjoyed sharing this video with other professionals working with him.

Steve could perform verbally with ease when MCing before his brain injury at a high tempo. He was able to perform at half the speed after his brain injury and what was effortless required significant concentration. To him, it felt like he was stuttering to get words out when speaking. Through a friend, he was offered a spot on a radio station to MC. His Mind then related, "I stutter when I speak" and "MCing is faster than speaking" to "if I stutter when I speak then I will stutter even more when MCing." He experienced nervousness about MCing on the radio. It would have been tempting to provide reassurance (experiential avoidance) around his stuttering and whether it would have been as bad as he imagined. However, from an ACT perspective I wanted him to approach the stimulus of 'stuttering,' rather than avoiding it. Drawing on what had been helpful before/what had worked, I suggested that we could intentionally get him to stutter as much as possible, by creating the character, 'MC Stutter.' Steve was willing to do this. At this time changed my Zoom background to decks in a radio studio and put my radio DJ headphones on. I showed this to Steve and suggested we have a name for the radio station. He suggested, "Jolty FM," with jolty having a similar relation to stutter, highlighting a lack of smoothness. Steve had recently talked about his value of 'freedom' that he could just turn up to a gig and jump on the stage. We recreated this context to some extent, by him being willing to just jump into the exercise without knowing we were going to do it, as it was a creative moment. Recording the exercise also added the context of performing and the function of entertaining. I stuttered in my role as DJ on "Jolty FM" and introduced "MC Stutter." Both Steve and I found it hard to intentionally try to stutter as much as possible. Steve used some past lyrics and added different performance gestures, as though he was engaging with the audience. We both smiled and laughed during the exercise, experiencing 'fun,' 'humour' and 'playfulness.' Steve reflected how he was able to use what he feared, 'stuttering,' and have a good time with it. He was willing to do something that really mattered to him: MCing on the radio, even with the fear of stuttering.

Sheila – walking 'towards' who matters

Sheila had had a stroke, which had left her with attention, memory, executive functioning and vestibular difficulties. She lived alone with support coming into the house. Sheila's husband had died several years before her stroke. Sheila used a four-wheel walker to get around the house, which she had been using since coming home from the hospital. Her physiotherapist was trying to increase Sheila's walking without her walker, which she would be able to do if there was support around.

Sheila was very anxious about walking without the walker and dismissive of any suggestions to do so.

I suggested a graded exposure approach to walking without the walker, which Sheila would not agree to, as she always wanted to have the walker in her sight, by the side of her bed. However, the sight of the walker acted as a powerful stimulus to use it. One day, Sheila said, "If my husband were alive, he would get rid of the walker and say, 'You'll be ok, I'll walk with you every step of the way.'"

In order to get rid of the stimulus of the four-wheel walker, without taking it out of the room and thinking about the ACT Matrix (Polk et al., 2016) and the power of people moving towards 'who' matters to them, I had the idea of covering the walker with a large black bag and having a laminated sign on the bag with a picture of Sheila and her husband together, with the words that Sheila's husband would say: "You'll be ok, I'll walk with you every step of the way." Unlike the suggestions of graded exposure, Sheila was willing to try this and agreed to me taking a photo of a picture of her and her husband that she had. We agreed to do this for a specific time (using a countdown clock that was visible) and when support was present. This had an immediate change in behaviour, with Sheila walking to the kitchen and back without her walker.

This idea can be seen as transforming the function of using the walker. The function was initially to reduce anxiety about falling (experiential avoidance). The function then changed to being in opposition to who was important to her. Not using the walker changed to moving closer towards her husband and his wishes/support. The function was now under appetitive control (see Herbert et al., 2021 for more details).

Although Sheila benefitted from this transformation of stimulus function when I was present, due to significant memory difficulties she needed Support Workers to adopt this approach outside of neuropsychology sessions. Due to how Sheila saw herself and Support Workers in the hierarchy, she dismissed Support Worker attempts to get her walking without the four-wheeled walker, unfortunately. Support Workers did not have the same confidence, due to their context. There were other ways that the behaviour, walking without the walker, could come under appetitive control with them. Examples included asking Sheila to waltz across the room with them. This added further variation and playfulness.

Tom – virtual body boarding

Tom sustained a severe traumatic brain injury as a result of a work accident. He had significant attention, memory, executive functioning and speech difficulties. Tom's main goals were to get back to swimming and running. When swimming, due to his difficulty with breath control, he found he would inhale water and therefore become very anxious about putting his head in water. Tom also struggled to get the explosive movement with high knees for running. Talking therapy was challenging for Tom. He didn't remember the difficulties he experienced and would also minimise any suggestion of difficulties outside of the context, saying, "I'm fine." I didn't really know what to do and where to start at the beginning.

As talking to him about the context wasn't working, I tried something different. I initially tried mindfulness of the breath, but with his difficulty with speech and breath control, he found this challenging. I then introduced some imagery work to see how he responded. I had done imagery exercises with previous clients that involved them closing their eyes, connecting with their body (touch of their body against the chair, rhythm of their breath, etc.) and then imagining getting up from their chair and walking across the room to a door that had appeared in the corner of the room, with a crack of light around it. I would then ask them to open the door and step through into a different scene, for example, being outdoors in nature somewhere.

I asked Tom if there was a beautiful place that he liked going to. He picked a beach that he would visit every year with his family and suggested I speak to his family about it. His family shared photos of the beach and described what it was like to me. I also found out that there was a live video feed of the beach, which I was able to watch online with Tom to talk about the key features of this beach. I then used the ideas to try to create an image of visiting the beach. I spoke with his SLT to incorporate imagery-based breathing exercises in the sea and with his physiotherapist to incorporate imagery-based running. This was based on the research that has shown that imagining doing an activity activates the same muscles as actually doing the activity (Yao et al., 2013).

I incorporated ACT processes (present-moment awareness, experiential acceptance, values and committed action), which culminated in imagining going body boarding and then jogging along the beach. I recorded the exercise, asking Tom to listen to it in between sessions, with his Support Workers and a Google Calendar entry to facilitate this practice. This created an opportunity for Tom to rest for a period of ten minutes, which was something he otherwise found difficult to do after his brain injury. Extracts of the imagery included:

> "Notice the freezing cold water on your toes and feet and gradually moving up inside your wetsuit to your calves and your knees…and up to your neck, and feel the cold water go down the back of your wetsuit."
>
> "As you are floating waiting to catch a wave, take your face and place it in the sea gently blowing out bubbles…as you do this a small wave gently washes over your face."
>
> "As you get out of the sea, you decide to go for a short jog along the beach to warm up, driving with your arms and keeping your knees high."

Subsequently, physically joining Tom in a swimming pool with his physiotherapist, he was able to relate the splash of the swimming pool to the waves of the sea. This transformed the function of the water in the pool, allowing it to wash over him. He was able to keep his head in the water and breathe through his nose. With the input of his physiotherapists, he spontaneously started running on the beach with his family and then went on to complete a sponsored run.

Geoff – I miss my books

Geoff sustained a severe traumatic brain injury as a result of a road traffic accident. He had attentional, memory and executive and visual difficulties. Prior to his accident he had enjoyed reading a range of books, including general knowledge, and had loved looking at maps, taking the lead in planning trips away with his wife. He was now unable to read books or make out information on maps. His wife was sad that this enjoyable activity together and their future was taken away from them. She felt anxious and stressed about going away together, when Geoff had always taken the lead in planning. She was understandably fused with thoughts, "It won't be the same," which was getting in the way of this values-based activity.

I considered 'knowledge' to be a key value that Geoff was now unable to put into action with planning holidays and came up with the idea of starting a 'knowledge project' with Geoff about their scheduled holiday in six months' time. I mentioned this to Geoff and his wife, and they were both keen for him to be involved in this, which hadn't always been the case with other suggestions for his rehabilitation.

I began by searching for audiobooks about the area where they were going to stay. I couldn't find any. I then wondered about me reading a book aloud to Geoff and recording it. I then had the idea to look on YouTube for videos with audio and found some about the specific area. The person in the video showed people around the area and talked about the history. They also had a dog they took with them everywhere, which was another way to connect with Geoff and his wife. As a result of the coronavirus, I had learnt the skill of sharing videos and sound via screenshare on Zoom.

I initially met with Geoff on Zoom and I shared the YouTube videos on screen. He could hear the information shared about the places they were going to visit. I adopted a curious, learning stance with him too, as they were places I had visited, but had not heard all the history behind them. Geoff was also able to see aspects of the video, which he responded to. We watched and listened to one video and then he wanted to watch and listen to more. At the end of the videos, I supported him with prompting for his memory to talk to his wife about what we had learnt. His wife then gained interest and joined us for future sessions, making it an enjoyable activity that we were also doing together.

His wife began to notice 'enjoyment' showing up in Geoff during this project. 'Enjoyment' was a key cue for her in doing activities with Geoff. She did not want to make him do anything he didn't enjoy, as the accident had taught her that life was too short. We even managed to use Street View on Google Maps to see the actual cottage they were going to and walk around the village. This helped with Geoff's wife's confidence of being able to find the cottage without Geoff's visual support and to go on holiday for the first time again together since Geoff's accident. They had a great time, and the reinforcement of the holiday led to further trips away, engaging in a valued activity together.

Metaphors with rehabilitation teams

It is very common for people I work with to need support from others and at the same time to not want that support. The driving forces of valuing independence in Western contexts and difficulty with awareness of difficulties following a severe brain injury often collide. Faced with the challenge of how do you help aversive functions of support develop some more appetitive functions, metaphors for the whole team have emerged.

Roxanne and the band

Roxanne sustained a severe brain injury and had been living in her own home with some daily support by her sister, until her sister had to move location. This meant that she needed a team of Support Workers instead. This was incredibly hard for her; she wanted things to stay as they had been and although she knew she needed support, she didn't want it. Roxanne was passionate about music. She attended gigs with her Support Workers and loved to sing. Talking with her one day and making room for how hard it was having support (acceptance), a metaphor naturally came to mind, that it was like she had been used to singing at home alone and then all of a sudden, this band turns up. To start off with, they are really annoying and you are singing and playing out of time and then something starts to happen and you start to play well together and go off on tour, rocking it where you go. Roxanne immediately related to this metaphor and was happy for me to share the metaphor with her Support Worker who was present. This then led to a creative energy between Roxanne, the Support Worker and myself about what instruments the different Support Workers might be playing in the band, e.g. the Lead Support Worker playing the drums and keeping the rhythm. Importantly, Roxanne would be Lead Singer, suggesting what songs they play next. The whole Support Worker team connected with this metaphor and it has been able to be played around with and added to, for example, linking to emotions and what type of music is being played, e.g., anger as punk and that just as Roxanne can be unhappy with support, bands also fall out with one another and there are some bands who navigate this and play music for a long time together.

Louise – the rally driver

Louise again was fiercely independent and also knew that she needed support. She had loved thrill-seeking before her injury and was passionate about cars. She did not like feeling other people were controlling her and would do the opposite if rules were imposed on her. She would try her best to make changes in her life and when these went wrong she would spiral downwards in mood and be very hard on herself. She was also very impulsive after her injury and struggled to regulate her behaviour. I have found the work of Mark Ylvisaker and Tim Feeney, introduced to me by an SLT colleague when I first qualified, so helpful when trying to engage people with rehabilitation. Ylvisaker and Feeney (2000) highlight the importance of metaphors in helping with developing self-regulation functions and a sense of control in the process. Louise's SLT had brought in different car metaphors already and Louise had really related to them.

Holding all of these functions of a metaphor in mind: self-regulation, control/choice, that mistakes are normal and are going to happen, that having a team is helpful, it all came together in vision when I was having a shower: Louise is a rally driver. She is driving the car but needs a navigator (Support Worker) sitting alongside to let her know what corner is coming up ahead, e.g., 'tight left.' It's also normal that she is going to go too fast around the corners and will crash and roll the car. When this happens, there is a whole rehabilitation team around her who can help her and the car get back on the course. When I introduced this to Louise, I presented it in visual form with images of rally cars with all four wheels off the ground, with images of the driver and navigator and a car rolling on a corner. Louise related to it straight away and suggested a particular rally driver who she really admired. I then changed the images to be of this particular rally driver. The whole team related to the metaphor too and has sparked off other creative ways of working with Louise and the whole team.

Project-based rehabilitation: Inspire others

Project-based rehabilitation (Ylvisaker & Feeney, 2000) was also introduced to me by an SLT colleague early in my career and has continued to inspire my work.

The website www.inspireothers.org.uk   literally started as a dream. I was working with a team with a client who couldn't go back to work and didn't want to do voluntary work, as they saw it as a 'crappy job.' We were really struggling to help them find meaningful long-term activity. Additionally, they had so much to share with the challenges they had faced that would be really helpful for other people with neurological conditions to hear. It was during rapid eye movement (REM) sleep where all the pieces came together and the name 'inspire others' and the vision to share stories from people with neurological conditions to hopefully help other people emerged. The psychological flexibility of ACT and contact with my values of creativity and connection allowed me to wake, register the domain name and email colleagues to see who wanted to co-create this project with me. A core stewarding group with therapists and clients developed. We used a ProSocial process (Atkins, Hayes, & Wilson, 2019) from the first meeting, to develop a clear shared identity and purpose using the ACT Matrix and psychological flexibility alongside it (see Figure 6.1):

We used the top right of the Matrix to take tiny, committed actions over months to create and launch the website in December 2021. This was something none of us had ever done before. For all of us, it is connecting with what matters to us. The project continues to create new opportunities and to develop all of us involved, from a client developing the logo, learning from each other about video editing and the client stories being so helpful in therapeutic work and teaching. Enjoy looking at the website to learn more.

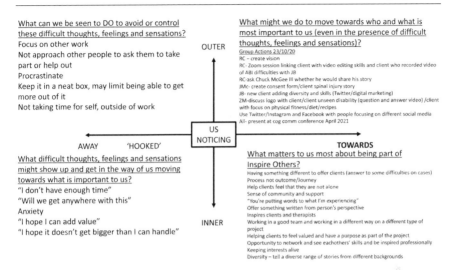

What can we be seen to DO to avoid or control these difficult thoughts, feelings and sensations?
Focus on other work
Not approach other people to ask them to take part or help out
Procrastinate
Keep it in a neat box, may limit being able to get more out of it
Not taking time for self, outside of work

OUTER

What might we do to move towards who and what is most important to us (even in the presence of difficult thoughts, feelings and sensations)?
Group Actions 23/10/20
RC – create vision
RC- Zoom session linking client with video editing skills and client who recorded video of ABI difficulties with JB
RC-ask Chuck McGee III whether he would share his story
JMc- create consent form/client spinal injury story
JB- new client adding diversity and skills (Twitter/digital marketing)
ZM-discuss logo with client/client unseen disability (question and answer video) /client with focus on physical fitness/diet/recipes
Use Twitter/Instagram and Facebook with people focusing on different social media
All- present at cog comm conference April 2021

US NOTICING

AWAY   'HOOKED'   TOWARDS

What difficult thoughts, feelings and sensations might show up and get in the way of us moving towards what is important to us?
"I don't have enough time"
"Will we get anywhere with this"
Anxiety
"I hope I can add value"
"I hope it doesn't get bigger than I can handle"

INNER

What matters to us most about being part of Inspire Others?
Having something different to offer clients (answer to some difficulties on cases)
Process not outcome/Journey
Help clients feel that they are not alone
Sense of community and support
"You're putting words to what I'm experiencing"
Offer something written from person's perspective
Inspires clients and therapists
Working in a good team and working in a different way on a different type of project
Helping clients to feel valued and have a purpose as part of the project
Opportunity to network and see eachothers' skills and be inspired professionally
Keeping interests alive
Diversity – tell a diverse range of stories from different backgrounds

Figure 6.1 ACT Matrix for Inspire Others

Continuing the creative process

Thank you for reading the chapter. My intention to you was to show the creative, helpful possibilities of using ACT with people with neurological conditions. I hope that I have inspired you to have fun and try different things out, even if you don't know whether it will work or not. These are examples that evolved in the contexts of my work and the clients I was working with. Enjoy finding your own ways that work for you and the specific client you are working with. I love that values, such as creativity can be expressed in millions of different ways. I am curious to see how you and others reading already put, or could put 'creativity' into action with neurorehabilitation. Enjoy the process. I'd love to hear how you get on.

References

Atkins, P. W. B., Wilson, D. S., & Hayes, S. C. (2019). *Prosocial: Using evolutionary science to build productive, equitable, and collaborative groups*. New Harbinger.

Hebert, E. R., Flynn, M. K., Wilson, K. G., & Kellum, K. K. (2021). Values intervention as an establishing operation for approach in the presence of aversive stimuli. *Journal of Contextual Behavioral Science*, *20*, 144–154. https://doi.org/10.1016/j.jcbs.2021.04.001

McGilchrist, I. (2021). *The matter with things*. Perspectiva Press.

Polk, K. L., Schoendorff, B., Webster, M., & Olaz, F. O. (2016). *The essential guide to the ACT matrix: A step-by-step approach to using the ACT matrix model in clinical practice*. New Harbinger.

Stoddard, J. A., & Afari, N. A. (2014). *The big book of ACT metaphors. A practitioner's guide to experiential exercises and metaphors in Acceptance and Commitment Therapy*. New Harbinger.

Törneke, N. (2017). *Metaphor in practice. A professional's guide to using the science of language and psychotherapy*. New Harbinger.

Törneke, N. (2020). Using metaphor in Acceptance and Commitment Therapy. Contextual Consulting Webinar, 15th May.

Whiting, D. L., Deane, F. P., Simpson, G. K., McLeod, H. M., & Ciarrochi, J. (2017). Cognitive and psychological flexibility after a traumatic brain injury and the implications for treatment in acceptance-based therapies: A conceptual review. *Neuropsychological Rehabilitation, 27*(2), 263–299. https://doi.org/10.1080/09602011.2015.1062115

Yao, W. X., Ranganathan, V. K., Allexandre, D., Siemionow, V., & Yue, G. H. (2013). Kinesthetic imagery training of forceful muscle contractions increases brain signal and muscle strength. *Frontiers in Human Neuroscience, 26*(7), 561. https://doi.org/10.3389/fnhum.2013.00561

Ylvisaker, M., & Feeney, T. (2000). Reflections on Dobermanns, poodles, and social rehabilitation for difficult-to-serve individuals with traumatic brain injury, *Aphasiology, 14*(4), 407–431. https://doi.org/10.1080/026870300401432

Chapter 7

Informing therapeutic practice after a traumatic brain injury

Values identification and achievement during engagement in Acceptance and Commitment Therapy

Diane Whiting, Grahame Simpson and Frank Deane

The chapter focusses on values for individuals with a traumatic brain injury. The chapter aims to provide greater clarification of the types of values that are important to people after they experience a brain injury. As part of this process, it also provides a review of a tool to assist in values identification and clarification. As evidence-based clinicians working with individuals who have experienced a traumatic brain injury (TBI), our values are to provide the most effective treatment to alleviate distress and facilitate emotional adjustment after the injury. We see values clarification and pursuit as a core process in the recovery journey after TBI that's intrinsically linked to goal-based rehabilitation. Unfortunately, there is limited research on values and valued action in this context. This chapter aims to address this gap and to contribute to the literature in order to assist other clinicians in pursuing evidence-based practice in working with values.

Traumatic brain injury is a global public health challenge, with 69 million people estimated to sustain a TBI every year (Dewan et al., 2019). In Australia, the incidence of TBI is estimated at 100 per 100,000 (Pozzato et al., 2019), with moderate and severe injuries comprising just under 12% of all TBIs. However, the lifetime costs for the moderate and severe TBI groups are estimated at $2.5 and $4.8 million per person (Australian dollars) respectively (Access Economics, 2009).

A TBI can result in a range of motor sensory (e.g., spasticity, tremor, reduced vision), cognitive (challenges with attention, speed of information processing, memory and executive functions) and emotional/behavioural (aggressive behaviours, lack of initiation, reduced self-awareness) impairments (Ponsford et al., 2014; Sabaz et al., 2014). These impairments can have an impact on a person's occupation with only 30–40% of people able to resume open employment post-injury (Simpson et al., 2020). Rates of relationship breakdown and/or social isolation can also increase post-injury (Winter et al., 2018; Wood & Yurdakul, 1997). Furthermore, a TBI can impact upon independent living skills in areas such as home management, transport, budgeting and community mobility, resulting in the need for support over the long term (Tate et al., 2020).

DOI: 10.4324/9781003193722-8

Not surprisingly, the above challenges can have a significant psychological impact upon individuals and their families. Psychological distress, including symptoms and disorders of anxiety, depression, hopelessness and suicide ideation, is elevated after TBI in comparison to the general population (Bahraini et al., 2013; Bombardier et al., 2010; Gould et al., 2011; Moore et al., 2006; Simpson & Tate, 2002). Although the majority of research focus to date has been on this psychological distress, there is also emerging evidence that resilience can play a role in buffering against negative outcomes and facilitating positive well-being after TBI (Elliott et al., 2019; Paasila et al., 2022; Rapport et al., 2020). Adjustment post-injury can involve cognitive, behavioural and emotional adaptation as well as a search for meaning (Freeman et al., 2015; Jones et al., 2018).

There has been growing evidence over the past decade for the efficacy of psychological therapies in treating psychological distress after TBI. Programs based on Cognitive Behavioural Therapy (CBT) have focussed on the treatment of symptoms of anger (Medd & Tate, 2000), social anxiety (Hodgson et al., 2005), anxiety and depression in combination (Ponsford et al., 2016) and hopelessness and suicide ideation (Brenner et al., 2018; Simpson et al., 2011). Treatments have been novel, integrating CBT with elements from motivational interviewing (Ponsford et al., 2016) or post-traumatic growth (Brenner et al., 2018; Simpson et al., 2011). However, the CBT-based treatments trialled to date have primarily focussed on the reduction of symptoms of psychological distress, but the efficacy of such approaches to promoting positive adjustment post-TBI is less clear.

As a therapeutic modality, Acceptance and Commitment Therapy (ACT) shows significant promise in being able to facilitate the post-TBI adjustment process, reducing feelings of psychological distress (Sander et al., 2021; Whiting, Deane, McLeod et al., 2020) and promoting meaningful engagement in life. Research in both civilian and military populations with a TBI has demonstrated the benefits of ACT being delivered in small groups (Whiting, Deane, Simpson et al., 2020), individually (Rauwenhoff et al., 2022; Sander et al., 2021; Whiting, Deane, McLeod et al., 2020) and in one-day workshops (Dindo et al., 2020). Furthermore, current research has expanded the mode of delivery to include the use of eHealth, with two clinical trials currently underway (Rauwenhoff et al., 2019; Whiting et al., 2021). In the context of these initial promising results, there is still a lot to learn about the features of the various therapeutic elements of ACT (i.e., contact with the present moment, acceptance, defusion, self-as-context, values and committed action, the core elements of psychological flexibility) when delivered in the context of TBI.

From among these elements, the focus of this chapter will be on the role and process of values identification. Values identification is a central component of ACT, providing the framework for committed action in the therapeutic process (Hayes et al., 1999). The use of values can play a dual role in guiding the therapeutic process after TBI, by both improving client-centred goal setting and motivation in rehabilitation, respectively. This may assist the person to move towards acceptance of their injury and improve their well-being as they engage in behaviour that is consistent with their identified values.

Values identification and clarification create an opportunity to define and personalise goals in relation to the client's preferred life directions. Client-centred goal setting is an important component of the rehabilitation process after brain injury (Prescott et al., 2015) with an increased focus on the use of SMART (specific, measurable, achievable, relevant and time-bound) goals (Hassett et al., 2014). The process of identifying and clarifying the importance of different valued life domains allows an individual to prioritise aspects of their lives that they wish to pursue and progress. In this way, values can be used to guide the establishment of SMART goals as they provide the opportunity for a client-centred approach to goal setting. Using a client-centred approach to setting goals is more likely to result in goal achievement (Prescott et al., 2019) as it also serves as a source of motivation for engagement in the rehabilitation process (Doig et al., 2009; Ellis et al., 2018), especially when discrepancies occur between identified values and current behaviour (Hayes et al., 1999).

Post-injury adjustment can be facilitated by client-centred goal planning and attainment, resulting in improved functioning and psychological well-being (Pais et al., 2019). In a broader sample of acquired brain injury (ABI), including both stroke and TBI, higher-rated valued living was associated with increased well-being and lower distress (Baseotto et al., 2022). Research has also indicated that living in accordance with your values promotes acceptance and mental health quality of life after an ABI. The relationship between acceptance and mental health quality of life was mediated by a higher match with their life values (Van Bost et al., 2017), further reinforcing the importance of values in an ABI population.

The process to identify meaningful values can be complex and metaphors are used to both facilitate values identification and demonstrate how values differentiate from goals and committed action. The direction or compass metaphor as used in the ACT-Adjust treatment protocol (Whiting, Deane, McLeod et al., 2020) explains the difference between setting a value and establishing a goal. A value is described as moving towards a point on the compass and while this gives a direction it is not a destination. Identifying a location that is in the same compass direction and moving towards that location is a goal. Metaphors allow abstract concepts to become more concrete and provide a pathway to understanding more abstract constructs for an individual with cognitive impairments.

Given the potentially important role of values in shaping goals within the rehabilitation context, understanding more about the value profile of clients is extremely important. A range of measures is currently used to identify and assess values in ACT, and a recent review identified the Valued Living Questionnaire (VLQ; Wilson et al., 2010) as the most commonly used measure in broader ACT research (Reilly et al., 2019). The review also found the current suite of values measures was not very sensitive to ACT treatment, and there was a need to validate the various values measures on different populations. In addition, there have been criticisms made about current values-measurement tools in their ability to facilitate clarification of values. It is proposed most values measures blur the concepts of value clarity (identification of the value) and valued action (behaviour moving the individual towards their identified value), and distinction is required between these two concepts (McLoughlin & Roche, 2022). Values card-sorting tools, where a value is presented to the person on a small card, allow values identification to occur, but assessment of valued action is also required to measure the behaviour of moving toward that value.

Considering the value profiles of various clinical populations, people with TBI need particular focus as the presence of cognitive difficulties including memory, attentional and executive impairments can potentially impact upon their capacity to adequately identify and assess values consistent behaviour. For individuals with a TBI, there are likely to be cognitive impairments resulting in (i) a lack of cognitive flexibility, in which the individual may become stuck or perseverate on one area of their life which is having the most significant impact at the time, for example, being unable to drive after their injury; (ii) poor generativity, in which the individual is unable to spontaneously provide ideas around their values without good scaffolding; and (iii) concrete thinking, which may prevent values identification around more abstract concepts or endeavours such as altruistic behaviours. These impairments may lead to difficulties in identifying relevant values to guide goal setting and the evaluation process of assessing values achievement. Therefore, understanding more about their values profiles within the context of their cognitive challenges is important.

Both questionnaires and card-sorting approaches have been trialled within TBI samples. In terms of questionnaires, Miller and colleagues (2022) recently reviewed the VLQ in individuals with an ABI. The VLQ covers ten life domains (family, couple relationships, parenting, friends/social life, work, education, recreation, spirituality and community life). The individual rates each domain on importance and then assesses how consistently they have been acting on their values in that domain over the previous week using a ten-point scale. Participants in the study reported struggling with comprehending some of the values due to their cognitive impairments (Miller et al., 2022). For example, participants found (i) it was hard to understand the abstract nature of some values; (ii) being able to recall how consistent their actions were with regard to their values was difficult; and (iii) difficulties with the rating scale indicating a need for modification of the VLQ with this population. These issues in using the VLQ were also reported in a series of individual case studies of people with an ABI undergoing an eight-week intervention using the VLQ (Sathananthan et al., 2022). Limited change in value attainment was achieved, and it was proposed participants struggled to accurately review their value attainment across the ten domains during the eight-week treatment program (Sathananthan et al., 2022).

As an alternative to questionnaires, a non-specified card-sorting device (Sander et al., 2021), as well as a therapy tool/outcome measure, namely the Survey of Guiding Principles (SGP: Whiting, Deane, McLeod et al., 2020; Whiting, Deane, Simpson et al., 2020) have been trialled in ACT treatments involving individuals with a TBI. The SGP (Ciarrochi & Bailey, 2008), using a series of 60 values cards (e.g., "maintaining the safety and security of my loved ones"), provides concrete examples of the values which can be presented both visually (written words) and verbally, with the administrator reading out the card to the client, as it is sorted. As a values-clarification exercise, this allows individuals to select those values they consider most important and provides a prompt for values that encompass all life domains. This is important for individuals who may struggle with generating appropriate and meaningful values due to cognitive impairments.

Overall, the literature pertaining to values identification and clarification for individuals with a TBI and the role of values work in rehabilitation goal striving is still in its infancy with difficulties in effectively identifying and classifying values and furthermore measuring values attainment following committed action. The current study investigated (i) the profile of values and domains identified and (ii) the rated behavioural consistency around those values (importance–success discrepancy) using the SGP, among individuals with a moderate-to-severe TBI who participated in a randomised controlled trial evaluating the efficacy of an ACT-based intervention to facilitate adjustment to the injury.

Methods

Setting and sample

This study undertook secondary analysis of SGP card-sort data from a previously reported randomised controlled trial. The trial tested the efficacy of an ACT-based intervention in facilitating adjustment post-TBI in comparison to an active control (Befriending) condition (Whiting, Deane, Simpson et al., 2020). The sample of individuals with a TBI (n=19) was recruited from the community rehabilitation service of the Liverpool Brain Injury Rehabilitation Unit (LBIRU), based in Sydney, Australia. The LBIRU also provides inpatient, vocational rehabilitation and transitional living programs (Tate et al., 2004). Participants were eligible for the clinical trial if they had (i) sustained a severe TBI (post-traumatic amnesia ≥7days) in the past five years and after the age of 18 years; and were (ii) currently between the ages of 18 and 65 years; (iii) reporting clinical levels of psychological distress (Depression>13 and/or Anxiety>9 and/or Stress>16) on the Depression Anxiety Stress Scale 21-item (DASS) (Lovibond & Lovibond, 1995); and (iv) had sufficient cognitive and linguistic abilities to complete self-report measures. Exclusion criteria included having a psychiatric illness including psychotic disorder or substance abuse, and currently undergoing psychological treatment. Ethical approval was received for the study from Sydney South West Local Health District Research Ethics Committee.

Measures

Survey of Guiding Principles

Values were identified using the Survey of Guiding Principles, a 60-item card-sort measure which guides participants through a three-stage process to identify their top ten values (Ciarrochi & Bailey, 2008). The 60 principles (values) map onto the ten dimensions identified in the Schwartz Values Survey (Schwartz, 2012) and include "Universalism and self-direction," "Relationships," "Achievement," "Sensation seeking," "Physical activity and health," "Spirituality and tradition," "Social restraint," "Security," "Power" and "Hedonism." In addition to these ten dimensions or domains, additional items were added to incorporate domains relevant to ACT, including *Negative experiential control* and *Positive experiential control*, and items related to the domains of *Spirituality*, *Sexuality* and *Career/ Vocational*, giving a total of 15 domains. There are a different number of values in each domain, ranging from two (*Popularity and courage*) to 11 (*Career/ Vocational*). Each card specifies one value/principle (e.g., "gaining wisdom," "maintaining the safety and security of my loved ones").

Participants are presented with the physical cards of the SGP and, following sorting, are asked to rate their top ten values. Each of the ten identified values is rated for Importance ("How important is this value?") and Success ("How consistently you are acting in accordance with this value?") on a five-point Likert scale where $0=$ "not very" and $4=$ "extremely." Discrepancy scores are then calculated between Importance and Success, where a negative score indicates success was lower than Importance. The SGP has been used to identify and rate values with regard to successful value achievement with health professionals (Veage et al., 2014) explored the relationship between values achievement and well-being. In adolescents/young adults, the SGP was found to have good internal consistency on the ratings of Importance ($\alpha=0.95$) and Success ($\alpha=0.96$) (Williams et al., 2015). Prior to the current trial, the SGP was trialled with two case studies assessing the feasibility of the ACT-Adjust program (Whiting, Deane, Simpson, et al., 2020).

Repeatable Battery of Neuropsychological Assessment (RBANS) (Randolph et al., 1998) is a brief battery of tests which assesses cognitive function across five cognitive domains: *Immediate memory*, *Visuospatial/constructional ability*, *Language and attention* and *Delayed memory*, as well as providing an overall Total Scale Index. It was initially developed for use in assessing individuals with dementia but has shown to be a reliable and valid instrument (Total Scale Index: $\alpha=0.84$) in identifying cognitive impairment in a moderate-to-severe TBI population (McKay et al., 2008).

Procedures

Study enrolment and completion of measures

Following informed consent, and the completion of the baseline assessment, participants enroled in the trial were randomly allocated to either the ACT treatment group (Act-Adjust) or the Befriending group. Participants were administered the SGP as a component of a larger test battery which included demographic information and measures pertaining to acceptance, psychological distress, motivation and mental health. The RBANS and SGP were administered by the principal researcher (DW) at baseline (Time 1) prior to randomisation, and then the SGP was administered by a psychologist blinded to the treatment condition at post-treatment (Time 2) and at the one-month follow-up (Time 3).

These principles are of the highest importance to me	These principles are of moderate importance to me	These principles are not very important to me
Maintaining the safety and security of my loved ones	Gaining wisdom	Having an exciting life
26	2	14

Figure 7.1 Survey of guiding principles layout. (Ciarrochi & Bailey, 2008).

The administration process for the SGP involved the presentation of the physical cards of the SGP to the participant. A brief explanation of the content of the cards was provided to the participant, and if required, the assessor read out the content of the cards to those clients who may have comprehension or reading challenges. The configuring of the cards is detailed in Figure 7.1.

In a three-stage process, the values were winnowed down to those of most salience to the participants. At Stage 1, participants were asked to classify each card according to one of three categories; (i) "These principles are of highest importance to me"; (ii) "These principles are of moderate importance to me"; or (iii) "These principles are not very important to me." Once all 60 cards were allocated, the ones categorised under, "These principles are not very important to me," are discarded. At Stage 2, the remaining two piles are shuffled and the participant was requested to go through the remaining cards and reclassify them again according to the three categories. If there were very few cards in the discarded pile, participants were prompted with the instruction, "Try to reduce the number of cards in each pile down as we need to find those that are most important to you." At Stage 3, only the cards remaining in the highest importance pile are retained and participants are requested to select ten cards from this pile and rank them from highest to lowest importance. This is undertaken by scattering all cards on the table, so they are visible to the participant and the participant is able to select ten cards they consider to be the most important. The selected cards were then ranked on the five-point Likert scale for Importance and Success.

ACT-Adjust and Befriending interventions

ACT-Adjust is a seven-session psychological treatment program using ACT which is delivered weekly with a one-month follow-up session. The program covers the six components on the ACT Hexaflex (*Defusion, Acceptance, Self-as-Context, Present-Moment Awareness, Values* and *Committed Action*), with mindfulness activities included in all sessions (Whiting, Deane, McLeod et al., 2020). Compensatory strategies to account for cognitive impairments after TBI include information presented both visually and verbally, the previous week's content being repeated at the beginning of each session and participants being provided with a workbook to assist with knowledge retention. Tasks are completed between sessions and the final session includes a review of the program.

Befriending (Bendall et al., 2003) is an active control which mimics the dosage of the ACT-Adjust treatment program (seven sessions). Participants are engaged in sessions with a clinician, and discussions are held around non-emotional topics such as hobbies or interests. If participants begin to discuss emotions, they are redirected by the clinician back to the targeted topic for the session. It has been used successfully to improve depressive symptomology in a number of different clinical populations (Mead et al., 2010).

Data analysis

Data were entered into SPSS 28 for data analysis (IBM Corp, Released 2021). Descriptives were generated for demographics and injury and psychosocial variables. Prior to analysis of the SGP data, between-groups tests (chi-square, t-test) were conducted to detect any differences between the ACT and Befriending groups using the baseline assessment (T1). The qualitative analysis of domains was analysed separately for each group (ACT and Befriending), but all time points (T1, T2 and T3) were combined. For the analysis of frequency of values identification, the ACT and the Befriending groups and all three time points (T1, T2 and T3) were combined. Discrepancy analysis (t-tests) between values Importance and Success for the top ten values and also across the domains was calculated for both groups combined, as previous analysis had indicated no group differences on these measures (Whiting, Deane, McLeod et al., 2020).

Results

The demographic and injury profile for the sample is detailed in Table 7.1, presented both as the total group and by each treatment group (ACT and Befriending). Participants were mainly male in both groups with an overall average age of 36.8 years (range 21–60) at the time of the study. Time post-injury for the sample fell between two and three years post-injury, with the ACT group being significantly less time post-injury compared to the Befriending group. The Befriending group had a significantly greater average number of days in post-traumatic amnesia (PTA, indicating a higher degree of injury severity) compared to the ACT group. However, both groups had extremely serious injuries, with the mean duration of PTA falling into the very severe (8–28 days PTA, ACT group) and extremely severe (greater than 28 days PTA, Befriending group) categories, respectively.

The two groups performed at a similar level on the RBANS, suggesting that there was not a large discrepancy in cognitive capacity across the sample as a whole. Both groups scored more than one standard deviation below the mean on the RBANS Total Index Score in the Borderline (70–79 Index Score) to Low Average (80–89 Index Score), indicating they were less than the 16th percentile

Table 7.1 Demographics of participants total and by treatment group allocation.

	All randomised participants		
	All participants (n = 19)	ACT (n = 10)	Befriending (n = 9)
Age (years), Mean (SD)	36.8 (12.6)	36.4 (13.5)	37.2 (12.5)
Time since injury (months), Mean (SD)	27.9 (19.8)	20.7 (17.5)	33.3 (21.5)[1]
Gender – Male, n (%)	15 (78.9%)	8 (80%)	7 (77.8%)
PTA (days), Mean (SD)	27.4 (19.2)	19.4 (13.7)	36.3 (21.2)[1]
Years of education, Mean (SD)	11.3 (1.5)	11.2 (2.0)	11.4 (1.0)
Relationship status, n (%)			
Married/De facto	13 (68.4%)	7 (70%)	6 (66.7%)
Single	5 (26.3%)	2 (20%)	3 (33.3%)
Separated/Divorced	1 (5.3%)	1 (10%)	0 (0%)
Lives with: n (%)			
Alone	1 (5.3%)	0 (0%)	1 (11.1%)
Parents	6 (31.6%)	3 (30.%)	3 (33.3%)
Spouse/partner	11 (57.9%)	7 (70%)	4 (44.4%)
Other family	1 (5.3%)	0 (0%)	1 (11.1%)
RBANS Total Index Score, Mean (SD)	80.1 (15.0)	79.4 (15.6)	80.8 (15.2)

Note: PTA: Post-traumatic amnesia; RBANS: Repeatable battery for the assessment of neuropsychological status. [1] Significant between-groups difference, $p < 0.05$.

of the population. This indicated the presence of mild-to-moderate cognitive impairment among the sample.

Though participants were directed to select ten values, two participants struggled to identify ten values at different time points. One participant identified eight values at pre-intervention (T1), one participant (not the same person) identified seven values at follow-up (T3). All participants identified ten values at post-intervention (T2).

Profile of values

Values frequency analysis

The frequency with which participants endorsed specific values and then the domains was analysed. The top five values nominated by participants across the total sample and across all time points were all focussed on connections with others, although the top values were spread across the three domains of *Security*, *Social restraint* and *Relationships* (see Table 7.2). The values spanned both family and broader social networks, as well as inter-generational dimensions. More specifically, the most frequently identified value "maintaining the safety and security of my loved ones" came from the *Security* domain. This was closely followed by

Table 7.2 Frequency of each value by group and time.

Value	Domain	Time 1		Time 2		Time 3		Time 1 + 2 + 3		Both groups
		ACT	Befr	ACT	Befr	ACT	Befr	ACT	Befr	
Maintaining the safety and security of my loved ones	Security	6	5	6	3	7	4	19	12	31
Showing respect for parents and elders	Social restraint	5	4	5	4	6	5	16	13	29
Being honest	Relationships	5	4	5	5	3	5	13	14	27
Having relationships involving love and affection	Relationships	4	4	4	5	2	6	10	15	25
Being loyal to friends, family and/or my group	Relationships	5	3	5	3	6	2	16	8	24
Having genuine and close friends	Relationships	4	3	3	1	3	2	10	6	16
Leading a stress-free life	Positive experiential control	2	2	4	2	2	3	8	7	15
Striving to be a better person	Creative self-direction	2	2	1	3	3	3	6	8	14
Feeling good about myself	Positive experiential control	3	3	2	2	1	3	6	8	14
Being safe from danger	Security	3	2	3	1	3	2	9	5	14
Being ambitious and hardworking	Achievement	3	1	4	2	2	0	9	3	12
Eating healthy food	Physical activity and health	1	3	1	4	0	2	2	9	11
Being at one with God	Spirituality and tradition	1	3	2	2	1	2	4	7	11
Accepting others as they are	Relationships	1	2	2	4	1	1	4	7	11
Having an enjoyable leisurely life	Hedonism	1	2	2	2	2	2	5	6	11
Being physically fit	Physical activity and health	1	2	2	1	1	3	4	6	10
Being self-disciplined and resisting temptation	Social Restraint	0	2	1	2	3	2	4	6	10
Showing respect for tradition	Spirituality and tradition	3	0	2	1	1	3	6	4	10
Acting consistently with my religious faith and beliefs	Spirituality and tradition	1	3	1	2	1	1	3	6	9
Making sure to repay favours and not be indebted	Security	1	3	1	1	1	2	3	6	9
Avoiding distress	Negative experiential control	1	2	2	1	1	2	4	5	9

(Continued)

Table 7.2 Continued

Value	Domain	Time 1		Time 2		Time 3		Time 1 + 2 + 3 Both groups	
		ACT	Befr	ACT	Befr	ACT	Befr	ACT	Befr
Being sexually active	Hedonism	2	2	1	1	2	1	5	4	9
Meeting my obligations	Social Restraint	1	2	1	2	0	2	2	6	8
Being wealthy	Power	0	1	1	1	3	2	4	4	8
Caring for others	Relationships	2	0	2	1	1	2	5	3	8
Being self-sufficient	Creative self-direction	0	1	0	4	0	2	0	7	7
Experiencing positive mood states	Positive experiential control	0	1	0	1	2	3	2	5	7
Promoting justice and caring for the weak	Universalism	0	0	2	2	1	2	3	4	7
Helping others	Relationships	2	1	0	1	2	1	4	3	7
Building and repairing things	Career-related	2	0	2	0	2	1	6	1	7
Working with my hands	Career-related	3	0	2	0	2	0	7	0	7
Having a sense of accomplishment and making a lasting contribution	Achievement	0	2	1	2	0	1	1	5	6
Connecting with nature	Universalism	1	1	1	1	0	2	2	4	6
Gaining Wisdom	Universalism	1	1	1	2	1	0	3	3	6
Having a life filled with adventure	Sensation seeking	1	1	0	1	2	1	3	3	6
Having an exciting life	Sensation seeking	0	1	1	3	0	0	1	4	5
Engaging in sporting activities	Physical activity and health	2	2	0	1	0	1	2	3	5
Having authority, being in charge	Power	2	1	1	1	0	0	3	2	5
Acting with courage	Popularity and courage	1	1	0	0	1	1	2	2	4
Figuring things out, solving problems	Creative self-direction	1	0	1	1	1	0	3	1	4
Seeking pleasure	Hedonism	0	1	0	2	0	0	0	3	3
Having a life filled with novelty and change	Sensation seeking	0	2	0	0	1	0	1	2	3
Being sexually desirable	Relationships	1	1	1	0	1	1	2	1	3
Engaging in clearly defined work	Career-related	0	0	0	0	1	1	2	1	3
Designing things	Career-related	1	0	1	0	1	0	3	0	3

(Continued)

Table 7.2 Continued

Value	Domain	Time 1		Time 2		Time 3		Time 1 + 2 + 3		Both groups
		ACT	Befr	ACT	Befr	ACT	Befr	ACT	Befr	
Organising things	Career-related	0	0	1	0	2	0	3	0	3
Researching things	Career-related	1	0	0	0	0	1	1	1	2
Avoiding self-doubt	Negative experiential control	1	0	0	1	0	0	1	1	2
Working on practical tasks	Career-related	1	0	0	0	1	0	2	0	2
Being competent and effective	Achievement	0	0	0	0	0	1	0	1	1
Being curious, discovering new things	Creative self-direction	0	1	0	0	0	0	0	1	1
Teaching others	Career-related	0	0	0	1	0	0	0	1	1
Creating beauty (in any domain)	Universalism	0	0	1	0	0	0	1	0	1
Enjoying food and drink	Hedonism	0	0	1	0	0	0	1	0	1
Being creative	Creative self-direction	0	0	0	0	1	0	1	0	1
Enjoying music art and/or drama	Career-related	1	0	0	0	0	0	1	0	1
Having influence over people	Power	0	0	0	0	0	0	0	0	0
Resolving disputes	Career-related	0	0	0	0	0	0	0	0	0
Competing with others	Career-related	0	0	0	0	0	0	0	0	0
Being admired by many people	Popularity and courage	0	0	0	0	0	0	0	0	0

a value from the *Social restraint* domain "showing respect for parents and elders." The next three highest selected values were all from the *Relationship* domain. These values could be understood as either focussing on or strengthening existing relationships, as well as aspiring to developing new relationships.

The next set of five most frequent values changed focus and were centred around personal development and well-being, once again falling across more than one domain. This included values such as "leading a stress-free life," "striving to be a better person" and "feeling good about myself." Other domains represented in the top third of selected values included *Physical activity and health* and *Spirituality and tradition*. Overall, values from the *Relationship* domain were the most frequently identified in each participant's top ten values (25%).

At the other end of the spectrum, four values were not endorsed at all ("having influence over people"; "resolving disputes"; "competing with others"; "being admired by many people"). A number of the least-frequently selected values seemed to be fairly abstract (e.g., "being creative," "being competent and effective"). In addition, nine of the 11 values in the *Career-related* domain were located in the bottom third of the endorsed values.

Domain frequency analysis

Values were categorised into their domains and an average number of values for each domain was calculated, as there are different numbers of values in each domain, ranging from two (*Popularity and courage*) to 11 (*Career-related* values) (see Figure 7.2). A visual inspection of the graph indicated differences between the two groups with regard to the value domains selected. Despite these differences, as can be seen from the graphs, these average numbers of values in each domain appear to remain consistent across the three time periods, indicating some stability in value identification over time.

The *Security* domain had the highest average for the sample as a whole, with all three constituent values selected with high levels of frequency, comprising three values ("maintaining the safety and security of my loves ones"; "being safe from danger"; and "making sure to repay favours and not be indebted"). As flagged in the previous section, values associated with the *Relationship* domain were also highly endorsed, with the exception of the value "being sexually desirable." *Social restraint* was the next most common domain endorsed, with values spanning again personal as well as social behaviour. Three other domains that were moderately endorsed were *Physical activity and health*, *Positive experiential control* and *Spirituality and tradition*.

Rated behaviour consistency (discrepancy analysis)

Average ratings, for the ten values selected, were calculated for Importance, Success and Discrepancy (difference between Importance and Success) at each assessment point (see Table 7.3). Analysis between time periods with both groups combined (ACT and Befriending) indicated increased success in working towards

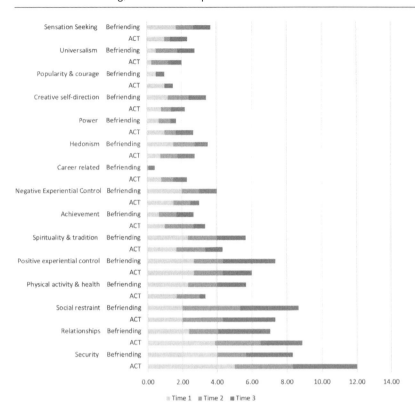

Figure 7.2 Average frequency for each value domain by treatment group

Table 7.3 Mean Importance, Success and Discrepancy for the top ten selected values at each time point (n = 16).

Value	Time 1 M (SD)	Time 2 M (SD)	Time 3 M (SD)	T1–T2 t value	T1–T3 t value
Importance	3.71 (0.21)	3.52 (0.44)	3.62 (0.42)	2.05*	1.09 ns
Success	2.62 (0.89)	2.74 (0.75)	2.69 (0.79)	0.96 ns	0.41 ns
Discrepancy	1.01 (0.95)	0.79 (0.78)	0.92 (0.82)	2.88**	0.91 ns

* $p<0.05$, **$p<0.01$

their values pre- to post-treatment, but this was not maintained at follow-up (T3). In addition to this, both groups significantly reduced their discrepancy scores pre to post-intervention but not at follow-up (one month later).

Average domain discrepancies, that is the difference between perceived importance and perceived success towards the values identified in that domain, was

Table 7.4 Average discrepancy between Importance and Success ratings by domain for Time 1 (pre-intervention), groups combined.

Domain	No. of values selected	No. of values in domain	Total discrepancy score	Average discrepancy
Positive experiential control	16	3	−46	−15.33
Negative experiential control	8	2	−21	−10.50
Security	25	3	−19	−6.33
Physical activity and health	11	3	−17	−5.67
Sensation seeking	7	3	−16	−5.33
Relationships	49	8	−40	−5.00
Power	5	3	−10	−3.33
Hedonism	10	4	−12	−3.00
Creative self-direction	10	5	−15	−3.00
Achievement	5	3	−9	−3.00
Spirituality and tradition	11	3	8	−2.00
Social restraint	14	3	−3	−1.00
Universalism	3	4	−1	−0.25
Career-related	9	11	−2	−0.22
Popularity and courage	3	2	0	0

Note: *Negative experiential control* values – "avoiding distress," "avoiding self-doubt."
Positive experiential control values – "experiencing positive mood states," "feeling good about myself," "leading a stress-free life."

calculated by calculating the total discrepancy score and dividing it by the number of values allocated to that domain. The most highly discrepant domains at pre-intervention were *Positive experiential control* and *Negative experiential control* (see Table 7.4).

Discussion

This study adds to the small extant literature documenting the values important to people who have sustained a moderate-to-severe TBI. It found a rich range of life areas that were of importance to participants, many of which have potential to be translated into rehabilitation goals and provide therapeutic opportunities for ACT intervention. However, the analysis found challenges with the scoring of the SGP. This involved measuring the discrepancy between value Importance and Success over the three study time points with a reduced discrepancy indicating improvements in valued action. Furthermore, group differences were not apparent with both groups indicating improvements between T1 and T2 (i.e., a main effect for time) by a reduction in their discrepancy, but this was not sustained at T3.

Values and domain profiles

The value profile found a high frequency selection of values from the *Relationship* domain, demonstrating the importance of psychosocial influences for individuals after experiencing a moderate-to-severe TBI. The importance of relationships and family over other areas of life has been reported in other values research for those with a mild-severe TBI (Pais et al., 2019). Relationships are influenced by multiple factors after a TBI (van den Broek et al., 2022) and are essential to well-being. As relationships deteriorate, social networks diminish and result in feelings of loneliness and isolation (Norup et al., 2020; Salas et al., 2022). Good social networks are also associated with increased activity resumption after a brain injury (Jellema et al., 2021). Thus, building and maintaining relationships with others provides an important scaffold for clients wanting to pursue activities consistent with their values resulting in both improved connection with others and feelings of well-being.

In the next tier of frequencies, a number of values highlighted the importance given to personal development and well-being. This may not be surprising given the significant levels of psychological distress reported within the group, but may also reflect a sample bias (i.e., participants were enroled in a trial for treatment to enhance psychological well-being). However, there is a growing understanding that well-being is broader than just a reduction of psychopathology or symptoms of psychological distress, but rather also incorporates enhanced quality of life (Rauen et al., 2020), positive self-esteem and flourishing (Paasila et al., 2022). Other values within this group included an emphasis on Physical activity and health, which has multiple benefits in both personal fitness, but also important for well-being (Johnson et al., 2023). Spirituality was also identified as an important value, and the limited research available to date has found that spirituality is related to a number of positive outcomes following TBI including psychological coping, physical health, mental health, productivity, life satisfaction, functional independence and post-traumatic growth (Jones et al., 2018).

At the domain level, the prominence of the *Security* domain may reflect increased awareness of danger or a perception the world is an unsafe place after experiencing an event which resulted in a TBI. Perception of threat and subsequent avoidance behaviour is often found after TBI, particularly for those who experience their injury as a result of an assault (Riley et al., 2004) or those more recently injured (Riley et al., 2010). It appears this increased threat perception may extend to close family members in addition to their own safety which closely links to the high endorsement of values in the Relationship domain.

Despite the large number of items relating to career within the SGP, there was low identification at the individual or domain level for career-related values. This may reflect a sample bias, in that people with TBI who had been able to return to work may have been less likely to sign up for the trial. However, Australian and international studies find only 30–40% of individuals with a moderate-to-severe TBI return to work post-injury, most commonly within the first two years (Hart et al., 2019; Sigurdardottir et al., 2020; Simpson et al., 2020). Given the timespan for the current trial was up to five years post-injury, the findings here might reflect the larger portion of people with TBI looking to invest their focus and energy into other domains, perceiving that they may not be able to return to work.

Behavioural consistency around values

There was a significant reduction in discrepancy between perceived importance of the value and successful achievement of the value for all participants pre to post-treatment, which was not maintained at one-month follow-up. This indicates both interventions resulted in improved perception of values achievement immediately after the interventions, but as different values were identified at later time points, then it was difficult to make comparisons to the original discrepancy scores. Repeated assessment of the values identified at baseline would provide a better opportunity to assess valued action, which was not adequately achieved in this study. The ability to effectively identify values and measure valued action is not restricted to the TBI literature and is a criticism of the current research in the broader ACT literature across other populations (McLoughlin & Roche, 2022).

With regard to analysis of domains, values from both Positive and Negative experiential control domains showed the highest discrepancies between importance and achievement pre-treatment. These domains were developed to reflect the clinical focus of ACT on experiential avoidance (Ciarrochi & Bailey, 2008). As the participants in this group were reporting elevated levels of distress which correlates highly to psychological inflexibility (Nemattavousi & Soltaninia, 2020; Whiting et al., 2015), it would be anticipated that high levels of discrepancy in these domains would be reported prior to the intervention. A highly distress population, therefore, is more likely to demonstrate discrepancy around the experiential control values both positive and negative.

There were a number of limitations to this study. The sample size was modest, and all participants displayed elevated levels of psychological distress. If a broader group of individuals with a TBI were sampled, it may present a different values profile. For the values achievement, the short time frame for the assessment and follow-up may not have been sufficient to detect changes in values Importance or Success indicating a lack of sensitivity. In addition, participants were able to select new values at each time point rather than focussing on addressing their achievement of the initially identified values, removing the opportunity to assess possible change in valued action on these initially identified values.

Clinical implications

Values have only been reported on the SGP, which itself may have some disadvantages over other values measures such as the VLQ (Wilson et al., 2010), which offers respondents the opportunity to rate their valued action in ten domains.

Some participants, due to their cognitive impairment, might perseverate on values in only a few life domains or become overwhelmed by choosing from 60 values available in the SGP. Some values which were more abstract received low levels of endorsement. This could reflect the impairments in abstract cognition commonly found after TBI and consistent with the RBANS results. Other factors such as low socio-economic status and lower levels of education typical of a proportion of people with TBI might also contribute to this finding.

Future research is needed to continue to identify the most effective ways of capturing data about the values that are of importance to people with TBI, and within the ACT treatment process, sensitive to change. Exploring alternative administration of the SGP to assist with cognitive overload and perseveration is a consideration as well as using alternative values identification measures. A larger sample not demonstrating psychological distress and reassessment over a longer time frame is also suggested. It would also be important to extend this research in future studies to people with mild or moderate injuries (up to seven days post-traumatic amnesia).

Values identification plays an integral role in ACT, and measurement of values achievement or valued action provides an important source of qualitative data in ACT efficacy trials. This extends existing outcomes such as increases in psychological flexibility and reductions in psychopathology, providing the opportunity to understand the broader benefits in life changes that participants with a TBI can experience through ACT.

References

Access Economics. (2009). *The ecomonic cost of spinal cord injury and traumatic brain injury in Australia*. Access Economics Pty Limited.

Bahraini, N. H., Simpson, G. K., Brenner, L. A., Hoffberg, A. S., & Schneider, A. L. (2013). Suicidal ideation and behaviours after traumatic brain injury: A systematic review. *Brain Impairment, 14*(1), 92–112. https://doi.org/10.1017/BrImp.2013.11

Baseotto, M. C., Morris, P. G., Gillespie, D. C., & Trevethan, C. T. (2022). Post-traumatic growth and value-directed living after acquired brain injury. *Neuropsychological Rehabilitation, 32*(1), 84–103. https://doi.org/10.1080/09602011.2020.1798254

Bendall, S., Killackey, E., Jackson, H., & Gleeson, J. (2003). *Befriending manual*. ORYGEN Research Centre.

Bombardier, C. H., Fann, J. R., Temkin, N. R., Esselman, P. C., Barber, J., & Dikmen, S. S. (2010). Rates of major depressive disorder and clinical outcomes following traumatic brain injury. *JAMA: Journal of the American Medical Association, 303*(19), 1938–1945. https://doi.org/10.1001/jama.2010.599

Brenner, L. A., Forster, J. E., Hoffberg, A. S., Matarazzo, B. B., Hostetter, T. A., Signoracci, G., & Simpson, G. K. (2018). Window to hope: A randomized controlled trial of a psychological intervention for the treatment of hopelessness among veterans with moderate to severe traumatic brain injury. *Journal of Head Trauma Rehabilitation, 33*(2), E64–E73. https://doi.org/10.1097/HTR.0000000000000351

Ciarrochi, J., & Bailey, A. (2008). *A CBT-practitioner's guide to ACT: How to bridge the gap between cognitive behavioral therapy and acceptance and commitment therapy*. New Harbinger Publications.

Dewan, M. C., Rattani, A., Gupta, S., Baticulon, R. E., Hung, Y.-C., Punchak, M., Agrawal, A., Adeleye, A. O., Shrime, M. G., Rubiano, A. M., Rosenfeld, J. V., & Park, K. B. (2019, April 1). Estimating the global incidence of traumatic brain injury. *Journal of Neurosurgery, 130*(4), 1080–1097. https://doi.org/10.3171/2017.10.JNS17352

Dindo, L., Johnson, A. L., Lang, B., Rodrigues, M., Martin, L., & Jorge, R. (2020). Development and evaluation of an 1-day Acceptance and Commitment Therapy workshop for Veterans with comorbid chronic pain, TBI, and psychological distress: Outcomes from a pilot study. *Contemporary Clinical Trials, 90*, 105954. https://doi.org /10.1016/j.cct.2020.105954

Doig, E., Fleming, J. M., Cornwell, P. L., & Kuipers, P. (2009). Qualitative exploration of a client-centered, goal-directed approach to community-based occupational therapy for adults with traumatic brain injury. *The American Journal of Occupational Therapy, 63*(5), 559–568. https://doi.org/10.5014/ajot.63.5.559

Elliott, T. R., Hsiao, Y.-Y., Kimbrel, N. A., DeBeer, B. B., Gulliver, S. B., Kwok, O.-M., Morissette, S. B., & Meyer, E. C. (2019). Resilience facilitates adjustment through greater psychological flexibility among Iraq/Afghanistan war veterans with and without mild traumatic brain injury. *Rehabilitation Psychology, 64*(4), 383–397. https://doi.org /10.1037/rep0000282

Ellis, J. M., Whited, M. C., Freeman, J. T., Corson, A. T., Jameson, J. P., Greenway, S., Sager, D. M., Midgette, E. P., & Varju, E. V. (2018). Life values as an intrinsic guide for cardiopulmonary rehabilitation program engagement: A qualitative analysis. *Journal of Cardiopulmonary Rehabilitation and Prevention, 38*(5), 309. https://doi.org/10.1097 /HCR.0000000000000295

Freeman, A., Adams, M., & Ashworth, F. (2015). An exploration of the experience of self in the social world for men following traumatic brain injury. *Neuropsychological Rehabilitation, 25*(2), 189–215. https://doi.org/10.1080/09602011.2014.917686

Gould, K. R., Ponsford, J. L., Johnston, L., & Schönberger, M. (2011). The nature, frequency and course of psychiatric disorders in the first year after traumatic brain injury: A prospective study. *Psychological Medicine, 41*(10), 2099–2109. https://doi.org/10.1017 /S003329171100033X

Hart, T., Ketchum, J. M., O'Neil-Pirozzi, T. M., Novack, T. A., Johnson-Greene, D., & Dams-O'Connor, K. (2019). Neurocognitive status and return to work after moderate to severe traumatic brain injury. *Rehabilitation Psychology, 64*(4), 435–444. https://doi.org /10.1037/rep0000290

Hassett, L., Simpson, G. K., Cotter, R., Whiting, D. L., Hodgkinson, A., & Martin, D. (2014). A prospective interrupted time series study of interventions to improve the quality, rating, framing and structure of goal-setting in community-based brain injury rehabilitation. *Clinical Rehabilitation, 29*(4),327–338. https://doi.org/10.1177/0269215514544040

Hayes, S. C., Strosahl, K. D., & Wilson, K. G. (1999). *Acceptance and commitment therapy: An experiential approach to behavior change.* Guilford Press.

Hodgson, J., McDonald, S., Tate, R. L., & Gertler, P. (2005). A randomised controlled trial of a cognitive-behavioural therapy program for managing social anxiety after acquired brain injury. *Brain Impairment, 6*(3), 169–180. https://doi.org/10.1375/brim.2005.6.3.169

IBM Corp. (Released 2021). *IBM SPSS statistics for windows.* In (Version 28.0) IBM Corp.

Jellema, S., van Erp, S., Nijhuis-van der Sanden, M. W., van der Sande, R., & Steultjens, E. M. (2021). Activity resumption after acquired brain injury: The influence of the social network as described by social workers. *Disability and Rehabilitation, 43*(8), 1137–1144. https://doi.org/10.1080/09638288.2019.1652855

Johnson, L., Williams, G., Sherrington, C., Pilli, K., Chagpar, S., Auchettl, A., Beard, J., Gill, R., Vassallo, G., & Rushworth, N. (2023). The effect of physical activity on health outcomes in people with moderate-to-severe traumatic brain injury: A rapid systematic review with meta-analysis. *BMC Public Health, 23*(1), 1–21. https://doi.org/10.1186/s12889-022-14935-7

Jones, K. F., Pryor, J., Care-Unger, C., & Simpson, G. K. (2018). Spirituality and its relationship with positive adjustment following traumatic brain injury: A scoping review. *Brain Injury, 32*(13–14), 1612–1622. https://doi.org/10.1080/02699052.2018.1511066

Lovibond, S. H., & Lovibond, P. F. (1995). *Manual for the depression anxiety stress scales* (2nd ed.). Psychology Foundation.

McKay, C., Wertheimer, J. C., Fichtenberg, N. L., & Casey, J. E. (2008). The Repeatable Battery for the Assessment of Neuropsychological Status (RBANS): Clinical utility in a traumatic brain injury sample. *The Clinical Neuropsychologist, 22*(2), 228–241. https://doi.org/10.1080/13854040701260370

McLoughlin, S., & Roche, B. T. (2022). ACT: A Process-Based Therapy in search of a process. *Behavior Therapy, 54*(6), 939–955. https://doi.org/10.1016/j.beth.2022.07.010

Mead, N., Lester, H., Chew-Graham, C., Gask, L., & Bower, P. (2010). Effects of befriending on depressive symptoms and distress: Systematic review and meta-analysis. *The British Journal of Psychiatry, 196*(2), 96–101. https://doi.org/10.1192/bjp.bp.109.064089

Medd, J., & Tate, R. L. (2000). Evaluation of an anger management therapy programme following acquired brain injury: A preliminary study. *Neuropsychological Rehabilitation, 10*(2), 185–201. https://doi.org/10.1080/096020100389246

Miller, H., Lawson, D. W., Power, E., Das Nair, R., Sathananthan, N., & Wong, D. (2022). How do people with acquired brain injury interpret the Valued Living Questionnaire? A cognitive interviewing study. *Journal of Contextual Behavioral Science, 23*, 125–136. https://doi.org/10.1016/j.jcbs.2022.01.003

Moore, E. L., Terryberry-Spohr, L., & Hope, D. A. (2006). Mild traumatic brain injury and anxiety sequelae: A review of the literature. *Brain Injury, 20*(2), 117–132. https://doi.org/10.1080/02699050500443558

Nemattavousi, M., & Soltaninia, S. (2020). The mediating role of experiential avoidance in the relationship between Alexithymia and emotion regulation in patients with major depression disorder after traumatic brain injury. *Shenakht Journal of Psychology and Psychiatry, 7*(2), 140–152. https://doi.org/10.52547/shenakht.7.2.140

Norup, A., Kruse, M., Soendergaard, P. L., Rasmussen, K. W., & Biering-Sørensen, F. (2020). Socioeconomic consequences of traumatic brain injury: A Danish nationwide register-based study. *Journal of Neurotrauma, 37*(24), 2694–2702. https://doi.org/10.1089/neu.2020.7064

Paasila, J. M., Smith, E., Daher, M., & Simpson, G. K. (2022). Reasons for living, positive psychological constructs and their relationship with suicide ideation in people with moderate to severe traumatic brain injury: A cross-sectional study. *Neuropsychological Rehabilitation, 32*(8), 2125–2146. https://doi.org/10.1080/09602011.2022.2100795

Pais, C., Ponsford, J. L., Gould, K. R., & Wong, D. (2019). Role of valued living and associations with functional outcome following traumatic brain injury. *Neuropsychological Rehabilitation, 29*(4), 625–637. https://doi.org/10.1080/09602011.2017.1313745

Ponsford, J. L., Downing, M., Olver, J., Ponsford, M., Acher, R., Carty, M., & Spitz, G. (2014). Longitudinal follow-up of patients with traumatic brain injury: Outcome at two, five, and ten years post-injury. *Journal of Neurotrauma, 31*(1), 64–77. https://doi.org/10.1089/neu.2013.2997

Ponsford, J. L., Lee, N., Wong, D., McKay, A., Haines, K., Alway, Y., Downing, M., Furtado, C., & O'Donnell, M. (2016). Efficacy of motivational interviewing and cognitive behavioral therapy for anxiety and depression symptoms following traumatic brain injury. *Psychological Medicine, 46*(5), 1079–1090. https://doi.org/10.1017/S0033291715002640

Pozzato, I., Tate, R. L., Rosenkoetter, U., & Cameron, I. D. (2019, August). Epidemiology of hospitalised traumatic brain injury in the state of New South Wales, Australia: A population-based study. *Australian and New Zealand Journal of Public Health, 43*(4), 382–388. https://doi.org/10.1111/1753-6405.12878

Prescott, S., Doig, E., Fleming, J., & Weir, N. (2019). Goal statements in brain injury rehabilitation: A cohort study of client-centredness and relationship with goal outcome. *Brain Impairment, 20*(3), 226–239. https://doi.org/10.1017/BrImp.2019.6

Prescott, S., Fleming, J., & Doig, E. (2015, December 6). Goal setting approaches and principles used in rehabilitation for people with acquired brain injury: A systematic scoping review. *Brain Injury, 29*(13–14), 1515–1529. https://doi.org/10.3109/02699052.2015.1075152

Randolph, C., Tierney, M. C., Mohr, E., & Chase, T. N. (1998). The Repeatable Battery for the Assessment of Neuropsychological Status (RBANS): Preliminary clinical validity. *Journal of Clinical and Experimental Neuropsychology, 20*(3), 310–319. https://doi.org/10.1076/jcen.20.3.310.823

Rapport, L. J., Wong, C. G., & Hanks, R. A. (2020). Resilience and well-being after traumatic brain injury. *Disability and Rehabilitation, 42*(14), 2049–2055. https://doi.org/10.1080/09638288.2018.1552327

Rauen, K., Reichelt, L., Probst, P., Schäpers, B., Müller, F., Jahn, K., & Plesnila, N. (2020). Quality of life up to 10 years after traumatic brain injury: A cross-sectional analysis. *Health and Quality of Life Outcomes, 18*, 166. https://doi.org/10.1186/s12955-020-01391-3

Rauwenhoff, J., Peeters, F., Bol, Y., & Van Heugten, C. (2019). The BrainACT study: Acceptance and commitment therapy for depressive and anxiety symptoms following acquired brain injury: Study protocol for a randomized controlled trial. *Trials, 20*(1), 1–10. https://doi.org/10.1186/s13063-019-3952-9

Rauwenhoff, J. C., Bol, Y., Peeters, F., van den Hout, A. J., Geusgens, C. A., & van Heugten, C. M. (2022). Acceptance and commitment therapy for individuals with depressive and anxiety symptoms following acquired brain injury: A non-concurrent multiple baseline design across four cases. *Neuropsychological Rehabilitation, 33*(6), 1018–1048. https://doi.org/10.1080/09602011.2022.2053169

Reilly, E. D., Ritzert, T. R., Scoglio, A. A., Mote, J., Fukuda, S. D., Ahern, M. E., & Kelly, M. M. (2019). A systematic review of values measures in acceptance and commitment therapy research. *Journal of Contextual Behavioral Science, 12*, 290–304. https://doi.org/10.1016/j.jcbs.2018.10.004

Riley, G. A., Brennan, A. J., & Powell, T. (2004). Threat appraisal and avoidance after traumatic brain injury: Why and how often are activities avoided? *Brain Injury, 18*(9), 871–888. https://doi.org/10.1080/02699050410001671829

Riley, G. A., Dennis, R. K., & Powell, T. (2010). Evaluation of coping resources and self-esteem as moderators of the relationship between threat appraisals and avoidance of activities after traumatic brain injury. *Neuropsychological Rehabilitation, 20*(6), 869–882. https://doi.org/10.1080/09602011.2010.503041

Sabaz, M., Simpson, G. K., Walker, A. J., Rogers, J. M., Gillis, I., & Strettles, B. (2014). Prevalence, comorbidities, and correlates of challenging behavior among community-dwelling adults with severe traumatic brain injury: A multicenter study. *Journal of Head Trauma Rehabilitation, 29*(2), E19–E30. https://doi.org/10.1097/HTR .0b013e31828dc590

Salas, C. E., Rojas-Líbano, D., Castro, O., Cruces, R., Evans, J., Radovic, D., Arévalo-Romero, C., Torres, J., & Aliaga, Á. (2022). Social isolation after acquired brain injury: Exploring the relationship between network size, functional support, loneliness and mental health. *Neuropsychological Rehabilitation, 32*(9), 2294–2318. https://doi.org/10 .1080/09602011.2021.1939062

Sander, A. M., Clark, A. N., Arciniegas, D. B., Tran, K., Leon-Novelo, L., Ngan, E., Bogaards, J., Sherer, M., & Walser, R. (2021, August). A randomized controlled trial of acceptance and commitment therapy for psychological distress among persons with traumatic brain injury. *Neuropsychological Rehabilitation, 31*(7), 1105–1129. https://doi .org/10.1080/09602011.2020.1762670

Sathananthan, N., Dimech-Betancourt, B., Morris, E., Vicendese, D., Knox, L., Gillanders, D., Das Nair, R., & Wong, D. (2022). A single-case experimental evaluation of a new group-based intervention to enhance adjustment to life with acquired brain injury: VaLiANT (valued living after neurological trauma). *Neuropsychological Rehabilitation, 32*(8), 2170–2202. https://doi.org/10.1080/09602011.2021.1971094

Schwartz, S. H. (2012). An overview of the Schwartz theory of basic values. *Online Readings in Psychology and Culture, 2*(1). https://doi.org/10.9707/2307-0919.1116

Sigurdardottir, S., Andelic, N., Wehling, E., Anke, A., Skandsen, T., Holthe, O. O., Manskow, U. S., & Roe, C. (2020). Return to work after severe traumatic brain injury: A national study with a one-year follow-up of neurocognitive and behavioural outcomes. *Neuropsychological Rehabilitation, 30*(2), 281–297. https://doi.org/10.1080/09602011 .2018.1462719

Simpson, G. K., McRae, P., Hallab, L., Daher, M., & Strettles, B. (2020). Participation in competitive employment after severe traumatic brain injury: New employment versus return to previous (pre-injury) employment. *Neuropsychological Rehabilitation, 30*(6), 995–1012. https://doi.org/10.1080/09602011.2018.1531769

Simpson, G. K., & Tate, R. (2002). Suicidality after traumatic brain injury: Demographic, injury and clinical correlates. *Psychological Medicine, 32*(4), 687–697. https://doi.org /10.1017/S0033291702005561

Simpson, G. K., Tate, R. L., Whiting, D. L., & Cotter, R. E. (2011). Suicide prevention after traumatic brain injury: A randomized controlled trial of a program for the psychological treatment of hopelessness. *Journal of Head Trauma Rehabilitation, 26*(4), 290–300. https://doi.org/10.1097/HTR.0b013e3182225250

Tate, R. L., Lane-Brown, A. T., Myles, B. M., & Cameron, I. D. (2020). A longitudinal study of support needs after severe traumatic brain injury. *Brain Injury, 34*(8), 991–1000. https://doi.org/10.1080/02699052.2020.1764101

Tate, R. L., Strettles, B., & Osoteo, T. (2004). The clinical practice of a community rehabilitation team for people with acquired brain injury. *Brain Impairment, 5*(1), 81–92. https://doi.org/10.1375/brim.5.1.81.35408

Van Bost, G., Van Damme, S., & Crombez, G. (2017). The role of acceptance and values in quality of life in patients with an acquired brain injury: A questionnaire study. *PeerJ, 5*, e3545. https://doi.org/10.7717/peerj.3545

van den Broek, B., Rijnen, S., Stiekema, A., van Heugten, C., & Bus, B. (2022). Factors related to the quality and stability of partner relationships after traumatic brain injury: A systematic literature review. *Archives of Physical Medicine and Rehabilitation.* https://doi.org/10.1016/j.apmr.2022.02.021

Veage, S., Ciarrochi, J., Deane, F. P., Andresen, R., Oades, L. G., & Crowe, T. P. (2014). Value congruence, importance and success and in the workplace: Links with well-being and burnout amongst mental health practitioners. *Journal of Contextual Behavioral Science, 3*(4), 258–264. https://doi.org/10.1016/j.jcbs.2014.06.004

Whiting, D. L., Deane, F. P., Ciarrochi, J., McLeod, H. J., & Simpson, G. K. (2015). Validating measures of psychological flexibility in a population with acquired brain injury. *Psychological Assessment, 23*(2), 415–423. https://doi.org/10.1037/pas0000050

Whiting, D. L., Deane, F., McLeod, H., Ciarrochi, J., & Simpson, G. K. (2020). Can acceptance and commitment therapy facilitate psychological adjustment after a severe traumatic brain injury? A pilot randomized controlled trial. *Neuropsychological Rehabilitation, 30*(7), 1348–1371. https://doi.org/10.1080/09602011.2019.1583582

Whiting, D. L., Deane, F. P., Simpson, G. K., Ciarrochi, J., & McLeod, H. J. (2020). Acceptance and Commitment Therapy delivered in a dyad after a severe traumatic brain injury: A feasibility study. *Clinical Psychologist, 22*(2), 230–240. https://doi.org/10.1111/cp.12118

Whiting, D. L., Simpson, G. K., Deane, F. P., Chuah, S. L., Maitz, M., & Weaver, J. (2021). Protocol for a phase two, parallel three-armed non-inferiority randomized controlled trial of Acceptance and Commitment Therapy (ACT-Adjust) comparing face-to-face and video conferencing delivery to individuals with traumatic brain injury experiencing psychological distress. *Frontiers in Psychology, 12*, 580. https://doi.org/10.3389/fpsyg.2021.652323

Williams, K. E., Ciarrochi, J., & Heaven, P. C. (2015). Relationships between valued action and well-being across the transition from high school to early adulthood. *The Journal of Positive Psychology, 10*(2), 127–140. https://doi.org/10.1080/17439760.2014.920404

Wilson, K. G., Sandoz, E. K., Kitchens, J., & Roberts, M. (2010). The valued living questionnaire: Defining and measuring valued action within a behavioral framework. *The Psychological Record, 60*(2), 249–272. https://doi.org/10.1007/BF03395706

Winter, L., Moriarty, H. J., & Short, T. H. (2018). Beyond anger: Emotion regulation and social connectedness in veterans with traumatic brain injury. *Brain Injury, 32*(5), 593–599. https://doi.org/10.1080/02699052.2018.1432895

Wood, R. L., & Yurdakul, L. K. (1997). Change in relationship status following traumatic brain injury. *Brain Injury, 11*(7), 491–501. https://doi.org/10.1080/bij.11.7.491.501

Chapter 8

Life asks you questions

Presence as process in Acceptance and Commitment Therapy for adults with aphasia

Fiona O'Neill

Life asks us questions. According to the behavioural psychologist, B.F. Skinner, the self is of social origin (1974). We come to know ourselves through being seen and known by others. Our capacity for psychological maturity, self-discovery and self-realisation are nurtured in *good enough* social contexts (Winnicott, 1958): negotiated and renegotiated through words, conversations and story exchange (Strong & Shadden, 2020).

The words we use to describe what we know of our world, both inner and outer, evolved in community. Without mutual agreement on what words mean, words don't work as words (for example, few English speakers today can parse or understand the original Anglo-Saxon of the words: "swylce ðær iu wæron"). This is as true of the words we use to describe what we know of the self as it is of things out in the world (Skinner, 1974, p. 30). Language is ever-evolving, generated and sustained by community: rooted in relationship (Hydén, 2013).

What happens when words fail, when there are no words? When someone asks how you are, and what falls out is a string of nonsense sounds? What happens when you try to say your son's name, but all others hear you say is "shit"? What is it like for you in the moment you realise recovery from a stroke is going to be nothing like recuperating from knee surgery: when it begins to slowly dawn on you that you won't be back at work in a few weeks, that perhaps you may never read your favourite books again, or write an email, say your daughter's name or tell your partner that you love them? How do you begin to meet that? How do you begin to rebuild, to balance recovery, acceptance and getting the most out of life as it is now, not as you would have chosen it to be (Meyerson & Zuckerman, 2019)? What does living in this new way mean *for* you, and what does it mean *about* you (Wilson, 2022)? Who are you now?

Such are living questions for many people experiencing aphasia, a language impairment associated with Acquired Brain Injury (ABI) that affects the ability to understand, talk, read, write and recognise and use numbers to varying degrees. The challenges of answering these questions suggest why a diagnosis of aphasia has been called "identity theft" (Shadden, 2005; Meyerson & Zuckerman, 2019), affecting the whole of a person's being.

DOI: 10.4324/9781003193722-9

The sudden onset of any disability can result in existential questions about life's meaning (Roos, 2014). However, people with aphasia can be hit with a "double whammy" – not only does the person with aphasia have to come to terms with a changed reality; they have to make sense of changes in who they are *in relation to others* in the absence of language and communication skills that once acted both as a means of making sense of their own experience and as the social glue to their every relationship, often with limited access to professional support to light their way forward on what can be a dark and isolating journey (Baker et al., 2018).

The repercussions for mental health and wellbeing can be significant. At all stages of recovery, individuals with aphasia experience poorer mental health and elevated risk of mood disorder relative to individuals with ABI without aphasia. Adults with aphasia are 7.408 times more likely to exhibit post-stroke depression symptoms than adults without aphasia, and 2.06 times more likely to experience these symptoms with every one-point increase in aphasia severity (Zanella et al., 2023).

Current mood screening for people with aphasia relates to depression and anxiety; however, in the broader stroke-survivor population, post-traumatic symptoms are present in one in four individuals the first year of recovery (Schultebraucks et al., 2020). High rates of anxiety documented in people with aphasia (Morris et al., 2017) may suggest a high likelihood of undiagnosed post-traumatic stress disorder (PTSD) in people with aphasia (Kristo & Mowll, 2022), reinforced by what people with aphasia share about the relevance of trauma to ongoing mood issues (Baker et al., 2020). Despite this level of need, it is estimated that less than 1% of adults with aphasia can access appropriate psychological support when needed (Townend et al., 2010) and people with aphasia are four times more likely to die by suicide than other survivors of brain injury.

In this context, there has been a call for increased interdisciplinary approaches to meeting the emotional needs of people with aphasia (Ryan et al., 2019) using evidence-based models of psychosocial and psychological support, including Acceptance and Commitment Therapy (ACT: Hayes, Wilson, & Strosahl, 2012). ACT aims to develop *psychological flexibility*, broadly defined as the capacity to be open, aware and responsive to the ups and downs of a human life and, in any given moment, step back, view the context as it is, not as it says it is, and from a calmer, wiser, steadier experience of conscious awareness, make wise choices that embody qualities of intrinsic worth to a person.

Psychological flexibility is nested within a broader approach to science known as Contextual Behavioural Science (CBS). CBS aims to design contextually sensitive interventions through identification of a small set of principles applicable across contexts and aligned with cross-disciplinary understanding of the best ways to create meaningful change (Hayes et al., 2012; Kashdan & Rottenberg, 2010; see Figure 8.1). The Psychological Flexibility model has also evolved with Process-Based Therapy and has been applied to the Evolutionary Extended Meta-Model. See Figure 8.2 (Ciarrochi et al., 2022).

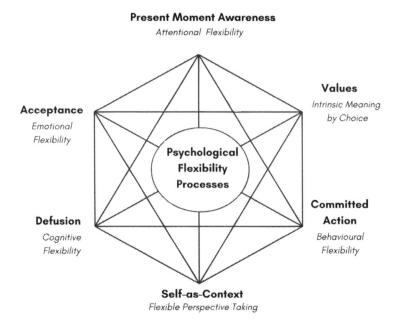

Present Moment Awareness
Attentional Flexibility

Values
Intrinsic Meaning
by Choice

Acceptance
Emotional
Flexibility

Psychological
Flexibility
Processes

Committed
Action
Behavioural
Flexibility

Defusion
Cognitive
Flexibility

Self-as-Context
Flexible Perspective Taking

Figure 8.1 The Psychological Flexibility Model or 'Hexaflex' (Copyright Steven C. Hayes, used by permission)

While at the time of writing no current published data exists to support the specific use of ACT with individuals with aphasia, promising findings have been reported with respect to post-stroke depression (Majumdar & Morris, 2019; Niu et al., 2022) and in the area of Traumatic Brain Injury (e.g. Whiting et al., 2020; Sander et al., 2020). In addition, a number of ACT protocols are in progress. Evans et al. (2022) are in the process of adapting a ten-week ACT protocol for people with aphasia focused on components hypothesised to be relevant and feasible. Mindfulness training that includes a) identification of core values; b) aphasia-friendly ACT education; c) individualised communication strategy training; and d) weekly "bold moves" for communication and life participation, consistent with core values.

Elsewhere in this volume, it has been suggested that the most relevant flexibility process to supporting psychological adjustment following ABI may be the development of **self as context**, considered particularly relevant to the treatment of trauma (Walser & Westrup, 2007). ACT Co-Founder Steven Hayes (2002) has suggested the importance of self as context therapeutically within ACT as it offers "at least one stable, unchangeable, immutable fact about oneself that has been experienced directly and is not just a belief or a hope or an idea". Hayes explains this can provide stability and constancy to support clients facing extreme psychological pain and trauma, offering contact with a knowing that, in some deep way,

Hexaflex Process Label	Flexibility Process Label	Extended Evolutionary Meta-Model	Aims to Develop:
Present Moment Awareness	Attentional Flexibility	• Attention • Affect • Physiological States and Responses	Ability to attend to what's happening here and now and remain open and aware when there are opportunities to close down or avoid.
Acceptance	Emotional Flexibility	• Attention • Affect • Physiological States and Responses	Ability to attend to what's happening *emotionally* here and now both in self and other, remaining open, aware and responsive when there are opportunities to close down or avoid.
Defusion	Cognitive Flexibility	• Cognition	Use of language to navigate context and disengage when language is not helpful
Self-as-Context	Flexible Perspective Taking	• Self	Self-awareness and the ability to take a broader perspective on own actions across time with compassion and acceptance in the service of making healthy life choices
Values	Intrinsic Meaning by Choice	• Motivation	Ability to clarify values, choose actions aligned with values and sustain these actions across times of adversity and challenge
Committed Action	Behavioural Flexibility	• Overt Behaviour	Skills through trial and error learning through trying out new and different behaviour to develop resources for self-management and enrich possibilities for living with meaning and purpose.

Figure 8.2 The Psychological Flexibility Model as applied to the Evolutionary Extended Meta Model with descriptors of functional aims

whatever arises, the deepest sense of one's being is not, and cannot, be threatened by any story that one may hold about the self, others, the world.

Potential support for self as context as an active ingredient in the successful working of ACT interventions has recently been indicated in a network analysis of the ACT model, in which it demonstrated the strongest associations across all components, overlapping in particular with present-moment awareness, but also acceptance and defusion (the mindfulness-informed components of the model; see Figure 8.1).

However, self as context has frequently been criticised for being too vague and abstract to allow for its effective operationalisation in clinical contexts, and too difficult to "quarantine" from other components in dismantling research (see Stockton et al., 2021). There is also limited empirical evidence for the efficacy of decontextualised practices relating to seeing oneself as a seer, removed from making contact with the specifics of life's difficult experiences, nor data to prove this repertoire functions to enhance access to conscious awareness as a stable, containing presence for exposure to painful content (Godbee & Kangas, 2020).

Given this, this chapter will explore challenges a person with aphasia may face with respect to self and identity more broadly, placing particular emphasis on the impacts of loss of language on a person's ability to access and express their "social self" given a restriction or reduction in access to validating social environments. The benefits of an individualised process-based approach and the necessity of deep, presenced listening to people's current concerns and unmet needs will also be considered.

Challenges to the social self: A CBS perspective on the role of the communication environment

ACT Co-Founder Kelly G. Wilson says that the self is "formed in a crucible of questions" (Wilson, 2022). The interest others show – or fail to show – in how we experience our inner world shapes our understanding of and ability to speak about it, with potentially important consequences for who we see ourselves as being in the world.

While we commonly think of the "self" as thing-like, a noun, in the tradition that ACT is a part of, it is more common to think of *selfing* as a verb. This aligns ACT with other modern psychotherapies, which typically emphasise process over substance (Wilson, 2022). On a common-sense level, we might reflect that we often describe ourselves and others in fixed terms rather than as a fluid or evolving process: "I am", "you are", "he is", "she is": "She is so kind", "He is a phenomenal worker", "She is troubled", "He is a loving father". Telling the story of the self in a "thing-like" way can increase suffering when a gap arises between a particular descriptor and life as it is lived: when a person no longer *measures up* to verbal rules they and others have derived over time that *make them who they are* (Meyerson & Zuckerman, 2019). When things change in life and a person encounters a painful struggle with some lost role or aspect of identity (a teacher, a friend, articulate, knowledgeable, credible) or betrayal of who they thought *someone else* was in relation to them (e.g. a partner has an affair) we can feel that something in us is missing, gone, absent – maybe shattered, maybe even destroyed (Baker et al., 2020; Meyerson & Zuckerman, 2019).

ACT is nested within a broader scientific approach with a specific interest in the creation of nurturing, validating environments (Biglan, 2015), in which selfing, like all human behaviour, can be understood as an act embedded and unfolding in the context of relationships and communities. In this way of thinking, when the answer to the question "who am I?" seems unclear, or suggests something deficient or absent, this may "suggest absence in the richness, nuance of the questioning environment" (Wilson, 2022). Intimacy in couples, for example, relies on connected authentic asking and answering of questions, which may be profoundly altered when experiences of trauma in the couple lead to a change or reduction in question types and responses, even without the added complication of language disability (Follette & Naugle, 2006). The questions we are asked by others, of ourselves, have transformational capacity to influence our understanding of ourselves and our relationships across our lives.

Stapleton and McHugh (2021), suggest a number of features shared by optimal environments that can effectively nurture "healthy selfing":

1. *The environment fosters sensitivity towards the individual,* cultivating and reinforcing the individual's capacity to identify and articulate their private experiences and emotions in the way that's right for them
2. *The environment supports the individual to be in contact with their internal experiences*
3. *The environment prevents the loss of selfing skills* (extinction) through ensuring ample opportunities to share internal experiences
4. *The environment honours the individual as a credible witness to their own experience,* avoiding any attempts to deliberately distort their response to their internal thoughts, feelings and bodily sensations
5. *The environment facilitates rich discussions regarding the "world within",* supporting effective and connected communication and self-expression across a range of situations

In Figure 8.3, these principles are reimagined and combined with commonly clinically adopted communicative practices currently utilised by Speech and Language Therapists in the context of working with adults with aphasia, aimed at supporting the individual to reveal their competence in interaction (Kagan, 1998; Simmons-Mackie, 1998; MacKenzie, 2017; Santo Pietro et al., 2019; van Rijssen et al., 2022).

Lack of access to a validating communication environment may risk inadequate rehabilitation of emotional language and the ability to engage in self-talk at times of trouble and stress, potentially contributing to a self-amplifying loop of rising emotional distress and reduced ability to make sense of and respond to difficult internal experience (Darrow & Follette, 2014). Resourcing a person and those who communicate with them to co-create a validating environment when language and communication capacities have been damaged or compromised is important work, and it can be challenging.

There is ample evidence that post-onset, people with aphasia are asked fewer questions about themselves across the contexts of their lives, and experience this as distressing and frustrating. As human beings, we have evolved to be sensitised to signs of loss of social value in the eyes of others. When our relational value to others seems in jeopardy we immediately and involuntarily feel a range of physiological sensations that evoke a range of socially oriented emotions that are typically uncomfortable and unwanted: jealousy, loneliness, shame, guilt, social anxiety and embarrassment (Leary & Asbury, 2022).

Facilitating Rich Discussions with Adults with Aphasia

Be there
Be aware,
Be ready

Affirm Capacity - Aphasia impacts language, not intellect - "I know you know".
Notice - eye contact, shifts in tone, facial expression, pauses
Name - curiously saying what you see: "I saw your face there, Mike! .."
Wonder - without imposing e.g. "Were you agreeing with Georgia, Mike?"
vs "you feel the same as Georgia on this..."
Remember - remember what matters to the person. "Chip is your older dog, right?"
Be ready - whiteboard for key words, objects, detailed photographs, video clips etc

Encourage
Safe
Exploration

Support Communication - write key words, use gesture, facial expressin
Slow down.. then slow down a little further. and give lots of time to respond
Model relaxed easy open pace and a steady trust that what needs to will emerge.
Encourage playfulness and risk-taking, make light-hearted fun of yourself at times
Offer interpretations choicefully - wonder aloud about meanings, "is that right?"
Repair quickly, responsibly, genuinely - "Oh I'm sorry I misunderstood you there"

Honour
experience

A person's experience is their experience - no toxic positivity OR lecturing on realistic hopes
Share what you think & feel but affirm differences e.g. "I haven't had that experience"
Co-construct social rules for the context - "some people find it useful when.. what do you think?"
Don't ask the person to disregard or override what they really feel for your approval
Ask permission before exploring painful areas (I wonder if it would be okay to stay here... is it okay if I ask you more about...). Leave a person in choice.
Be genuinely interested - listen to people's stories of their lives with wonder and appreciation.

Reclaim
words
for life inside
the skin

Affirm emotional talk is welcome and important here
Explore feelings, develop and refine a shared vocabulary and understanding
Support a wide range of ways to explore inner worlds- offer visual supports eetc
Enrich complex topics through multiple modalities e.g. videos, photographs, objects, literature, poetry, art, music
Help a person reclaim words that are important to them e.g. forgiveness, doubt, rage.
Develop word grids with examples and develop these as you explore together

Figure 8.3 Creating contexts to support 'healthy selfing' in adults with aphasia

The Need-Threat model of ostracism (Williams & Zadro 2001; Williams, 2009) suggests this can threaten fundamental human needs for belonging, control, self-esteem and meaningful existence. Many people with aphasia experience chronic, repeating experiences of being ignored or not responded to by those around them, excluded from conversations of relevance to their lives and reduced opportunities to participate fully in valued domains of living (Harmon, 2020; Fotiadou et al., 2014). Effective strategies to manage experiences of ostracism in the general population include the use of cognitive strategies to reappraise the event's meaning, but even in psychotherapeutic interventions with people with aphasia, it seems that these are rarely trained explicitly (Kneebone, 2016; Kneebone & Jeffries, 2013; Thomas et al., 2013).

A qualitative study by Harmon (2020) suggested that some individuals with mild to moderate aphasia organically learn to use cognitive strategies to cope with challenging communication situations as they adjust to life with a language disability; however, further investigation of psychotherapeutic intervention kernels such as **cognitive restructuring** (changing one's thoughts) and **cognitive defusion** (separating one's self from one's thoughts) may provide benefits for some individuals (Larsson et al., 2016).

When interactional processes *repeatedly* and *chronically* fail across communication partners and contexts, particularly at times of elevated stress and need, vicious cycles of interpersonal misunderstanding and communication breakdown can dismantle a person's sense of their stake or influence in two-way interaction, diminishing what seems possible in the realm of meaningful interpersonal connection, with inevitable consequences for a sense of self (Haun et al., 2008; Crielesi et al., 2019). Psychological resources become depleted and hope is lost, often leading to aggression and irritability, or social withdrawal (Williams, 2009). Chronic ostracism has been positively associated with severe psychological distress (Waldeck et al., 2017; Williams & Zadro, 2001).

Even in the hospital environment, in comparison to how they interact with other patients, when nurses interact with patients with aphasia, they do not usually interact about issues other than physical care and rarely attempt to "repair" incidences of conversational breakdown (e.g. they may ignore a patient or walk away, rather than work with the patient to understand what they are communicating). Interactions instead tend to fall into a pattern of closed questions and simple responses (Haun, Rittman & Sberna, 2008), potentially elevating traumatic stress (Chang et al., 2016, 2018).

Qualitative research with partners of people with aphasia suggests reduced patterns of communication contribute to misunderstanding, frustration, anxiety and withdrawal in couples, creating relationship-threatening "we-stress" (Croteau et al., 2020; Falconier & Kuhn, 2019) in which one or both partners may feel the need to mask their own emotions and "stay positive" in challenging communicative encounters. Consistent with the predictions of the Need-Threat model, people with aphasia report feeling intense feelings when faced with repeating communication breakdown (Harmon, 2020; Harmon et al., 2019) and can become self-conscious about their impairments (Cavanaugh & Haley, 2020), leading to an increased focus on the self and reduced ability to take the perspective of and empathise with the struggles also faced by their communication partners (Harmon, 2020). Over time, a lack of authentic connection can lead to withdrawal from the interaction by both or either partner, either physically or in terms of the types and quality of responses that they engage with (Follette & Naugle, 2006; Croteau et al., 2020). As relationships and friendships end, social networks shrink (Azios et al., 2022). Over time, as many as half of people with aphasia may begin to avoid social settings altogether, often contributing to or exacerbating experiences of low mood and social exclusion (Baker et al., 2018; Baylor et al., 2011; Le Dorze et al., 2014; Garcia et al., 2000).

When this vicious cycle of communication breakdown persists, some people may experience persisting, pervasive aversive internal experiences associated with ostracism and/or invalidating social environments, including **existential loneliness**

(Nyström, 2006; Nilsson, Jannson & Norberg, 1997) and **chronic sorrow** (Roos, 2014). Bolmsjö et al. (2018) define existential loneliness as

> the immediate awareness of being fundamentally separated from other people and from the universe, primarily through experiencing oneself as mortal, or, *especially when in a crisis, experiencing not being met (communicated with) at a deep human (i.e. authentic) level, and typically therefore experiencing negative feelings, that is, emotions or moods, such as sadness, hopelessness, grief, meaninglessness or anguish.*
>
> (p. 219)

Chronic sorrow is an experience of complex grief particularly associated with disability, with a tendency to resurge across the lifespan at moments where there is renewed contact with "lost self", e.g. renewed grief as their young children grow, and keeping up with them in conversation becomes harder over time (Parr, Duchan & Pound, 2003). Existential loneliness has been described by people with aphasia as a loneliness of a depth and kind never known before: feelings of wordless inferiority, being imprisoned in the body, distrustful of others, living through harrowing moments of feeling entirely alone and hollow, in a world where even close loved ones felt masked and unreachably distant (Nyström, 2006; Bolmsjö et al., 2018; van Tilburg, 2021). Chronic sorrow is associated with the "severe life narrative interruption" of sudden onset of disability that necessitates constructing and relearning the world in such a way as to make the new reality "believable as well as bearable" (Roos, 2014, p.181). Both are frequently associated with social contexts that are invalidating and unresponsive, with little or no social recognition of either the loss or the person who is experiencing loss (Roos, 2014).

Every obstacle is an opportunity for growth

How can these deep emotional and existential needs of people with aphasia be addressed? While developing individual and communication partner skills and restoring access to a social network might be the first responses that come to mind for many health and social care professionals when faced with a client sharing existential concerns related to belonging, usually when people are asked about what they are most troubled by, they talk about the problem in relationship to *how it feels* – their yearning for closeness and intimacy, or wish to escape a sense of meaninglessness and purpose in life (van Tilburg, 2021), the psychological impact of which may not be addressed by skills building or environmental manipulation alone. Existential concerns ("life has no meaning") may not even be directly addressed in specialist mental health services (Søberg et al., 2022).

At the same time, individual differences across people with aphasia remind us that recovery of a social self in the wake of sudden onset of disability is not an outcome but a process of human growth and adaptation, and as such, as potentially creative and variable as any human life. Like the self itself, social recovery is not rule-governed,

Figure 8.4 Individual and social factors impacting recovery trajectories

"thing-like" or fixed, but an unfolding experienced reality on a continuum from connectedness to social isolation, influenced by life history and the qualities of the communication environment (Haun et al., 2008). The degree to which a person recovers an optimal sense of connectedness *in the time and in the manner that is right for them* depends on a diverse range of personal and social factors, including early learning history and attachment style, the impact of disability, access to emotional, psychological and instrumental support, as well as personal factors such as attitude, life philosophy and capacity for emotional expression (see Figure 8.4).

While some of these factors are within a person's sphere of control and influence to modify, some are not, and some may never be (Haun et al., 2008). Here, ACT with its process-based emphasis on valued living and developing a broader, more spiritual sense of self in relation to life's challenges appears to have good potential to support individuals struggling to "accept life on life's terms" and explore new possibilities even in contexts of severe constraint (Walser & O'Connell, 2021, 2023).

It begins by listening: Addressing individual differences through a process-based approach

Effective implementation of ACT involves understanding and seeking to predict and influence **processes of change** (pathways to change) proven to predict healthy psychosocial outcomes. In choosing the most relevant pathway to change, ACT therapists work closely with a person to understand their needs in context, combining and iteratively tracking the impact of "evidence based kernels" (Embry & Biglan, 2008) that are:

- Based on research and theory
- Tailored to an individual's specific context
- Connected to related processes
- Modifiable

- Evolving over time
- Predicted to work at multiple levels (e.g., sociocultural and biopsychosocial)
- Predictably patterned in a way that can be reasonably hypothesised to produce desirable outcomes (Hofmann & Hayes, 2019)

The relative success or failure of this approach depends on the clinician accurately understanding and analysing idiographic contextual variables (Walser & O'Connell, 2023) – in other words, appreciating the person's current concerns and unmet needs in the specific context of their life as it is being lived.

Interventions based on known processes of change should be designed to meet the *specific* needs of a specific person in a specific time, place and context, considered across different dimensions important for meaningful behavioural change and growth (thinking and feeling; feelings and emotions; self; attention; motivation; acting in the world) and levels (biopsychosocial and sociocultural). This approach to intervention design recognises that people adjust in different ways related to their deep needs and evolve strategies for managing the problems of living over time shaped by the interaction of their learning history and constraints and possibilities afforded by their current context.

As such, successful working in a process-based approach begins with listening and *progresses* through listening. As the intervention unfolds, in a single session and over time, the practitioner must work closely with the person to track pathways to change that reliably produce desirable outcomes for them. To facilitate this, practitioners remain open, curious and analytically aware of what might be going on for a person, considering how to support a person's evolution in *their desired direction* through **varying, selecting and retaining behaviours** with the greatest potential to meet their needs successfully (see Figure 8.5).

An ACT practitioner therefore does not need to, and indeed is discouraged from, using a pre-scripted or prescriptive protocol, or viewing a person from within a

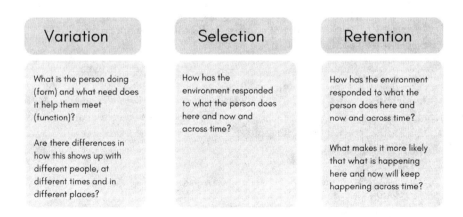

Figure 8.5 Variation, selection and retention

restrictive, attention-narrowing noun-like approach to understanding the problems they are facing in living, e.g. "Broca's aphasia", "depressive" or even sneakier rules like "likely to suffer depression if they withdraw from social activity" or "needs to drop attachment to a story of who they used to be and develop a more realistic view of what is possible now". At present, work is ongoing to refine how best to support this not only in ACT but across rehabilitation modalities, with the advent of a process-based approach, which will facilitate measurement of pathways for change for an individual through automated statistical analysis of high-density, longitudinal data obtained from an assessment pool based on processes of change associated with healthy outcomes (Ciarrochi et al., 2022). Practitioners are welcome, within their professional scope and competence, to adapt the Process-Based Assessment Tool (PBAT) for the purposes of meeting the specific needs of their working context and the needs of the individuals they work. Current items included in the PBAT are available to download from https://pbatsupport.com/free-download/, including a comprehension-adapted version of a set of cards with visual cues to support understanding and discussion (see Figure 8.6).

This has the potential to be an exciting development within the aphasia rehabilitation context for individual tailoring of measurement of psychosocial interventions aligned with the principles of person-centred care (Jesus et al., 2022):

1. Respectful of and tailored to the needs of the whole person
2. Reflexive and responsive to the situation
3. Relational – genuine, supportive, trustful and compassionate

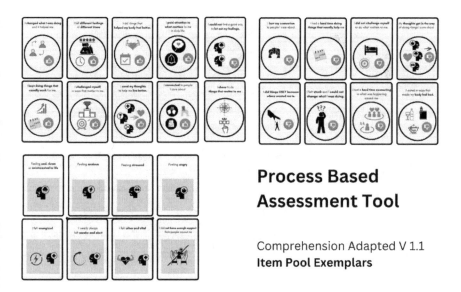

Figure 8.6 Comprehension adapted Process-Based Assessment Tool item exemplars (adapted and used with permission from Joseph Ciarrochi)

4. Focused on meanings, hopes and strengths
5. Collaborative, empowering and co-constructed

Of specific relevance to aphasia rehabilitation, adopting a process-based focus to measurement aligns with the SMARTER framework for aphasia goals, which encourages a *shared, monitored, accessible, relevant, transparent, evolving* and *relationship-centred* process of collaborative goal setting (Hersh et al., 2012).

Case formulation

What might this look like in practice? The diagram below shows a process-based formulation of a simple network-based data shared by a single (real!) individual in a trial of high-density longitudinal data over a month (Hayes, 2022). For the purposes of this chapter, this has been "reimagined" to include learning from clinical experience working with people with aphasia experiencing challenges with sadness that are distressing to them. The story below is not specific to an individual but an amalgamation of the stories of individuals with aphasia whose challenges with sadness are well reflected by this process diagram (see Figure 8.7).

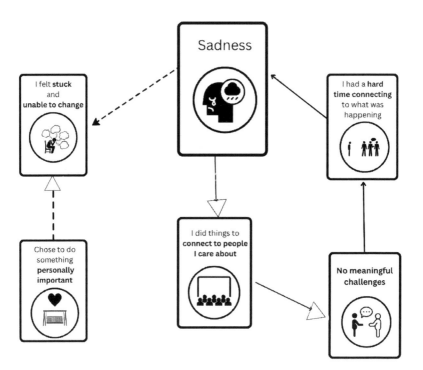

Figure 8.7 Process-based formulation for Mike (used with permission from Joseph Ciarrochi)

Meet "Mike" (details have been changed to maintain confidentiality)

Mike is a man in his early 60's who had a stroke four years ago. He has severe expressive aphasia and mild-moderate challenges with understanding, which can be significantly challenging in noisy, busy environments and fast, free-flowing conversations.

Prior to his stroke, Mike was working in a fast-paced corporate environment in a large city. Recently he has become aware he will be unable to return to that role. Mike is currently participating in a locally funded back-to-work programme and hopes to find some voluntary work a few hours a week over the next year, perhaps working outdoors or with animals at a local co-operative. He is determined to achieve this goal and committed to engaging with rehabilitation, but over the last few months, he has been struggling more and more with low mood and most days avoids leaving the house.

Since an earlier consultation meeting where he shared, Mike has been experimenting with getting out and about, beginning with contexts that don't require much conversation. At that meeting, he agreed to go to the cinema with his partner Linda twice a week. Mike is surprised to find that the more he goes out with Linda, the more sad he seems to feel.

Analysis of Mike's daily data relating to his mood using the PBAT revealed the above network. In dialogue with Mike using a Talking Mat (Murphy & Boa, 2012) using aphasia-friendly icons of the processes that emerged as important, he indicates that when he gets to the cinema he usually feels spaced out and uncomfortable, and has a hard time connecting to what's going on. This surprises and worries him because he can follow films at home well enough, and can't see why it should be any different in the cinema. Although he indicates awareness that some of his struggles to follow the film reflect background noises like the rustling of popcorn and incidental noises like coughing, nonetheless he is still disappointed and concerned he feels sad, which makes him feel more sad, yet redoubles his determination to make this work as spending time with Linda is so important to him. However, every week, it seems to be the same old story. He feels pretty stuck with it.

Slowly, Mike identifies that while getting out with Linda is something he values, the noisiness and busyness of the cinema are also extremely overwhelming and flood him with a felt sense of panic and thoughts it will always be like this.

The therapist then probes times that Mike and Linda do things together that are important for them, wondering if there is a time that they are together that feels a little sweeter and more comfortable ("the Sweet Spot" exercise, Wilson, 2022). Mike's face lights up after a moment, and he shares photos from his phone taken by their adult daughter. The photograph shows Linda and Mike, arms around each other on a porch swing, looking at a sunset. Mike says, "This. Quiet and calm and peace and love. Stillness".

The therapist and Mike do an additional activities card sort, exploring other moments that match any or all of the descriptors "quiet", "calm and peace", "love".

Pictures related to time in nature, and pictures of being with his pets or holding his new grandchild often match all three. "This", he repeats and points. "Alone, this…" smiling. "Alone", gesturing back and forth between pictures. "You are alone here? Not together?" "No no… TOGETHER (with emphasis)". "Alone together?" "Yes! YES!" Mike replies emphatically. "Happy together, alone together!"

Therapist: "What do you like most about those moments?"
Mike: "Us. Just us".
Therapist: "Just you, alone together, happy?"
Mike: "Yes. Quiet… warm… together… alone together…"

Using visual support materials, the therapist asks Mike how he feels in his body now when he remembers those times then. Mike gestures to an outline map of a body and says, "Warm", "happy sad, sad happy".

Therapist (Writing on a whiteboard, summarising): "Alone together, warm and quiet, is happy and sad".

(pausing while Mike looks at the words).

Therapist: "Anything else?"
Mike: "No pressure".
Therapist: "No pressure?"

Mike then picks up a pen and writes "Move forward", "cinema". He pauses and slumps in the chair, saying heavily, with constriction in his throat.

Mike: "No, no, no, no. Too much" (louder voice, constricted throat, rising intonation).
Therapist: "No, no, no, no. Too much" (gentler volume, easy voice, rising and falling intonation, soft and easy).

They sit for a moment, looking at the words.
   Mike looks again at the photo of him and his wife. He pauses and sighs.

Mike: "Just shitty. Move forward and… shitty. Angry sad. Slowly, slowly. So much so slowly… Frustring (sic)… Useless… Get in bin, Mike".

Mike's eyes moisten and he lets out a deep sigh, and the therapist wordlessly reaches out and puts her hand on Mike's. Together, they just sit alone together *with sadness*: welcoming it, and not pushing it away.

It begins with listening: Listening to story, hearing process

The quality of frustrated grief in Mike's story will be familiar terrain for many clinicians working with people with severe aphasia. Aphasia brings many deep losses, alongside distress that is considerably challenging for a person to express, often at many levels. Listening deeply to people with aphasia requires a listener with time and willingness to sit with the person and listen actively with persistence and gentleness to the stories clients tell of their lives (Strong & Shadden, 2020).

In the rehabilitation context, where time is a critical resource, facilitating effective therapy with individuals with severe communication challenges also makes extra demands on time:

1. Developing accessible materials, e.g. aphasia summary documents
2. Making materials relevant for an individual, e.g., topic-specific pictures, icons, videos, etc.
3. Allocating sufficient time to ensure a person has shared their true meaning (taking up to 15 minutes, at times, to establish one point to shared agreement)

Interactionally, the therapist is required to slow down sufficiently to allow a person to explore new repertoires while ensuring that the deep thread of conversation is not lost, balancing her own attention to offering embodied presence and sensitivity to nonverbal shifts in interaction with holding the arch of the client's narrative in mind, ensuring that she fully understands the literal meanings the client is sharing, as well as the feelings underneath them.

The case example above shows how a process-based approach could potentially help focus the instrumental requirements of listening to people with aphasia, e.g. creation of appropriate person-specific visual supports for use with a Talking Mat, freeing up the time a clinician has to spend with a client, empowering them to listen with a more embodied presence to a client's efforts to express *what will be most helpful to them* in moving forward in ways that matter *to them.*

A process-based approach supported by automated data collection of high-density longitudinal data may have the potential to allow a therapist to think more broadly and deeply about the needs of the person in front of her, allowing her to take her foot off her own accelerator and defuse from jumping to conclusions about the primary processes most relevant to bringing change. Potentially, a clinician's initial interpretation of Mike's low mood and social withdrawal might lead to rigid fusion with issues relating to his own emotional capacity to sit with distress, professional competence or premature "problem solving" that misses the heart of what Mike wants to make seen and known; for example, the clinician might ignore the emotional content in the room and suggest that he wears ear defenders to the cinema or attend a sensory-supported screening, or alternatively hypothesise that he is rigidly attached to an outdated or unrealistic story of who he is and might benefit from a brief intervention to see himself as "more than his story" or an "observer" of his lost life, which, especially in a rushed format in a short session, could be inadvertently invalidating of Mike's current pain (Walser & O'Connell, 2023).

By adopting a process-based focus, not only have Mike's feelings of grief and frustration at the slow journey of rehabilitation been expressed in a helpful, healing context *within the session*, but he has been supported to explore greater variability in the *quality* of his sadness and social withdrawal: there have been opportunities to express sadness, anger and a desire for quiet, peace, calm and warmth, including time that he can be "alone together" with those that he loves – not only with Linda, but also his granddaughter and pet – *without needing to push "just shitty" down and away.*

In Mike's case, further exploration and expansion of meanings of the feeling of "just shitty" were facilitated with visual and textual supports over a number of sessions, leading to a co-developed intervention including a brief acceptance practice, in which Mike made a commitment to practice bringing more gentleness to his struggle, as physicalised by a rock from a nearby hiking trail as a symbolic representation of his loss and stress (see Figure 8.8 for adapted visual support for homework).

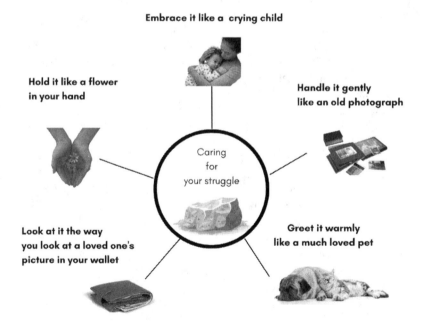

Figure 8.8 Supporting Mike's struggle: Visual acceptance map (adapted from Hayes, 2019)

Deep presence and healing relationships: We as context

The intervention chosen in this case example combines acceptance and defusion practices in this brief practice, in the service of supporting Mike with viewing *himself* and the role changes he has experienced in relation to disability more flexibly, defusing from thoughts like "get in bin, Mike" and a behavioural tendency to just keep going with rehabilitation activities that he is finding overwhelming, both of which we might hypothesise could have potential to lower his mood over time.

When considered in the context of interventions to develop a more flexible sense of self, we can see how, broadly speaking, we might think of this as a self-as-context intervention, supporting Mike to develop a more expansive perspective on the problems he is facing at the moment.

Walser and Westrup (2007) suggest four important functions of self-as-context work in adjusting to adverse life experiences that may include traumatic adjustment:

- It helps defuse from thoughts that intensify suffering, e.g. "I am useless", "I am broken" (get in bin)
- It helps defuse from thoughts that action is controlled by thoughts and feelings (feeling sad means it is *important* to persist, even when overwhelmed)
- It can release the anxiety of carrying thoughts that feel unacceptable or wrong, e.g. "I know she loves it, but I hate going to the cinema with Linda"
- It affirms the self as whole and intact despite the trauma

Interestingly, a recent network analysis to determine the theoretical structure of the ACT model and the interrelations between its components (Christodoulou et al., 2023) unexpectedly found self as context to have the strongest associations across most components, with self-as-context items merging with other processes, particularly present-moment awareness, defusion and acceptance. Self as context and present-moment awareness also had higher associations for people with high perceived stress.

Bunting and Hayes (2008) suggested that the ACT flexibility processes, self as context and present-moment awareness align well with the Existentialist-Integrationist construct of **presence**, the fundamental quality of the therapeutic relationship in the Existentialist-Integrationist model (Schneider, 2008). Therapist presence in ACT, they suggest, creates a psychologically flexible facilitative atmosphere, which has been called in other modalities a "holding environment" fostering an engaged and emotionally accepting environment for the client. This allows the client the freedom to express themselves more fully and choose more freely towards a "more experientially liberated life" (Bunting & Hayes, 2008).

If, as suggested, the function of developing a self-as-context repertoire is to facilitate people to experience stability and a sense of safeness in the face of co-existing with disturbing and challenging thoughts, feelings and remembered experiences, understanding the interpersonal, social functions of developing a self-as-context/we-as-context repertoire might be useful. Conceptualising self as context as a repertoire facilitative of access to an introjected felt experience of a less individualistic, more social, caring hierarchical presence would align with the sense of self as context outlined in Hayes' *Making Sense of Spirituality,* an early paper pre-dating ACT (1984).

To clarify what we mean here, we might consider the structure of brief exercises that address a sense of safety in the presence of difficulty, e.g. "Notice, Name, Refocus" as adapted from the WHO's (2020) *Doing What Matters in Times of Stress* protocol created by Russ Harris and adapted by Hayes (2022) (see Figures 8.9 and 8.10).

Notice, Name, Refocus (Hayes, 2022)

Here are three steps to apply when you're struggling, when you're facing something that's really challenging and really stretches your capacity...

(Offer 2-3 relevant, specific examples for the context and situation)

Step 1 is to **notice.**

Notice your difficult thoughts and feelings. Don't let them slip by.
Don't let them just go into the woodwork.

Why? Because the habits of mind that lead us away from what we care about tend to be automatic.

If we can simply notice that this hurts, that worry is there, that pain is there... if we can just take that microsecond we have a little chance to break the cycle of automatic amplification, as we get hooked by our experiences and then before we know it, and often not even knowing it, we're avoiding our experiences.

Step 2 is to **name** it.

This is a powerful step. Just call it out. When you notice it, name it. Give it a name. "I'm feeling anxious", "there's tightness in my stomach", "my heart is pounding", "I have the thought that there's nothing I can do it."

Simply naming your experience gives you a little bit of separation but it also brings that awareness in, because of how we are, as this strange amalgam of learning that is nonverbal, and learning that is verbal, it gives us a chance to carry forward our awareness. This helps us deploy our skills and to catch ourselves when we start to hide from our own experience.

You might even just the words that "I notice..". "I notice I'm having the thought that, I'm having the feeling that.." "I notice there's anxiety..". "I notice there's a thought.."

Having done that, having taken on board and even given it a name, you can move to step 3.

Step 3 is to **refocus on what matters to you.**

Focus on what you care about.

Be careful, don't use it as a subtraction. Don't use it as a distancing move to minimise or eliminate of what you have noticed and named.

Do it much as you might if you took something heavy and you put it on your back and then you looked at where you were going and you took a step forward: *"With this pain, and with this history, with this thing that I just named, I am taking this step".*

In that refocusing forward is that mental step that you take that lets you know that you're safe, let's you know that you're able, even though there are hard feelings, that you're not incapacitated.

You can do things. You can focus on the things that you care about.

That defines this situation as safe and useful. Safe in the sense of it's okay to be aware in this way even of something that painful, and useful because often in that very moment, as we carry it forward, often you'll see a link, you'll notice, that in a way, this action of caring sometimes is deepened by your own openness to feel, and to think, and to remember: to notice and name what's going on with you.

Figure 8.9 Notice, Name and Refocus script (Adapted from Hayes 2022, used with permission)

Notice, Name, Refocus   (adapted from Hayes (2022)

 Notice: Pay attention to the hard feelings and thoughts.
                    Just notice that they're there.

 Name: Give those feelings and thoughts a name.
                    For example, "I'm feeling worried" or "I'm feeling sad."

 Refocus: Think about what you care about
                    and step forward towards it.

 Do it like you are carrying something heavy on your back
and you can still look ahead
and take a step forward **towards what matters to you.**

 Taking this step lets you know **you are safe**.
It is safe to be aware in this way of something that painful.
This **helps** you **move forward** with **difficult feelings.**

Figure 8.10 Notice, Name and Refocus: Aphasia friendly reminder card (Adapted from Hayes 2022, used with permission)

This exercise touches on a range of different potential processes – attentional, emotional and behavioural flexibility and self-regulation, with an overarching emphasis on regulating a sense of down-regulating threat and offering care. The specific instruction in the Hayes (2022) adaptation of this exercise evokes the "visual cliff" experiment (Gibson & Walk, 1960), in which one-year-olds were encouraged to crawl across a constructed "pretend cliff" that was perfectly safe to their mother on the other side (see Figure 8.11).

The infants of mothers who expressed fear or distress would not explore the edges of the boundary or attempt to crawl forward.

In this exercise, the listener is, in a sense, being guided to become an encouraging caregiver to themselves, creating a physiological, attentional, emotional and motivational context (*"this lets you know* that you are safe to move forward"), in the service of facilitating an increase in positive approach behaviour in the presence of uncertainty that is being experienced as distressing.

Paul Gilbert (in Gilbert & Simos, 2022) suggests it's important to consider a distinction in human behaviour between environments that lead to adult *safety*-seeking and *safeness*-seeking. He explains the distinction as follows: safety is regulated by threat monitoring and control focused on the prevention of harm. Safeness and

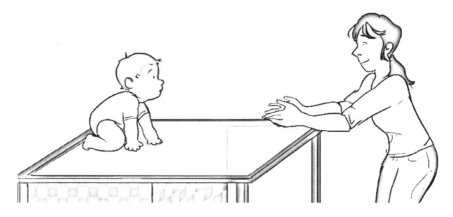

Figure 8.11 The Visual Cliff (Gibson & Walk, 1960)

safeness cues, on the other hand, relate to noticing sources of support and helpful-ness that reduce threat emotions and responses and encourage exploration and play.

Thought of in this way, the consciousness we experience as a secure base and safe haven where we can rest, before we return to exploration and play, is more akin to that of a compassionate carer than a distant, omnipresent, dispassionate observing God. Making contact with a sense of self, suffused with safeness, can support a person's ability to be *lovingly with* difficult and disturbing thoughts, emo-tions and bodily sensations, rather *about* them in a way that constricts attentional, emotional and behavioural flexibility.

What if *presence* (physical or emotional, or both) were foundational to our ability to learn and to explore with confidence (with fidelity to ourselves)? The therapeutic relationship is considered the "bedrock" of ACT therapy (Walser & O'Connell, 2023). In Figure 8.12, self as context and present-moment awareness are seen connected by a double-headed arrow, visualised as the "backbone" of the socially extended Hexaflex (Hayes, 2019, 2022). Hayes (2019) provided general suggestions for how to conceptualise the six processes of the Hexaflex as they might be socially extended and how these relate to the Psychological Flexibility model (Hayes, 2022). In Figure 8.13, these are related to the Extended Evolutionary Meta-Model as outlined by Hayes et al. (2020).

What might this mean in the context of developing ACT for aphasia?

While a full discussion of the implications of adopting such an approach more broadly is outside the scope of this chapter, we would suggest that listening with presence may have particular relevance to meeting the emotional needs of people with aphasia. Clarke (2003), a counsellor with aphasia, speaks of the importance of *doing less, being more* in addressing emotions in aphasia rehabilitation:

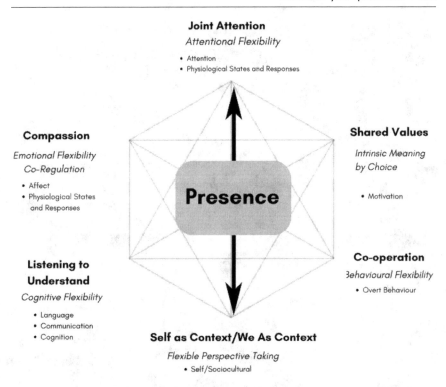

Joint Attention

Attentional Flexibility

- Attention
- Physiological States and Responses

Compassion

Emotional Flexibility
Co-Regulation

- Affect
- Physiological States and Responses

Shared Values

Intrinsic Meaning
by Choice

- Motivation

Presence

Listening to Understand

Cognitive Flexibility

- Language
- Communication
- Cognition

Co-operation

Behavioural Flexibility
- Overt Behaviour

Self as Context/We As Context

Flexible Perspective Taking
- Self/Sociocultural

Figure 8.12 Presence: linking We as Context, Joint Attention, Self as Context and Present Moment Awareness (Adapted from Hayes (2019). Used with permission).

I poured out my angry and confused feelings. This demonstration of emotion needed [the therapist's] presence. I needed her acknowledgement of my predicament and she gave me this by giving me the time and space to express myself. When later I asked myself what she had done, the answer I arrived at was "not that much". I cannot recall her saying one single word. What she silently gave me though was precious time and space… This was an early example of doing less I have learned from.

(Clarke, 2003)

We have seen that coming to terms with living with aphasia often provokes deep questions of both personal and social identity, nested within profound experiences of contact with grief and loss. Across our lives, when we are threatened or distressed, we will seek a sense of *felt security* with interested, available (and often stronger, wiser others) as safe havens in times of need from which to explore and develop new skills and experience suffering when we find that there is no one near, interested or responsive (Shaver & Mikulincer, 2014).

Socially Extended Hexaflex Labels	Flexibility Process Label	Extended Evolutionary Meta-Model	Purpose
Joint Attention	Attentional Flexibility	• Attention • Affect • Physiological States and Responses	Ability to attend to what's happening here and now *in both self and other* and remain open and aware when there are opportunities to close down or avoid.
Compassion	Emotional Flexibility	• Attention • Affect • Physiological States and Responses	Ability to attend to what's happening *emotionally* here and now *in both self and other* remaining open, aware and responsive when there are opportunities to close down or avoid.
Listening to Understand	Cognitive Flexibility	• Cognition	Use of language to explore and navigate context with another person to reach a shared understanding, disengaging when language is not helpful (both from own thoughts and literal or rigid attachment to the meaning of the other person's words or communication).
We-as-Context	Flexible Perspective Taking	• Self	Self-awareness *in the context of the relationship* and the ability to take a broader perspective on own actions across time with compassion and acceptance in the service of making healthy *choices that support the relationship*
Shared Values	Intrinsic Meaning by Choice	• Motivation	Ability to clarify shared values, choose actions aligned with values and sustain these actions across times of adversity and challenge
Co-operation	Behavioural Flexibility	• Overt Behaviour	Working together to learn more about eachother through trial and error learning – trying out new and different behaviour to develop shared resources for effective communication *in this relationship*, that honour what each person finds personally meaningful and important.

Figure 8.13 The Socially-Extended Hexaflex related to the Extended Evolutionary Meta Model (Hayes et al. 2020)

To allow new repertoires to emerge in any therapeutic context, slowing the pace and waiting is important (Wilson, 2022); however, uncontrolled pace, silence without presence and communication "trouble spots" that create a lengthy period of uncertainty can interfere with the natural rhythms and routines of interaction, hindering the ability of both parties to attend to and follow the thread of conversation and explore a topic in depth. This can create threats not only to communication partners understanding the literal content of what is being said and its deeper personal meanings but also, more broadly, the context in which it is being said: the therapeutic relationship or working alliance. This can increase the likelihood of ruptures and invalidation in the unfolding of an intervention through reciprocal interaction of inflexibility processes across therapist and client (Walser & O'Connell, 2021).

Relationship-centred care is fundamental to aphasia rehabilitation (Worrall et al., 2017) but can be complicated by the time pressures of the working environment, specifically with reference to the creation of communication environments that adequately protect rehabilitation of emotional language. People with long-term conditions, including people with aphasia, repeatedly ask to be met with dignity as a whole person in a genuine, warm relationship. Care in the context of any long-term condition involves caring for people who are facing anguish, grief, despair, existential loneliness and chronic sorrow. Care in such contexts needs to be *loving care*, emphasising warmth, companionship, humour and space for touch and tears (Beach et al., 2006), and also professionally skilful care. In the case of aphasia, this means care that is appropriately tailored to the specific communication needs of the individual in such a way as to facilitate deep conversations around meaning, purpose, love, life and loss. Adopting a process-based focus on tailoring psychosocial interventions to the individual, combined with opportunities for deep listening and therapeutic presence, may yet have the potential to revolutionise our understanding of how best to meet the emotional, psychosocial and spiritual needs of people with aphasia, including people with severe aphasia. Life asks you questions. Perhaps we already know the answer:

The fish trap exists because of the fish.
Once you've got the fish, you can forget the trap.
The rabbit snare exists because of the rabbit.
Once you've got the rabbit, you can forget the snare.
Words exist because of meaning.
Once you've got the meaning, you can forget the words.
Where can I find a man who has forgotten words so I can have a word with him?
Chuang Tse (in Sekhon, 2022)

References

Azios, J. H., Strong, K. A., Archer, B., Douglas, N. F., Simmons-Mackie, N., & Worrall, L. (2022). Friendship matters: A research agenda for aphasia. *Aphasiology*, *36*(3), 317–336.

Baker, C., Rose, M., Ryan, B., & Worrall, L. (2020). Barriers and facilitators to implementing stepped psychological care for people with aphasia: Perspectives of stroke health professionals. *Topics in Stroke Rehabilitation*, 1–13. https://doi.org/10.1080/10749357.2020.1849952

Baker, C., Worrall, L., Rose, M., & Ryan, B. (2018). Experiences of mood changes and depression after post-stroke aphasia. *Aphasiology*, *32*(sup1), 11–12.

Baylor, C., Burns, M., Eadie, T., Britton, D., & Yorkston, K. (2011). A qualitative study of interference with communicative participation across communication disorders in adults. *American Journal of Speech-Language Pathology, 20*(4), 269–287. https://doi.org/10.1044/1058-0360(2011/10-0084

Beach, M. C., Inui, T., & Relationship-Centered Care Research Network. (2006). Relationship-centered care: A constructive reframing. *Journal of General Internal Medicine, 21,* 3–8.

Biglan, A. (2015). *The nurture effect: How the science of human behavior can improve our lives and our world.* New Harbinger.

Bolmsjö, I., Tengland, P.A., & Rämgård M. (2018). Existential loneliness: An attempt at an analysis of the concept and the phenomenon. *Nursing Ethics, 26*(5), 1310–1325. https://doi.org/10.1177/0969733017748480

Bunting, K., & Hayes, S. C. (2008). Language and meaning: Acceptance and commitment therapy and the EI model. In K. J. Schneider (Ed.), *Existential-integrative psychotherapy: Guideposts to the core of practice* (pp. 217–234). Routledge/Taylor &Francis Group.

Cavanaugh, R., & Haley, K. L. (2020). Subjective communication difficulties in very mild aphasia. *American Journal of Speech-Language Pathology, 29*(1S), 437–448. https://doi.org/10.1044/2019_AJSLP-CAC48-18-0222

Chang, B. P., Carter, E., Ng, N., Flynn, C., & Tan, T. (2018). Association of clinician burnout and perceived clinician-patient communication in the Emergency Department. *The American Journal of Emergency Medicine, 36*(1), 156.

Chang, B. P., Sumner, J. A., Haerizadeh, M., Carter, E., & Edmondson, D. (2016). Perceived clinician–patient communication in the emergency department and subsequent post-traumatic stress symptoms in patients evaluated for acute coronary syndrome. *Emergency Medicine Journal, 33*(9), 626–631.

Christodoulou, A., Karekla, M., Costantini, G., & Michaelides, M. P. (2023). A network analysis approach on the Psychological Flexibility/Inflexibility model. *Behavior Therapy, 54*(5), 719–733.

Ciarrochi, J., Sahrda, B., Hofmann, S., & Hayes, S. C. (2022). Developing an item pool to assess processes of change in psychological interventions. The process-based assessment tool (PBAT). *Journal of Contextual Behavioral Science, 23,* 200–213.

Clarke, H. (2003). Doing less, being more. In S. Parr, J. Duchan, & C. Pound (Eds.). *Aphasia inside out: Reflections on communication disability.* (pp.80-90). Open University Press.

Crielesi, M., Roche, L., Monopoli, G., Yeates, G. N., & Monte, S. (2019). Mindfulness interventions for people with aphasia–case evidence from individual and group therapy formats. In K. Meredith & G.N. Yeates (Eds.), *Psychotherapy and aphasia* (pp. 107–135). Routledge.

Croteau, C., McMahon-Morin, P., Le Dorze, G., & Baril, G. (2020). Impact of aphasia on communication in couples. *International Journal of Language & Communication Disorders, 55*(4), 547–557.

Darrow, S. M., & Follette, W. C. (2014). A behavior analytic interpretation of alexithymia. *Journal of Contextual Behavioral Science, 3*(2), 98–108.

Embry, D. D., & Biglan, A. (2008). Evidence-based kernels: Fundamental units of behavioral influence. *Clinical Child and Family Psychology Review, 11*(3), 75–113. https://doi.org/10.1007/s10567-008-0036-x

Evans, W. S., Meyer, E., & Hunting Pompon, R. (2022). Introduction to Acceptance and Commitment Therapy for SLPs. Abstract for platform presentation, Annual American Speech-Language-Hearing Association Conference (November 2022).

Falconier, M. K., & Kuhn, R. (2019). Dyadic coping in couples: A conceptual integration and a review of the empirical literature. *Frontiers in Psychology*, *10*, 571.

Follette, W. C., & Naugle, A. E. (2006). Functional analytic clinical assessment in trauma treatment. In V. M. Follette & J. I. Ruzek (Eds.), *Cognitive-behavioral therapies for trauma* (2nd ed., pp. 17–33). Guilford Press.

Fotiadou, D., Northcott, S., Chatzidaki, A., & Hilari, K. (2014). Aphasia blog talk: How does stroke and aphasia affect a person's social relationships? *Aphasiology*, *28*(11), 1281–1300.

Garcia, L. J., Barrette, J., & Laroche, C. (2000). Perceptions of the obstacles to work reintegration for persons with aphasia. *Aphasiology*, *14*(3), 269–290.

Gibson, E. J., & Walk, R. D. (1960). The "visual cliff." *Scientific American, 202*(4), 64–71. https://doi.org/10.1038/scientificamerican0460-64

Gilbert, P., & Simos, G. (Eds.). (2022). *Compassion focused therapy: Clinical practice and applications*. Routledge.

Godbee, M., & Kangas, M. (2020). The relationship between flexible perspective taking and emotional well-being: A systematic review of the "self-as-context" component of acceptance and commitment therapy. *Behavior Therapy*, *51*(6), 917–932.

Harmon, T. G. (2020). Everyday communication challenges in aphasia: descriptions of experiences and coping strategies. *Aphasiology*, *34*(10), 1270–1290. https://doi.org/10.1080/02687038.2020.1752906

Harmon, T. G., Jacks, A., Haley, K. L., & Bailliard, A. (2019). How responsiveness from a communication partner affects story retell in aphasia: Quantitative and qualitative findings. *American Journal of Speech-Language Pathology*, *29*(1), 142–156. https://doi.org/10.1044/2019_AJSLP-19-0091

Haun, J., Rittman, M., & Sberna, M. (2008). The continuum of connectedness and social isolation during post stroke recovery. *Journal of Aging Studies*, *22*(1), 54–64. https://doi.org/10.1016/j.jaging.2007.03.001

Hayes, S. C. (1984). Making sense of spirituality. *Behaviorism, 12*(2), 99–110.

Hayes, S. C. (2002). Buddhism and acceptance and commitment therapy. *Cognitive and Behavioral Practice*, *9*(1), 58–66.

Hayes, S. C. (2019). *A liberated mind: The essential guide to ACT*. Random House.

Hayes, S. C. (2022, August 17). How change happens: Why improvement in our mental health will require going beyond mental illness categories [Webinar]. Alan Hu Platform. https://www.youtube.com/watch?v=pDp0KLvatlU

Hayes, S. C., Ciarrochi, J., Hofmann, S. G., Chin, F., & Sahdra, B. (2022). Evolving an idionomic approach to processes of change: Towards a unified personalized science of human improvement. *Behaviour Research and Therapy*, *156,* 104155.

Hayes, S. C., Hofmann, S. G., & Ciarrochi, J. (2020). A process-based approach to psychological diagnosis and treatment: The conceptual and treatment utility of an extended evolutionary model. *Clinical Psychology Review*, *82,* 101908. https://doi.org/10.1016/j.cpr.2020.101908

Hayes, S. C., Strosahl, K. D., & Wilson, K. G. (2012). *Acceptance and commitment therapy: The process and practice of mindful change* (2nd ed.). Guilford Press.

Hersh, D., Worrall, L., Howe, T., Sherratt, S., & Davidson, B. (2012). SMARTER goal setting in aphasia rehabilitation. *Aphasiology*, *26*(2), 220–233.

Hofmann, S. G., & Hayes, S. C. (2019). The future of intervention science: Process-based therapy. *Clinical Psychological Science: A Journal of the Association for Psychological Science*, *7*(1), 37–50. https://doi.org/10.1177/2167702618772296

Hydén, M. (2013). Narrating sensitive topics. In M. Andrews, C. Squire, & M. Tamboukou (Eds.), *Doing narrative research* (2nd ed., Kindle loc. 5145–5510). Sage.

Jesus, T. S., Papadimitriou, C., Bright, F. A., Kayes, N. M., Pinho, C. S., & Cott, C. A. (2022). Person-centered rehabilitation model: Framing the concept and practice of person-centered adult physical rehabilitation based on a scoping review and thematic analysis of the literature. *Archives of Physical Medicine and Rehabilitation, 103*(1), 106–120.

Kagan, A. (1998). Supported conversation for adults with aphasia: Methods and resources for training conversation partners. *Aphasiology, 12*(9), 816–830.

Kashdan, T. B., & Rottenberg, J. (2010). Psychological flexibility as a fundamental aspect of health. *Clinical Psychology Review, 30*(7), 865–878.

Kneebone, I. I. (2016). Stepped psychological care after stroke. *Disability and Rehabilitation, 38*(18), 1836–1843. https://doi.org/10.3109/09638288.2015.1107764

Kneebone, I.I., & Jeffries, F.W. (2013). Treating anxiety after stroke using cognitive-behaviour therapy: Two cases. *Neuropsychological Rehabilitation, 23*(6), 798–810. https://doi.org/10.1080/09602011.2013.820135

Kristo, I., & Mowll, J. (2022). Voicing the perspectives of stroke survivors with aphasia: A rapid evidence review of post-stroke mental health, screening practices and lived experiences. *Health & Social Care in the Community, 30*(4), e898–e908.

Larsson, A., Hooper, N., Osborne, L. A., Bennett, P., & McHugh, L. (2016). Using brief cognitive restructuring and cognitive defusion techniques to cope with negative thoughts. *Behavior Modification, 40*(3), 452–482.

Leary, R., & Asbury, K. (2022). Alone in the COVID-19 lockdown: An exploratory study. *Analyses of Social Issues and Public Policy, 22*, 536–559. https://doi.org/10.1111/asap.12317

Le Dorze, G., Salois-Bellerose, É., Alepins, M., Croteau, C., & Hallé, M. C. (2014). A description of the personal and environmental determinants of participation several years post-stroke according to the views of people who have aphasia. *Aphasiology, 28*(4), 421–439.

MacKenzie, S. (2017). Mosaics, ambiguity and quest: constructing stories of spirituality with people with expressive aphasia. Canterbury Christ Church University (United Kingdom).

Majumdar, S., & Morris, R. (2019). Brief group-based acceptance and commitment therapy for stroke survivors. *British Journal of Clinical Psychology, 58*(1), 70–90.

Meyerson, D. E., & Zuckerman, D. (2019). *Identity theft: Rediscovering ourselves after stroke*. Andrews McMeel Publishing.

Morris, R., Eccles, A., Ryan, B., & Kneebone, I. I. (2017). Prevalence of anxiety in people with aphasia after stroke. *Aphasiology, 31*(12), 1410–1415.

Murphy, J., & Boa, S. (2012). Using the WHO-ICF with talking mats to enable adults with long-term communication difficulties to participate in goal setting. *Augmentative and Alternative Communication, 28*(1), 52–60.

Nilsson, I., Jansson, L., & Norberg, A. (1997). To meet with a stroke: Patients' experiences and aspects seen through a screen of crises. *Journal of Advanced Nursing, 25*(5), 953–963. https://doi.org/10.1046/j.1365-2648.1997.1997025953.x

Niu, Y., Sheng, S., Chen, Y., Ding, J., Li, H., Shi, S., ... Ye, D. (2022). The efficacy of group acceptance and commitment therapy for preventing post-stroke depression: A randomized controlled trial. *Journal of Stroke and Cerebrovascular Diseases, 31*(2), 106225.

Nyström, M. (2006). Aphasia–an existential loneliness: A study on the loss of the world of symbols. *International Journal of Qualitative Studies on Health and Well-being, 1*(1), 38–49.

Parr, S., Duchan, J., & Pound, C. (2003). *Aphasia inside out: Reflections on communication disability*. Open University Press.

Roos, S. (2014). *Chronic sorrow: A living loss*. Routledge.

Ryan, B., Bohan, J., & Kneebone, I. (2019). Help-seeking and people with aphasia who have mood problems after stroke: perspectives of speech–language pathologists. *International Journal of Language & Communication Disorders, 54*(5), 779–793.

Sander, A. M., Clark, A. N., Arciniegas, D. B., Tran, K., Leon-Novelo, L., Ngan, E., & Walser, R. (2020). A randomized controlled trial of acceptance and commitment therapy for psychological distress among persons with traumatic brain injury. *Neuropsychological Rehabilitation, Early Online,* 1–25. https://doi.org/10.1080/09602011.2020.1762670

Santo Pietro, M. J., Marks, D. R., & Mullen, A. (2019). When words fail: Providing effective psychological treatment for depression in persons with aphasia. *Journal of Clinical Psychology in Medical Settings, 26*(4), 483–494.

Schneider, K. J. (Ed.). (2008). Existential-integrative psychotherapy: Guideposts to the core of practice. Routledge/Taylor & Francis Group.

Schultebraucks, K., Wen, T., Kronish, I. M., Willey, J., & Chang, B. P. (2020). Post-traumatic stress disorder following acute stroke. *Current Emergency and Hospital Medicine Reports, 8,* 1–8.

Sekhon, J. (2022). *Enabling Speech-Language Pathologists to feel confident and competent in counselling for supporting psychological wellbeing in people affected by post-stroke aphasia* (Doctoral dissertation, La Trobe University).

Shadden, B. (2005). Aphasia as identity theft: Theory and practice. *Aphasiology, 19*(3–5), 211–223. https://doi.org/10.1080/02687930444000697

Shaver, P. R., & Mikulincer, M. (2014). Adult attachment and emotion regulation. In J. J. Gross (Ed.), *Handbook of emotion regulation* (2nd ed., pp. 237–250). Guilford Press.

Simmons-Mackie, N. (1998). In support of supported conversation for adults with aphasia. *Aphasiology, 12*(9), 831–838.

Skinner, B. F. (1974). *About behaviorism*. Random House.

Søberg, A. I. B., Danbolt, L. J., Sørensen, T., & Haug, S. H. K. (2022). Patients at risk of suicide and their meaning in life experiences. *Archive for the Psychology of Religion,* 00846724221137620.

Stapleton, A., & McHugh, L. (2021). Healthy selfing: Theoretically optimal environments for the development of tacting and deictic relational responding. *Perspectivas em Análise do Comportamento, 12*(1), 125–137. https://doi.org/10.18761/PAC.2021.v12.RFT.10

Stockton, D., Kellett, S., Wilkinson, N., Hague, J., Bliss, P., Heaver, M., & Devine, A. (2021). A feasibility and pilot randomised dismantling trial of the efficacy of self-as-context during acceptance and commitment therapy. *International Journal of Cognitive Therapy, 14*(4), 704–723. https://doi.org/10.1007/s41811-021-00118-6

Strong, K. A., & Shadden, B. B. (2020). The power of story in identity renegotiation: Clinical approaches to supporting persons living with aphasia. *Perspectives of the ASHA Special Interest Groups, 5*(2), 371–383.2681-2692.

Thomas, S. A., Walker, M. F., Macniven, J. A., Haworth, H., & Lincoln, N. B. (2013). Communication and Low Mood (CALM): A randomized controlled trial of behavioural therapy for stroke patients with aphasia. *Clinical Rehabilitation, 27*(5), 398–408. https://doi.org/10.1177/0269215512462227

Townend, E., Tinson, D., Kwan, J., & Sharpe, M. (2010). "Feeling sad and useless": An investigation into personal acceptance of disability and its association with depression following stroke. *Clinical Rehabilitation, 24,* 555–564.

van Rijssen, M.N., Veldkamp, M., Bryon, E., Remijn, L., Visser-Meily, J.M.A., Gerrits,E., & van Ewijk, L. (2022). How do healthcare professionals experience communication with people with aphasia and what content should communication partner training entail?. *Disability and Rehabilitation, 44*(14), 3671–3678.

van Tilburg, T. G. (2021). Social, emotional, and existential loneliness: A test of the multidimensional concept. *The Gerontologist, 61*(7), e335–e344.

Waldeck, D., Tyndall, I., Riva, P., & Chmiel, N. (2017). How do we cope with ostracism? Psychological flexibility moderates the relationship between everyday ostracism experiences and psychological distress. *Journal of Contextual Behavioral Science, 6*(4), 425–432.

Walser, R. D., & O'Connell, M. (2021). Acceptance and commitment therapy and the therapeutic relationship: Rupture and repair. *Journal of Clinical Psychology, 77*(2), 429–440.

Walser, R. D., & O'Connell, M. (2023). Alliance rupture and repair in acceptance and commitment therapy. In C. F. Eubanks, L. W. Samstag, & J. C. Muran (Eds.), *Rupture and repair in psychotherapy: A critical process for change* (pp. 165–186). American Psychological Association. https://doi.org/10.1037/0000306-008

Walser, R. D., & Westrup, D. (2007). *Acceptance and commitment therapy for the treatment of post-traumatic stress disorder and trauma-related problems: A practitioner's guide to using mindfulness and acceptance strategies.* New Harbinger.

Whiting, D. L., Deane, F., McLeod, H., Ciarrochi, J., & Simpson, G. K. (2020). Can acceptance and commitment therapy facilitate psychological adjustment after a severe traumatic brain injury? A pilot randomized controlled trial. *Neuropsychological Rehabilitation, 30*(7), 1348–1371. http://dx.doi.org/10.1080/09602011.2019.1583582

Williams, K. D. (2009). Ostracism: A temporal need-threat model. *Advances in Experimental Social Psychology, 41,* 275–314.

Williams, K. D., & Zadro, L. (2001). Ostracism: On being ignored, excluded, and rejected. In M. R. Leary (Ed.), *Interpersonal rejection* (pp. 21–53). Oxford University Press.

Wilson, K. G. (2022). *Working with self and identity in ACT.* Praxis Education. https://www.praxiscet.com/working-with-self-and-identity-evergreen-signup/

Winnicott, D. W. (1958). The capacity to be alone. *The International Journal of Psychoanalysis, 39,* 416.

World Health Organisation (WHO). (2020). *Doing what matters in times of stress.* https://www.who.int/publications/i/item/9789240003927

Worrall, L. E., Hudson, K., Khan, A., Ryan, B., & Simmons-Mackie, N. (2017). Determinants of living well with aphasia in the first year poststroke: A prospective cohort study. *Archives of Physical Medicine and Rehabilitation, 98*(2), 235–240.

Zanella, C., Laures-Gore, J., Dotson, V. M., & Belagaje, S. R. (2023). Incidence of post-stroke depression symptoms and potential risk factors in adults with aphasia in a comprehensive stroke center. *Topics in Stroke Rehabilitation, 30*(5), 448–458. https://doi.org/10.1080/10749357.2022.2070363

Chapter 9

Applying the relational frame theory account of the self to self-related issues following a traumatic brain injury

Alison Stapleton, Richard Coates, Fergus Gracey and Louise McHugh

Imagine you wake up in a hospital and people tell you that you have sustained something you'd never heard of before, a 'traumatic brain injury' (TBI). You can't remember the accident and you can't remember a few days leading up to it. You can't move your arms and your legs as you used to. Your vision is blurry, you can't smell, things don't taste the same, and noise is overwhelming to you. You find it hard to concentrate on what is going on around you. You struggle to remember your experience after the accident. You say or do things that you wouldn't usually have done. You can't say the words you want to say. You find it hard to understand the perspective of people around you and you are having difficult interactions with those people closest to you. People tell you that you are doing these things and you are not aware of it. When you do eventually go home, you can't fulfil your usual roles around the house; you can't do things that matter to you, and you can't go back to work. Your relationships with your family have completely changed. Your partner says that they feel more like your carer than your partner. Your children seem scared of you and you find it hard to be around them when they are making so much noise. You shout at them over the slightest thing, which isn't like you at all. Your partner may well tell professionals, "They are not the same person that I married." So many aspects that make you 'you' can be altered following brain injury. It can be very painful to realize this for you and your family. When you do become aware that you are not the same person, you and your family may then become preoccupied with getting you back to the 'you' you were before the brain injury.

'Self-as-context' is one of the six components of the acceptance and commitment therapy (ACT; Hayes et al., 1999) 'hexaflex' model of psychological flexibility. Given its focus on a stable sense of self, self-as-context seems like a vital skill to consider when helping people adjust to the impacts of TBI. In addition, relational frame theory (RFT), an ACT-compatible theory of human language and cognition, may have valuable insights for understanding the 'self' and helping people with TBI develop an ongoing, evolving, (relatively) more flexible sense of self; more an action/behaviour (selfing) than a thing (self).

DOI: 10.4324/9781003193722-10

The relational frame theory account of the self

From an RFT perspective, the 'self' is the result of particular patterns of behaviour called 'relational framing' that develop from an early age (Hayes et al., 2001; McHugh et al., 2019). Simply put, children learn to relate different aspects of their experience in ways that allow them to respond more effectively to the world and themselves. As a child interacts with others, relational framing becomes increasingly fluent, the ultimate outcome being the emergence of the relatively complex sense of self that is seen in most adults (McHugh et al., 2004). With this come skills of perspective-taking, self-rules, mindful experience, spirituality, and even transcendence (McHugh & Stewart, 2012).

Once an individual begins to relationally frame through their interactions with the socio-verbal community, as they elaborate their relational networks, the functions of their environment will be transformed in increasingly complex and diverse ways. Thus, in theory, the world becomes increasingly verbal and language becomes virtually 'inescapable'. Naturally, an individual's own behaviour becomes part of this network of relationally transformed stimuli. Thus, given how much access we have to it, both directly through our own experience as well as through the reflection of that experience by other members of the verbal community, verbally responding to one's own responding becomes a core aspect of our world. For example, we might note improved running skills (e.g., "I'm getting faster"), which makes the running club we have joined more reinforcing. We might notice a tendency to procrastinate with work when feeling overwhelmed (e.g., "I keep avoiding writing because there is so much to do") and make plans next time we have a big task to complete.

We also might develop 'stories' about who we are (e.g., "I'm just not a maths person"; "I am unlovable"; "I am a shell of my former self"). We can also derive more generalized functions of 'self'. Returning to the example of running skills, if an individual's learning history led them to derive that being fast meant being good, then the faster they get, the better and better they are. Verbal responding to one's own responding is how the self is conceptualized from an RFT perspective. This conceptualization reflects important aspects of mainstream theories but also, by facilitating research and intervention, represents an important advancement both theoretically and empirically on previous approaches (see Montoya-Rodríguez et al., 2017 for a review).

The three selves

In accordance with RFT, an extended relational repertoire combined with perspective-taking establishes three functionally different types of self, namely self-as-content, self-as-process, and self-as-context (Hayes, 1995). We will now describe each self, how it relates to TBI, and its associated processes and outcome measures. For brevity, we will describe one core skill that may be a useful target for each pattern of selfing. Readers are directed to Kangas and McDonald (2011) for a more detailed overview of additional relevant processes for working with acquired brain injury. See Table 9.1 for a summary of the three self repertoires.

Table 9.1 A summary of the three self repertoires in accordance with relational frame theory.

Self Repertoire	Definition	Example	Question Prompts
Self-as-content	Conceptualized stories, evaluations, and descriptions about the self	"I am damaged"; " I am not enough"; " I am a burden."	"List things about yourself. How do you describe yourself? What descriptions of yourself limit you?"
Self-as-process	Ongoing knowing self attuned to current experience	"I am having the thought that 'I am burdensome' and feeling guilty."	"What were you feeling then? And what are you feeling now?"
Self-as-context	Stable and consistent perspective from which to view self-related experiences (observer/container self)	"I notice that my thoughts and feelings are part of me, and I am more than these parts. I am the witness of all my experiences across my life."	"Who is noticing? Notice you are having the thought that you are burdensome. Who is having that thought?"

Self-as-content

Self-as-content consists of descriptive and evaluative relational networks that a person constructs about themselves and their histories over time (e.g., "I am kind," "I am bad at writing manuscripts," etc.). As soon as verbal humans become self-aware, they begin to interpret, explain, evaluate, predict, and rationalize their behaviour. They organize these descriptions and evaluations of their own histories and tendencies into a coherent network that results in the construction of a presentation of 'self' that generally persists across time and contexts. According to ACT, difficulties can occur when these products of relational responding (e.g., thoughts, judgments, comparisons, beliefs, etc.) are treated as objectively 'true' and inherent aspects of the real world, i.e., when we become 'fused' (Hayes et al., 1999). This is especially problematic when self-evaluations appear as historically rooted and unchangeable; that is, our self-stories/conceptualized self may become rigid and no longer simply describe our past behaviour, but also guide our future behaviour in directions that maintain the coherence of the content (story) we've constructed. This may result in us ignoring or discounting contradictory evidence, selectively attending to and amplifying confirmatory evidence, and acting in ways that are consistent with our story about who we are and how we came to be that way, regardless of whether doing so best serves our needs, wants, and desires.

For example, imagine an individual with TBI has formed a rigid self-story post-injury (e.g., "I am burdensome to my friends and family"). This individual may begin to behave in ways that align with this story about themselves (e.g., opting out of social events) despite the apparent consequences (e.g., strained relationships), exacerbating issues long-term. As individuals are learning to navigate the world post-injury and noticing changes in their functioning, they may form new stories about themselves that become rigid and self-limiting over time (see Nochi, 1997 for a relevant discussion of 'void' self-stories in TBI patients). For example, if someone tightly held the self-story "I am incapable," they may avoid engaging in treatment and rehabilitation activities, becoming trapped in a self-amplifying feedback loop.

In line with ACT and RFT, reducing cognitive fusion by teaching individuals with TBI to gently defuse from self-limiting self-stories (i.e., deliteralization; to recognize that they are distinct from the labels they assign themselves and that thoughts are not objective truths) both pre- and post-injury may enable them to live more effectively (Kangas & McDonald, 2011). Defusion makes (metaphorical) space for individuals to view their self-content from a different perspective, transforming any problematic functions. Numerous evidence-informed defusion techniques may be useful in this regard – for example, Titchener's repetition, singing self-stories to the tune of "Happy Birthday," and the Passengers on the Bus metaphor (Hayes et al., 1999; Stoddard & Afari, 2014). Cognitive fusion/defusion may be measured over time via self-report measures such as the seven-item Cognitive Fusion Questionnaire (Gillanders et al., 2014) or the four-item Target Thought Measure (Larsson et al., 2016), in addition to individualized behavioural measures (e.g., assessing engagement in valued actions previously inhibited by fusion with rigid self-content).

Importantly, self-report measures require interoception (i.e., require the individual to access information about their experiences and 'self'), which may be challenging depending on the nature of the TBI. In addition, self-report measures require making a generalized rating. Often, in the context of self-change processes, rehabilitation begins by addressing context-specific experiences of self, rather than more generalized self-as-content, meaning generalizations may be particularly challenging in the early phases. Moreover, different phases of rehabilitation may occasion changes in some selfing repertoires and not others (e.g., targeting self-as-process before self-as-content). Therefore, while self-report measures can be useful tools, in addition to ensuring that the outcome measures are aligned to the 'right type' of outcome, it is important to meet the individual where they are at. In many cases, it may make more sense to target/measure self-as-process first, then self-as-content later, after probably some years of reinforcing experiences and support to verbally label and describe these. We ask readers to keep these points in mind throughout this chapter.

Self-as-process

Self-as-process is the ongoing, verbal discrimination of psychological events as they occur in the moment. Statements that reflect self-as-process often begin with phrases such as "I feel...," "I think...," "I wonder...," etc. Self-as-process feeds the conceptualized self (e.g., in order to know that "I am an anxious person," I must first know that I frequently feel fear and have nervous energy across many contexts). Self-as-process is also necessary to contact a transcendent sense of self-as-context since a self-monitoring repertoire is required to observe the observer. Self-as-process functions as a crucial guide for the individual themselves. For example, understanding and responding to thoughts and feelings about other people's behaviours in a fluid and flexible manner is critical in the context of establishing and maintaining personal relationships.

In the context of TBI, self-as-process can be viewed as crucial in facilitating the development of updated, realistic self-representations, in addition to allowing individuals to adapt these representations in line with their ongoing experience. Self-as-process is also important for responding effectively to emotional states and other private events. Noticing private events as they occur enables an individual to better predict how particular contexts will impact them, providing them with space to optimize their behaviour (McHugh et al., 2019). Self-as-process is also useful for self-rules, allowing individuals to better respond in accordance with shifting environmental contingencies (Stapleton et al., 2023). For individuals with TBI, targeting self-as-process is theorized to facilitate the development of attuned self-awareness, decreasing psychological rigidity (Sylvester, 2011; Whiting et al., 2012).

Given that self-as-process focuses on an individual's ongoing experience, present-moment awareness is a relevant process to target. For example, in an eyes-closed exercise, individuals with TBI could be encouraged not to 'struggle against' their internal experiences related to TBI, allowing them to experientially contact that their world and 'self' comprises more than just their diagnosis (Kangas & McDonald, 2011). When facilitating present-moment awareness, it is important to manage the potential dominance of a conceptualized past and future wherein the present moment is lost to worry and rumination (e.g., gently orienting away from rigid conceptualizations of pre-injury experiences that undermine contact with the here and now); scaffolding interoception and willingness while adopting a harm-reduction approach and endorsing judicious use of safety behaviours.

Self-as-context

Self-as-context is invariant in all self-discriminations. If someone answers many different questions about themselves and their behaviour then the only aspect of their answering that will be consistent across time is the context (perspective) from which the answer is given, that is, 'I, HERE and NOW'. Since self-as-context is an abstraction from the content of verbal responding it is 'contentless' and is thus constant and unchanging from the time it first emerges. Self-as-context is a product of verbal responding yet, as a verbal category that applies to everything that a person has ever done, it incorporates both the non-verbal self (as a behavioural stream resulting from direct psychological processes) and the verbal self (as both object and process of knowledge gained through relational framing). Therefore, self-as-context can provide the experiential link between non-verbal and verbal self-knowledge.

Self-as-context is the stable perspective from which all self-related processes can be seen, including problematic self-storying and helpful values (i.e., life directions that are meaningful to the individual). Self-as-context is used to help individuals disentangle themselves from their descriptions and evaluations (i.e., to hold their self-stories lightly; to flexibly respond to self-content). Self-as-context involves seeing yourself as the thinker, not the thoughts; the feeler, not the feelings (McHugh et al., 2019).

Of the three selves, self-as-context is most relevant to post-TBI adjustment (Whiting et al., 2017). In accordance with RFT, through recognizing that they are not their stories about themselves (i.e., defusing from self-content), individuals can begin to decrease their metaphorical attachment to their stories, seeing themselves as both the stable observer of their inner world and container of their experiences (Hayes et al., 1999; Whiting et al., 2017). Furthermore, given apparent challenges with traditional perspective-taking and perspective-shifting associated with TBI, self-as-context seems important to target. Self-as-context provides a 'safe place' from which to view self-related experiences, enabling beneficial perspective shifts. To illustrate this, consider an individual with TBI who, pre-injury, conceptualized themselves as 'the caregiver' in their social circles, talking friends through challenging situations. Post-injury, depending on which regions of the brain are impacted, this individual may not be able to offer the same level of support to their friends, resulting in them withdrawing socially and experiencing loss (e.g., "Who am I?"). Emphasizing self-as-context, we can begin to notice that while our self-stories and inner experiences are constantly changing (i.e., we are not just the 'caregiver' in all contexts at all times; wanted and unwanted emotions will come and go), our stance as the observer and container is stable and consistent (i.e., "I am not my content; I am the person noticing my self-content and having my experiences").

Self-as-context is a core component of the ACT model of psychological flexibility that can be facilitated and contacted in a myriad of ways, including the Observer exercise (Hayes et al., 1999), the Classroom Metaphor (Stoddard & Afari, 2014), and the Stage Show Metaphor (Harris, 2019). Self-as-context may be measured using self-report measures, such as the ten-item Self-as-Context Scale (Zettle et al., 2018) and 15-item Self-Experiences Questionnaire (Yu et al., 2016), or behavioural measures, such as the Functional Self-Discrimination Measure (FSDM; Atkins & Styles, 2016). See McHugh and Stapleton (2021) for an overview.

Evidence underlying the relational frame theory account of the self

There is growing empirical support for looking pragmatically at the three selves from an RFT perspective. For example, in an examination of the relationships between the three selves and mental health, Moran et al. (2018) found that low self-as-content, high self-as-process, and high self-as-context predicted lesser depression, anxiety, and stress. Self-reported self-as-context is positively correlated with better work adjustment, social adjustment (Yu et al., 2016), and mindfulness (Zettle et al., 2018). Self-reported self-as-context is also negatively correlated with depressive symptomatology (Moran et al., 2018; Yu et al., 2016, 2017), suicidal thoughts (McCracken et al., 2018), and pain interference (Yu et al., 2016). Extending beyond quantitative self-report, qualitative studies employing a behavioural measure, namely the FSDM, found that higher occurrences of self-as-content were related to lower levels of well-being, while higher occurrences of self-as-context were related to increased well-being and psychological flexibility (Atkins & Styles, 2016; Eswara Murthy et al., 2021; García-Zambrano et al., 2019; Moran & McHugh, 2020; Styles & Atkins, 2018).

A number of studies have also looked at the benefit of training self-as-context where this repertoire is not present or lacks fluency. Given that the malleability of this repertoire is of particular interest in the area of TBI, we will provide a brief overview of this work. Studies in this area have demonstrated that brief self-as-context interventions improve tolerance to aversive external stimuli (Carrasquillo & Zettle, 2014; Gil-Luciano et al., 2017; Hayes et al., 1999; Luciano et al., 2011) and reduce impaired memory for self-threatening information (Saunders et al., 2013). Recent work by Hashimoto et al. (2020) examined whether a self-as-context intervention could reduce the impact of age-related stereotypes on older adults' cognitive performance (performance on a Block Design task from the Wechsler Adult Intelligence Scale-III). Results indicated that the self-as-context intervention successfully reduced interference from age-related stereotypes, increasing cognitive performance.

Beyond the contextual behavioural science literature, there is also neuroscience evidence supporting the self-as-content and self-as-process distinction at the level of neural processing. For example, Farb et al. (2007) found evidence for two distinct neural modes of self-reference that map onto self-as-content and self-as-process (referred to as narrative and momentary/'experiential' modes of self-reference, respectively). Using functional magnetic resonance imaging, Farb et al. (2007) monitored these distinct forms of self-reference in mindfulness novices and non-novices (participants that had attended an eight-week mindfulness course). Findings revealed that, in novices, narrative focus was associated with focal reductions in self-referential cortical midline regions (medial prefrontal cortex; mPFC) whereas for the non-novices narrative focus resulted in more marked and pervasive reductions in the mPFC and increased engagement of a right-lateralized network comprising the lateral PFC and viscerosomatic areas. Furthermore, through functional connectivity analyses, Farb et al. (2007) observed that novices displayed a strong coupling between the mPFC and right insula that was not observed in non-novices. Overall, findings indicated that there are two neurally distinct selves that are integrated but can be dissociated through mindfulness training.

There is increasing empirical evidence both at a basic scientific level (e.g., Farb et al., 2007) as well as via practitioner research (e.g., Meili & Kabat-Zinn, 2004) that both mindfulness and self-as-context can promote psychological health as well as provide the basis for increasing insight into one's psychological processes. From the current perspective, mindfulness involves deliberate ongoing responding in accordance with self-as-process which strengthens the operant of perspective-taking on one's own behaviour as well as weakens the functional context for cognitive fusion with the kinds of ongoing thoughts that might otherwise simply become part of the increasingly expansive self-as-content relational network. Both these processes make the temporary contentless perspective of self-as-context more likely. What is perhaps particularly important about descriptions such as this is that they involve specification in technical terms supported by an empirical program of research of the processes involved in mindfulness and self-as-context in a way that can facilitate further research into and refinement of these concepts, and this is arguably unique to the current approach. At the same time, there are some important caveats identified in the literature. For example, clients can find self-as-context confusing (Dalrymple et al., 2020) and the utility of self-as-context depends on contextual factors, few of which have been identified (Brockman et al., 2023).

Reflections on the convergence between RFT and the 'Y-Shaped' process model of rehabilitation

Gracey et al.'s (2009) 'Y-Shaped' process model of rehabilitation has some notable similarities to the RFT account of the self. Integrating these accounts will enable researchers, practitioners, and other interested parties to benefit from both, informing treatment and increasing available resources (e.g., exercises, outcome measures, etc.). A complete account of Gracey et al.'s (2009) model is beyond the scope of this chapter. However, we will provide a brief overview of its conceptual basis and key components. The Y-Shaped model may be subdivided into three phases focused on identity: (i) understanding social and interpersonal discrepancies, (ii) reducing threat to self and the impact of self-discrepancies, and (iii) promoting psychological growth and lifespan development. The model depicts social and psychological discrepancies (e.g., stories about the self pre-injury versus post-injury) ultimately converging (the lines of the 'V' at the top of the 'Y' giving rise to the unified trunk of the 'Y') across rehabilitation as a client moves from struggling with self-concept toward regaining a realistic sense of self that is adaptively tuned to their ongoing experience. When entering the psychological growth and flourishing phase, clients are encouraged to discover and develop aspects of continuity with their pre-injury self while engaging in meaningful actions.

Conceptual basis for the Y-Shaped model relevant to convergence with RFT

The conceptual basis of the Y-Shaped model was heavily influenced by a particular cognitive process theory applied to common mental health problems, Teasdale and Barnard's (1993) Interacting Cognitive Subsystems (ICS) model. The clinical and research development of this model led to the development and evaluation of mindfulness-based cognitive therapy for depressive relapse (Segal et al., 2002). Perhaps as a result, this provides a rich context for conceptual convergence between the Y-Shaped model and RFT. One tenet of the ICS model is that the Beckian view of cognitive restructuring or cognitive change should be revised as the focus of change here is, incorrectly, on what they describe as focusing on 'propositional' (semantic, logical) cognitive content or meanings. They note that a separate meaning-related system that deals with 'implicational' (multi-sensory, subjective, metaphorical, felt) aspects of meaning is the key process involved in vulnerability to, and maintenance of, distress, for example in depression and depressive relapse. A further critical aspect of the ICS account is the distinction between different processing modes, specifically between 'automatic' and 'buffered' processing. In automatic processing mode, cognitive/sensory material from the implicational (felt sense, demeanour, metaphors, etc.) and propositional (e.g., specific negative thoughts) subsystems is processed without reflection and drives behavioural and other subsystems, resulting in maintenance of the 'mind in place' or 'depressive interlock'.

Shifting the processing of meaning to 'buffered mode', wherein the automatic recycling of meanings is disrupted by activity in other subsystems while capacity for reflection on implicational meanings is in operation, provides the basis to change the state, and is hypothesized to allow someone, for example, to have a negative experience without this tipping into becoming a prolonged episode of depression. A variety of techniques are proposed by Teasdale (1999) as plausible means within cognitive behavioural therapy (CBT) of generating this 'buffered' processing mode, including mindfulness meditation, attention control training, and the Gestalt 'two-chair technique'. Later, the same hypothesis was used to reformulate how behavioural experiments operate (Bennett-Levy et al., 2004), where the process of making predictions and engaging in behavioural tasks to 'test' predictions, followed by reflection on this, serve to 'buffer' the processing of meanings and allow changes in sensory and motor subsystems that further support cognitive (process) changes. This conceptual background to the Y-Shaped model helpfully outlines processes that appear convergent with how RFT conceptualizes self in terms of content, process, and context, which we will now consider.

The three selves considered within the Y-Shaped model

The rehabilitation process mapped out through the Y-Shaped model entails first acknowledging the existential 'threat' to self people might be experiencing, as illustrated in the opening lines of this chapter. The processes that follow can be readily described in terms of the three selves outlined in RFT. Reduction in threat/ increasing safety is seen as a necessary condition to engage neurocognitive abilities to self-reflect, think flexibly, and access a broader repertoire of past and current experiences not constrained by a particular 'story' about the self. Furthermore, in keeping with Ben-Yishay's and Diller's (1993) description of the setting of holistic rehabilitation, and Ylvisaker and Feeney's Vygotsky-informed approach to 'scaffolding' learning and change, the rehabilitation setting should be appropriately adapted to take into account the challenges of attending rehabilitation, within which specific threats to self can be explored and addressed (Ylvisaker et al., 2003, 2008). There is potential here then for aspects of the Y-Shaped model to bring additional techniques to the RFT-informed repertoire of techniques, addressing contextual aspects of the setting which are specific to the needs of those experiencing the range of cognitive, emotional, and other changes caused by TBI.

Self-as-content and self-discrepancy

Within this safe, rehabilitative context, the next step in the process is to understand the person's views about their current, pre-injury, and ideal aspects of self, i.e., self-as-content in RFT terms. This aspect of the model concerned with the content of psychological discrepancies was developed in the context of evidence indicating the association between higher levels of distress and greater levels of discrepancy of beliefs about current self versus pre-injury self (Cantor et al., 2005; Tyerman & Humphrey, 1984). Measures used in this research probe the 'content' of beliefs about different aspects of self, be that past, present, future, or ideal. In addition, qualitative inquiry has noted that the experience of self-discrepancy is heavily rooted in specific meaningful contexts (Gracey et al., 2009), and that the continuity of self is positively experienced (Ellis-Hill et al., 2008). Understanding and, in due course, reflecting to the client about the 'content' of their (different) selves, especially with a focus on felt sense/metaphor or 'story', flows from this, with these processes in therapy or rehabilitation then converging with the notions of self-as-context and self-as-process in RFT terms.

Self-as-process, scaffolding, and experiments

Prompts and scaffolding are provided for the injured person to become aware of (reflect on) these different 'selves' and develop and nurture an updated sense. This appears closely related to the motion of self-as-process (i.e., the need to contact the ongoing experience). A range of methods are described in the Y-Shaped approach that align with work on self-as-process. Initially the therapist's reflections back to the injured person about their self 'content' will carefully label experiences so as to shift content to process by emphasizing thoughts, feelings, etc. Development of rehabilitative behavioural experiments entails labelling the person's assumptions about a particular context with which they are 'fused' as a 'prediction', as something open to scrutiny, and which a trusted professional believes is open to scrutiny. This is compatible with the ACT approach of holding thoughts 'lightly'; noticing what one's mind says and evaluating whether following that thought serves you rather than becoming caught in a debate or responding to your thoughts as literal truths. While undergoing the experiment, the person is prompted to reflect on and report what is happening in the moment. Records are kept and referred back to (including written but also video), providing a concrete substrate for reflection on self and on private events, which might otherwise be difficult given cognitive change to memory, shifting, etc.

In addition, the importance of present-moment focus is described in the original paper on the Y-Shaped model: "focusing on the here-and-now may provide an adaptive way of reducing pre- to post-injury discrepancy, or altering expectations about speed of recovery so as to be less concerned about slow progress" (Gracey et al., 2009, p. 879). The conceptualization of behavioural experiments within the Y-Shaped process model is heavily oriented toward generating a 'buffered' processing mode in which the person is both experiencing *and* reflecting, to pivot away from overly rigid and generalized rules and assumptions, and to facilitate openness to future experience. A common response in practice from service users has been less about reporting alternative assumptions, and more about saying they are more confident to try things to learn, perhaps indicating a shift away from self-as-content toward self-as-process. Here the RFT account has the potential to enrich the Y-Shaped model by providing additional means of conceptualizing the change process and additional techniques for supporting change. In addition, the convergent account provided here indicates the potential for a form of rehabilitative behavioural experiment aimed at 'self-as-process' to be a viable tool when supporting change with people following brain injury, in keeping with suggestions that such behavioural approaches are more accessible to those with cognitive changes resulting from TBI.

Self-as-context and continuity

Through building repertoires for responding from self-as-context, individuals can notice their inner experiences constantly changing while their 'self' as the observer and container remains constant. This stable sense of self aligns with processes earlier on in the Y-Shaped model, where people are asked to reflect on different aspects of self. Reflections on the part of the therapist, along with documented records of ever-changing experiences observed by the injured person provide a further substrate for self-as-context. At the point where the arms of the 'Y' 'join', the injured person often reflects on some sense of reconnection with 'self' but in a new way, a sense of connection or continuity thus emerges. This continuity across pre- and post-injury selves forms the foundation of work on 'nourishing' and growing post-injury identity as realized in the person's participation in activities in their everyday life, which resonates with enduring aspects of self. Recent work on valued living following brain injury integrating ACT with rehabilitation

(Sathananthan et al., 2022) closely aligns with this and brings additional techniques and measures for supporting this phase of the rehabilitative or therapeutic endeavour, for example, the development of a brain-injury-friendly version of the valued living questionnaire (Miller et al., 2022).

The RFT account of the self may therefore enhance the Y-Shaped model and approaches to 'self' following TBI in a number of ways, stemming from explicitly recognizing the importance of providing a safe and consistent 'self' by observing and reflecting on experiences in life post-injury (including rehabilitation) and steering clients away from forming new rigid self-stories that have the high potentiality to become problematic over time. Furthermore, the structure and organization of the Y-Shaped model (particularly in providing a framework for integrated multidisciplinary rehabilitation that places identity or self at the heart and offers more accessible, behavioural methods for addressing self-as-process and self-as-content) indicate new avenues for synergizing RFT and the Y-Shaped model in brain injury contexts.

Future research

In an effort to catalyze future research, we will now present some viable avenues. First, theorists, practitioners, and researchers should explore the utility of integrating the RFT account of the self with the Y-Shaped model. While some research has examined the usefulness of training self-as-context for individuals with TBI, more work needs to be done across a variety of contexts and populations, with particular emphasis on and reference to the type and severity of the TBIs. Second, there is a serious need to explore the kinds of metaphors used to present self-as-context to clients, whether tailoring metaphors to enhance salience impacts on comprehensibility, and whether experiential or didactic delivery results in better outcomes. This is particularly important for self-as-context because people can find it confusing initially (Dalrymple et al., 2020) and many individuals living with TBI reportedly experience challenges with high-verbal content. Third, it is important to identify and understand contextual considerations for teaching self-as-context. For example, Brockman et al. (2023) found that cognitive reappraisal outperformed a self-as-context-type strategy (integrating experiences into one's sense of self and meaning) in beneficially impacting affect for clients who reported not having their connection needs met. Brockman et al. (2023) suggest that "many clients may lack access to social connection and supportive 'external' voices and need to compensate by developing their own supportive 'internal' voice through reappraisal" (p. 123). Thus, there are likely numerous contextual factors that are important for co-evaluating the utility of teaching self-as-context and should be further researched. Finally, there is a need to explore additional means of measuring self-as-context, particularly biophysiological methods. While there are existing self-report measures and qualitative coding frameworks that tap into self-as-context, ecological momentary assessment, neurological, and single-item indicators of self-as-context would undoubtedly be useful in clinical and experimental contexts. Given that self-as-context is essentially a fluid perspective-taking repertoire, recent empirical work on deictics may offer insights into developing such measures (Montoya-Rodríguez et al., 2017).

Concluding remarks

The RFT account of the self may be useful for both understanding and managing individuals' experiences of TBI with regard to its impact on selfing. Throughout this paper, we have argued that targeting self-as-context may produce positive outcomes for patients after sustaining a TBI. We have signposted means of measuring and training the three selves, while also describing how the RFT account of the self relates to Gracey et al.'s (2009) 'Y-Shaped' model of the change process in rehabilitation. In theory, self-as-context provides a unique perspective that allows individuals to recognize both perpetual change (i.e., thoughts, feelings, stories, etc.) and continuity (i.e., the consistent observer/container). The most important relationship we have is the one with ourselves. If we can foster flexible self-as-context repertoires, then we can create profound change, empowering people and their many selves to move closer toward who and where they want to be.

References

Atkins, P., & Styles, R. (2016). Measuring self and rules in what people say: Exploring whether self-discrimination predicts long-term wellbeing. *Journal of Contextual Behavioural Science, 5*(2), 71–79. https://doi.org/10.1016/j.jcbs.2016.05.001

Bennett-Levy, J., Butler, G., Fennell, M., Hackman, A., Mueller, M., & Westbrook, D. (Eds.). (2004). *Oxford guide to behavioural experiments in cognitive therapy*. Oxford University Press. https://doi.org/10.1093/med:psych/9780198529163.001.0001

Ben-Yishay, Y., & Diller, L. (1993). Cognitive remediation in traumatic brain injury: Update and issues. *Archives of Physical Medicine and Rehabilitation, 74*(2), 204–213. https://doi.org/10.5555/uri:pii:000399939390363F

Brockman, R., Ciarrochi, J., Parker, P., & Kashdan, T. B. (2023). Behaving versus thinking positively: When the benefits of cognitive reappraisal are contingent on satisfying basic psychological needs. *Journal of Contextual Behavioral Science, 27*(1), 120–125. https://doi.org/10.1016/j.jcbs.2023.01.005

Cantor, J. B., Ashman, T. A., Schwartz, M. E., Gordon, W. A., Hibbard, M. R., Brown, M., Spielman, L., Charatz, H. J., & Cheng, Z. (2005). The role of self-discrepancy theory in understanding post–traumatic brain injury affective disorders: A pilot study. *The Journal of Head Trauma Rehabilitation, 20*(6), 527–543.

Carrasquillo, N., & Zettle, R. D. (2014). Comparing a brief self-as-context exercise to control-based and attention placebo protocols for coping with induced pain. *The Psychological Record, 64*, 659–669. https://doi.org/10.1007/s40732-014-0074-3

Dalrymple, K. L., D'Avanzato, C., & Morgan, T. (2020). Implementing ACT in a partial hospitalization program. In M. E. Levin, M. P. Twohig, & J. Krafft (Eds.), *Innovations in acceptance and commitment therapy: Clinical advancements and applications in ACT* (pp. 188–202). New Harbinger.

Ellis-Hill, C., Payne, S., & Ward, C. (2008). Using stroke to explore the life thread model: An alternative approach to understanding rehabilitation following an acquired disability. *Disability and Rehabilitation, 30*(2), 150–159. https://doi.org/10.1080/09638280701195462

Eswara Murthy, V., Stapleton, A., & McHugh, L. (2021). Self and rules in a sample of adults experiencing homelessness: Relationships to shame, well-being, and psychological inflexibility. *Journal of Contextual Behavioral Science, 21*(1), 88–97. https://doi.org/10.1016/j.jcbs.2021.06.003

Farb, N. A., Segal, Z. V., Mayberg, H., Bean, J., McKeon, D., Fatima, Z., & Anderson, A. K. (2007). Attending to the present: Mindfulness meditation reveals distinct neural modes of self-reference. *Social Cognitive and Affective Neuroscience, 2*(4), 313–322. https://doi.org/10.1093/scan/nsm030

García-Zambrano, S., Rehfeldt, R. A., Hertel, I. P., & Boehmert, R. (2019). Effects of deictic framing and defusion on the development of self-as-context in individuals with disabilities. *Journal of Contextual Behavioral Science, 12*, 55–58. https://doi.org/10.1016/j.jcbs.2019.01.007

Gillanders, D. T., Bolderston, H., Bond, F. W., Dempster, M., Flaxman, P. E., Campbell, L., Kerr, S., Tansey, L., Noel, P., Ferenbach, C., Masley, S., Roach, L., Lloyd, J., May, L., Clarke, S., & Remington, R. (2014). The development and initial validation of The Cognitive Fusion Questionnaire. *Behavior Therapy, 45*, 83–101. http://dx.doi.org/10.1016/j.beth.2013.09.001

Gil-Luciano, B., Ruiz, F. J., Valdivia-Salas, S., & Suárez-Falcón, J. C. (2017). Promoting psychological flexibility on tolerance tasks: Framing behavior through deictic/hierarchical relations and specifying augmental functions. *The Psychological Record, 67*, 1–9. https://doi.org/10.1007/s40732-016-0200-5

Gracey, F., Evans, J. J., & Malley, D. (2009). Capturing process and outcome in complex rehabilitation interventions: A 'Y-shaped' model. *Neuropsychological Rehabilitation, 19*(6), 867–890. https://doi.org/10.1080/09602010903027763

Harris, R. (2019). *ACT made simple: An easy-to-read primer on acceptance and commitment therapy* (2nd ed.). New Harbinger.

Hashimoto, K., Muto, T., Spencer, S. D., & Masuda, A. (2020). Mitigating behavioral assimilation to age stereotypes: A preliminary analogue investigation of a contextual behavioral science approach. *Journal of Contextual Behavioral Science, 18*, 48–52. https://doi.org/10.1016/j.jcbs.2020.08.006

Hayes, S. C. (1995). Knowing selves. *The Behavior Therapist, 18*, 94–96.

Hayes, S. C., Barnes-Holmes, D., & Roche, B. (Eds.). (2001). *Relational frame theory: A post-Skinnerian account of human language and cognition.* Plenum Publishers.

Hayes, S. C., Strosahl, K. D., & Wilson, K. G. (1999). *Acceptance and commitment therapy: An experiential approach to behavior change.* Guilford Press.

Kangas, M., & McDonald, S. (2011). Is it time to act? The potential of acceptance and commitment therapy for psychological problems following acquired brain injury. *Neuropsychological Rehabilitation, 21*(2), 250–276. https://doi.org/10.1080/09602011.2010.540920

Larsson, A., Hooper, N., Osborne, L. A., Bennett, P., & McHugh, L. (2016). Using brief cognitive restructuring and cognitive defusion techniques to cope with negative thoughts. *Behavior Modification, 40*(3), 1–31. https://doi.org/10.1177/0145445515621488

Luciano, C., Ruiz, F. J., Vizcaíno Torres, R., Sánchez Martín, V., Gutiérrez Martínez, O., & López, J. C. (2011). A relational frame analysis of defusion interactions in acceptance and commitment therapy: A preliminary and quasiexperimental study with at-risk adolescents. *International Journal of Psychology and Psychological Therapy, 11*, 165–182.

McCracken, L., Patel, S., & Scott, W. (2018). The role of psychological flexibility in relation to suicidal thinking in chronic pain. *European Journal of Pain, 22*(10), 1774–1781. https://doi.org/10.1002/ejp.1273

McHugh, L., Barnes-Holmes, Y., & Barnes-Holmes, D. (2004). Perspective-taking as relational responding: A developmental profile. *The Psychological Record, 54*(1), 115–144. https://doi.org/10.1007/BF03395465

McHugh, L., & Stapleton, A. (2021). Self-as-context. In M. P. Twohig, M. E. Levin, & J. M. Petersen (Eds.), *The Oxford handbook of acceptance and commitment therapy* (pp. 249–270). Oxford University Press. https://doi.org/10.1093/oxfordhb/9780197550076 .013.11

McHugh, L., & Stewart, I. (2012). *The self and perspective taking: Contributions and applications from modern behavioral science.* New Harbinger.

McHugh, L., Stewart, I., & Almada, P. (2019). *A contextual behavioral guide to the self: Theory and practice.* New Harbinger.

Meili, T., & Kabat-Zinn, J. (2004). The power of the human heart: A story of trauma and recovery and its implications for rehabilitation and healing. *Advances in Mind-Body Medicine, 20*(1), 6–15.

Miller, H., Lawson, D., Power, E., das Nair, R., Sathananthan, N., & Wong, D. (2022). How do people with acquired brain injury interpret the Valued Living Questionnaire? A cognitive interviewing study. *Journal of Contextual Behavioral Science, 23*, 125–136. https://doi.org/10.1016/j.jcbs.2022.01.003

Montoya-Rodríguez, M. M., Molina, F. J., & McHugh, L. (2017). A review of relational frame theory research into deictic relational responding. *The Psychological Record, 67*(4), 569–579. https://doi.org/10.1007/s40732-016-0216-x

Moran, O., Almada, P., & McHugh, L. (2018). An investigation into the relationship between the three selves (self-as-content, self-as-process and self-as-context) and mental health in adolescents. *Journal of Contextual Behavioral Science, 7*, 55–62. https://doi .org/10.1016/j.jcbs.2018.01.002

Moran, O., & McHugh, L. (2020). Measuring occurrences of self and other discriminations in relation to mental health in adolescent textual responses. *Journal of Contextual Behavioral Science, 15*, 253–263. https://doi.org/10.1016/j.jcbs.2020.01.010

Nochi, M. (1997). Dealing with the 'Void': Traumatic brain injury as a story. *Disability & Society, 12*(4), 533–555. https://doi.org/10.1080/09687599727119

Sathananthan, N., Dimech-Betancourt, B., Morris, E., Vicendese, D., Knox, L., Gillanders, D., Das Nair, R., & Wong, D. (2022). A single-case experimental evaluation of a new group-based intervention to enhance adjustment to life with acquired brain injury: VaLiANT (valued living after neurological trauma). *Neuropsychological Rehabilitation, 32*(8), 2170–2202. https://doi.org/10.1080/09602011.2021.1971094

Saunders, J., Barawi, K., & McHugh, L. (2013). Mindfulness increases recall of self-threatening information. *Consciousness and Cognition, 22*(4), 1375–1383. https://doi .org/10.1016/j.concog.2013.09.001

Segal, Z. V., Williams, J. M. G., & Teasdale, J. D. (2002). *Mindfulness-based cognitive therapy for depression: A new approach to preventing relapse.* Guilford Press.

Stapleton, A., Stynes, G., Cassidy, S., & McHugh, L. (2023). Assessing acceptance and commitment therapy for adolescent mental health: Single-case A-B design with high temporal density assessments. *Journal of Contextual Behavioral Science, 29*(1), 147–159. https://doi.org/10.1016/j.jcbs.2023.06.011

Stoddard, J. A., & Afari, N. (2014). *The Big Book of ACT Metaphors: A practitioner's guide to experiential exercises and metaphors in acceptance and commitment therapy.* New Harbinger.

Styles, R. G., & Atkins, P. W. (2018). Measuring perceptions of self and others in what people say: A replication and extension of the functional self-discrimination measure. *Journal of Contextual Behavioral Science, 9*, 45–52. https://doi.org/10.1016/j.jcbs.2018.06.005

Sylvester, M. (2011). *Acceptance and commitment therapy for improving adaptive functioning in persons with a history of pediatric acquired brain injury* [Doctoral thesis, University of Nevada]. Reno.

Teasdale, J. D. (1999). Emotional processing, three modes of mind and the prevention of relapse in depression. *Behaviour Research Therapy, 37*(S1), S53–S77. https://doi.org/10.1016/S0005-7967(99)00050-9

Teasdale, J. D., & Barnard, P. J. (1993). *Affect, cognition and change: Re-modelling depressive thought.* Lawrence Erlbaum Associates.

Tyerman, A., & Humphrey, M. (1984). Changes in self-concept following severe head injury. *International Journal of Rehabilitation Research, 7*(1), 11–24.

Whiting, D. L., Deane, F. P., Simpson, G. K., McLeod, H. J., & Ciarrochi, J. (2017). Cognitive and psychological flexibility after a traumatic brain injury and the implications for treatment in acceptance-based therapies: A conceptual review. *Neuropsychological Rehabilitation, 27*(2), 263–299. https://doi.org/10.1080/09602011.2015.1062115

Whiting, D. L., Simpson, G. K., Ciarrochi, J., & McLeod, H. J. (2012). Assessing the feasibility of acceptance and commitment therapy in promoting psychological adjustment after severe traumatic brain injury. *Brain Injury, 26*(4–5), 588–589.

Ylvisaker, M., Jacobs, H. E., & Feeney, T. (2003). Positive supports for people who experience behavioral and cognitive disability after brain injury: A review. *The Journal of Head Trauma Rehabilitation, 18*(1), 7–32.

Ylvisaker, M., McPherson, K., Kayes, N., & Pellett, E. (2008). Metaphoric identity mapping: Facilitating goal setting and engagement in rehabilitation after traumatic brain injury. *Neuropsychological Rehabilitation, 18*(5–6), 713–741. https://doi.org/10.1080/09602010802201832

Yu, L., McCracken, L., & Norton, S. (2016). The Self Experiences Questionnaire (SEQ): Preliminary analyses for a measure of self in people with chronic pain. *Journal of Contextual Behavioural Science, 5*(3), 127–133. https://doi.org/10.1016/j.jcbs.2016.07.006

Yu, L., Norton, S., Almarzooqi, S., & McCracken, L. M. (2017). Preliminary investigation of self-as-context in people with fibromyalgia. *British Journal of Pain, 11*, 134–143. https://doi.org/10.1177/2049463717708962

Zettle, R. D., Gird, S., Webster, B., Carrasquillo-Richardson, N., Swails, J., & Burdsal, C. (2018). The self-as-context scale: Development and preliminary psychometric properties. *Journal of Contextual Behavioural Science, 10*, 64–74. https://doi.org/10.1016/j.jcbs.2018.08.010

Evaluating a novel, online Acceptance and Commitment Therapy intervention for allied healthcare professionals in a neurorehabilitation setting

Karen Kinsella, Marcia Ward and Sharon Houghton

The concept for this study evolved over many, many years, since I started studying psychology part-time in 2005. Perhaps the concept evolved even further back if I think of who I am as a person. One of my earliest known values was a strong, natural desire to help other people. Compassion for others was strongly nurtured in our busy household with five children. In a historical time when there was a perception of less awareness, presence or acceptance of diverse cultures, ethnicities and beliefs in Ireland, I vividly remember my parents welcoming students from various countries into our home every summer and accepting them just as they were. There was a modelling of behaviour from our parents of what it truly meant to be open to accepting others. I laugh now when I reflect on those fun and chaotic summers, as those experiences, together with a nurtured sense of 'all for one and one for all' attitudes that my parents were committed to develop as a family, shaped me significantly in my continuing need to help others feel understood and heard.

Nurturing 'all for one and one for all' is a guiding star for me years later in my work at the brain injury organisation, Headway Ireland. I became keenly aware of supporting the needs of survivors of Acquired Brain Injury (ABI) and Allied Healthcare Professionals (AHCPs) supporting them. Within my clinical training, I had an opportunity to do a small-scale study as part of the course requirements.

With that in mind, I intentionally involved clients who took part in that study and who live with ABI as stakeholders in this research, reflecting Public Patient Involvement (PPI). This is to aid and work with individual clients so that they are involved in their healthcare pathway. In the neurorehabilitation setting, clients work with AHCPs to make decisions about their healthcare needs. This is understood as advancing future health systems. This has been identified as a first step in adjusting care to become more patient-centred (Florin & Dixon, 2004). Moreover, in the 'Sharing the Vision' mental health policy for everyone in Ireland, the focus is on developing a broad-based, whole-system policy. Its aim is to promote, prevent and provide early intervention, as well as address service access, co-ordination and continuity of care. It also aims to be socially inclusive and provide accountability

DOI: 10.4324/9781003193722-11

while demonstrating continuous improvement (Department of Health, 2020). By addressing this whole-system policy for everyone, I was very excited to explore the use of Acceptance and Commitment Therapy (ACT) with staff, while also involving clients as 'co-producers' of their health at this stage of my career. It also sat well with my personal and professional values in 'all for one and one for all' advocacy, empathy and helping others. Subsequently, I enrolled in an ACT training workshop specifically targeted for use in a workplace.

Together with my field supervisor, an ACT therapist, we designed and implemented an organisational intervention online. While we had hoped to deliver the intervention in person, to a range of AHCPs in different settings, we also had to adjust to the health and safety restrictions imposed by the arrival of Covid-19 in March 2020 in Ireland. The impact on health service delivery was significant, as the focus was to address the needs of the general population during a pandemic by protecting them. Unfortunately, this meant that we had to sacrifice a control group due to accessibility issues to other AHCPs as they experienced disruptions to their service delivery.

Taking all of these factors into account, the established goals of the research were to enhance the AHCPs' wellbeing, psychological flexibility (PF) and understanding of clients' needs. While clinicians in the ABI setting had used a variety of resources and frameworks over the years, the ACT model was chosen as the most appropriate. It addressed the needs of the research aim and it had worked well in this neurorehabilitation location previously with clients and family previously. This model had not been used with AHCPs here. An online, group intervention was designed to meet the research needs and founded on practice-based evidence. This study sought to examine and explore the experiences of AHCPs who engaged with the ACT group, using a mixed-methods approach.

Traditionally mental health care has predominantly focused on treating symptoms of mental disorders with less emphasis on promoting wellbeing, as more than the absence of symptoms of mental illness (Diener et al., 2009; Diener et al., 1999; Ryff, 1989; Seligman & Csikszentmihalyi, 2014). Wellbeing is embedded in the field of positive psychology, examining the psychological resources that promote optimal functioning and allow individuals to flourish (Seligman & Csikszentmihalyi, 2014). Importantly, low levels or changes in wellbeing were significantly associated with depression longitudinally, and to the prevalence and incidence of mental illness symptoms (Keyes, 2005, 2010; Wood & Joseph, 2010). Wellbeing has been enhanced by increasing PF, reducing symptoms of depression and anxiety and mediating the effects of perceived stress on the quality of life (Lappalainen et al., 2014, 2015; Nyklíček & Kuijpers, 2008; Puolakanaho et al., 2020; Räsänen et al., 2016). Accordingly, the ACT model is suitable as a framework promoting mental health and wellbeing (Hayes et al., 2012; Keyes, 2007). Studies using ACT have illustrated improvement in employees' mental and overall psychological health and demonstrated AHCP abilities to be innovative (Bond & Bunce, 2000; Bond et al., 2016a, 2016b; Flaxman & Bond, 2010a, 2010b; Kashdan & Rottenberg, 2010).

Promoting mental health and wellbeing amongst AHCPs is an important area to consider, as there were 259,000 employees in this sector in Ireland in 2018 (Mikulic, 2020). AHCPs use scientific principles to promote wellness, while supporting healthcare systems in a variety of settings (TTM Healthcare, n.d.). Importantly, the level of caring given by an AHCP has been shown to impact the degree of a person's suffering (Kret, 2011).

However, the Irish Congress of Trade Unions reported that 90% of voluntary sector employees considered their job to be stressful and 82% of the employees in the health service reported high levels of stress (Clarke, n.d.). This contributed to AHCPs being vulnerable to compassion fatigue, stress overload and burnout, negatively impacting their ability for self-care and to 'bear with the suffering of others' (Figley, 2002a, 2002b; Moore & Cooper, 1996; Sharkey & Sharples, 2003; Wall et al., 1997; Wollenburg, 2004; Yadavaia et al., 2014). Importantly, Waters et al. (2018) showed evidence of preliminary support for providing brief ACT interventions for distressed healthcare workers.

However, effective communication between clients and healthcare providers, as a factor contributing to person-centred care, has become a primary topic globally (Gremigni et al., 2008; Hemsley & Balandin, 2014). Indeed, the information provided in acute settings has been experienced by patients and clients as conflicting, insufficient and incorrect at times (HSE & HIQA, 2019). Notwithstanding this finding, patient-centredness is recognised as a primary component of quality care, which is under-developed and not universally recognised (European Patients Forum, 2017; EXPH, 2014). Evidence illustrated that when patients are transparently involved in their own healthcare decisions as 'co-producers' of their health with clinicians, outcomes are more positive, such as better health, more engaged patients and lower costs, reflecting best evidence-based practice (Arterburn et al., 2012; European Patients Forum, n.d.; Mulley et al., 2012; Veroff et al., 2013). This co-production and PPI has been identified as a first step in adjusting care to become more patient-centred (Florin & Dixon, 2004). In fact, in an ACT intervention to support physical therapists in their practice with clients in the UK, results indicated promising findings compared to usual care, resulting in fewer but longer sessions (Godfrey et al., 2016, 2020). There have also been positive outcomes in various ACT interventions involving social workers, intellectual disability services and rehabilitation professionals (Brinkborg et al., 2011; Kurtz et al., 2014; McCracken & Yang, 2008; Noone & Hastings, 2010).

In an ABI rehabilitation setting, AHCPs work with clients whose brain injury was acquired during their lifetime. Causes include stroke, brain haemorrhage or infections, tumours, lack of oxygen, falls or other traumatic accidents. Although there are no exact statistics for Ireland, epidemiological studies in Europe propose ABI incidence rates occur at 235 hospitalised cases (including fatalities) per 100,000 population (Torner & Schootman, 1996). ABI of any severity in humans can result in a multitude of cognitive deficits and communication issues which may individually or collectively interact to impact behaviour (Arciniegas et al., 2002; Dikmen et al., 1995; Lyon, 2002). Importantly, research has demonstrated significant negative changes in self-esteem and self-concept and an increase in symptoms of depression and anxiety after an ABI (Ponsford et al., 2014). Consequently, adjusting to ABI often means a willingness to adjust to a new reality and identity before recovery can begin in a more holistic manner (Soo et al., 2014).

Studies investigating the factors that impacted recovery found that the expectations of ABI clients were incongruent with the expectations of AHCPs they worked with. Specifically, adults with ABI yearned to return to their pre-injury functioning. In contrast, AHCPs in a rehabilitation setting would look for "small, but notable change in function" (Lutz et al., 2011). In fact, ABI adult survivors often experience long-term disability, with considerable personal and public societal costs. Global incidence rates for ABI range from 180 to 500 cases per 100,000 population per annum (CDC, 2001), with trauma-related ABI set to become the third-leading cause of death and disability worldwide by 2020 (Povlishock & Katz, 2005). Therefore, understanding the needs of ABI survivors represents an expanding public health concern. There is an awareness that a partnership between clients, families and AHCPs is warranted in their recovery (Institute for Patient- and Family-Centered Care, 2015).

This importance of patient-centredness is addressed in Klonoff's (2010) seven-stage model of recovery in the Patient Experiential Model model of care for survivors of ABI. At each successive vulnerable stage, AHCPs have an opportunity to help clients in their understanding of adjustment to their 'new normal' reality. By teaching ACT skills to AHCPS, communication skills and PF could be enhanced, meeting a stated Health Service Executive (HSE) need and addressing a 'triple aim' to improve patient experiences, outcomes and cost efficiency and 'quadruple aim' by caring for the AHCPs at the same time to provide a 'whole-system healthy workplace intervention' (Bodenheimer & Sinsky, 2014; Brand et al., 2017; Sikka et al., 2015). In this study, PPI promoted collaborative roles for the clinicians and clients.

More recently, COVID-19, a novel coronavirus, resulted in a global public health crisis. Over 3.4 billion people in 84 countries were confined to their homes due to 'social distancing' restrictions, meaning millions of employees have been working remotely online at home, resulting in both benefits and risks to wellbeing (Bouziri et al., 2020). Notably, research has shown that AHCPs and the general population have experienced high levels of anxiety, stress and depression during this crisis (Braquehais et al., 2020; Wang et al., 2020; Zhu et al., 2020). To address the benefits and risks to wellbeing, online programmes were developed. However, evidence has illustrated that few e-teaching approaches met the need for learners to feel competent in skill acquisition or impacted their delivery of person-centred care (Lawn et al., 2017). However, evidence illustrated that if AHCPs are more psychologically flexible, both personal and professional outcomes with clients could be positively influenced (Mischel, 1969; Miller et al., 1999; Platania et al., 2015; Runco, 2014). Significantly, by building PF using ACT, interventions have performed as well as or better than work-related stress interventions; Cognitive Behavioural Therapy (CBT) stress management training; personal development workshops and mindfulness training (Bond & Bunce, 2000; Flaxman & Bond, 2010a; Flaxman & Bond, 2010b; Frögéli et al., 2016). Consequently, this ACT study would aim to support AHCPs in their support of clients, based on the clients highlighting their unmet needs, which were integrated into this intervention.

Aim and questions

The main aim of this research was to evaluate the effectiveness of an online ACT intervention for AHCPs in an ABI setting, informed by PPI. A further goal was to establish aspects of the programme that could be developed for future AHCPs. In addition, by using a mixed-methods approach, a richer understanding of the processes of change within the intervention could be understood, during and after Covid-19. For the purpose of this chapter, the main focus will be on the qualitative component, as this provided rich insights into how and why the learning took place.

Methods

Participants consisted of 38 AHCPs, aged between 18–65 years, working in an ABI neurorehabilitation setting in Ireland. Eight of those participants consented to take part in the qualitative focus group. The qualitative research aim was an effective way to explore 'how or why' an intervention was experienced. Instructions to access the intervention and online measures were shared. All data collection for the quantitative component took place between 17th December 2020–11th March 2021.

The ACT intervention was online from 17th December 2020. The field supervisor was an ACT therapist. The researcher was a certified trainer in this manualised ACT programme, adapted from Hayes et al. (2013, p. 25) for community delivery (Flaxman et al., 2019; McIntosh & Gascoyne, 2020). I also brought my first career as a graphic designer and my value of 'creativity' into developing this training. The organisational staff learning platform hosted the pre-recorded intervention, called 'Psychological Flexibility and Wellbeing Training Programme.' Participants could self-enrol. The skills modules taught the six core ACT processes in a user-friendly three-pillar framework. The pillars were called 'Open,' 'Noticing' and 'Active.' The 'Open' pillar reflected skilfully relating to the inner world with acceptance and defusion skills. Building on this, the 'Noticing' pillar reflected teaching a strengthened awareness by paying flexible attention to the present moment and learning how to see the self in context. Lastly, the 'Active' pillar reflected learning how to use identified values as a guide to actively commit to identified goals. The intervention consisted of a ten-minute introduction and four 40-minute skills modules, with guided narration. Outcome measures evaluated relational components to the ACT processes. Participants were instructed to allow a minimum of thee days between modules. This formed the quantitative component of the study with pre- and post-outcome data. Online webinars were delivered in late February 2021, consisting of a summary of skills learned and discussion. Each webinar finished with an invitation to participants to share their experience of the intervention.

Eight participants consented to take part in a focus group online. This discussion lasted one and a half hours. Questions were semi-structured, guided by the research questions and phrased in an open-ended way, aiming to elicit more descriptive responses. The researcher and the field supervisor facilitated the discussion.

Measures and outcomes

The study aimed to corroborate results from different methods of data collection reflecting quantitative questionnaires and qualitative semi-structured focus group interviews. The qualitative component of this study used Braun and Clarke's (2006) six-step thematic analysis framework, driven by the research question to identify, analyse and report patterns (themes) within data. Using a realist and semantic approach, data was coded at an explicit, surface level, for meanings and patterns. An inductive data-driven approach identified themes strongly linked to the data, to gain insight into experience, without a pre-existing coding frame.

Results

Qualitative results

Qualitative results are presented in main themes and related subthemes. Themes emerged from the analysis of one focus group. These themes and subthemes are illustrated in Table 10.1.

Covid-19 impact

Staff spoke of the "*new norm*" impacting on their wellbeing personally in their living environments, relationships and social activities and professionally in adapting to new work practices, such as working online at home. Staff fluctuated

Table 10.1   Summary of themes and subthemes that emerged from the focus group.

Theme	Subtheme
Covid-19 Impact	• Role of technology • Impact on wellbeing • Online flexibility enhanced learning
Positive Online ACT Experience	• Helpful, user-friendly framework • Multi-media enhanced learning • Variety of skills enjoyed and learned
Lifelong Skills	• Personal and professional scope • Active and future use of skills
Reflections and Hopes	• Organisational role in staff wellbeing • Future staff needs

in their experience and coping capacity with "*Covid stuff,*" due to the enduring nature of the pandemic and multiple "*lockdowns*" and restrictions. Significantly, all staff discussed the helpfulness of the ACT training in coping with the impact of Covid-19. Some staff described missing the pre-Covid work environment and "*the kind of social interaction of the clients coming in and out, and the kind of buzz with that and with... the team itself.*" However, staff also described some positive effects of Covid-19 and "*there are parts, elements that are really, really good*" and "*Covid has affected my life positively actually, as opposed to negatively,*" while acknowledging the "*heightened awareness*" and "*Covid precautions*" due to health and safety guidelines: "*Jesus, did I clean the trolley, did I wash my hands after I cleaned the trolley?*" To a degree, staff discussed a sense of wellbeing and time-frames, "*before Covid,*" "*when Covid came,*" "*management of Covid*" and "*after Covid*" and implications for their lives moving forward. Below, the subthemes 'role of technology,' 'impact on wellbeing' and 'online flexibility enhanced learning' are discussed in more detail.

ROLE OF TECHNOLOGY

Staff identified the importance of technology impacting their wellbeing personally and professionally as a result of Covid-19 health and safety restrictions. Most staff members experienced some anxiety and frustration around it. Staff reflected on their confidence using technology and accessibility issues for themselves and clients. Staff conveyed an awareness of equipment needed, such as headphones, familiarity with different platforms and improving abilities to resolve common technical issues such as hearing "*you are on mute*" or swapping equipment between computers and phones to maintain connectivity. As a result, some staff found that their window of tolerance and flexibility with others was lower when specific issues arose.

> "*Any little quirky thing, like that drives me mad.*"
> "*Like my fear would be technology.*"
> "*Getting all clients up online, so it was a very challenging time.*"
> "*There can be so much frustration there when you're helping people online.*"

Staff also identified technology as a new way of maintaining wellbeing while meeting family and friends safely. Importantly, staff highlighted their gratefulness for having the technical equipment necessary during Covid-19 with an awareness that others were less fortunate.

> "*Connecting with people... be it at the weekends on Zoom calls, Zoom quizzes, connecting with family, connecting with friends in a different way.*"

> "*We have all the stuff, we've all the technology we need right, so we're very fortunate.*"

IMPACT ON WELLBEING

Staff recognised changes in their wellbeing as a result of Covid-19. Feelings of heightened worry, anxiety and stress emerged, due to changes in household organisation and structure and adapting to the changes.

> *"I got really caught up in this Covid stuff… and looking at the numbers and worrying about the numbers."*
> *"The first two lockdowns I would say, very similarly to Speaker 1 and Speaker 6 there, they were fine, far from ideal… the second one, I suppose I was just so grateful… to be working… the third one, it's just a bit harder… it's just going on a long time now."*
> *"The whole routine of the house was up-skuttled in that respect."*

Professionally, it emerged that some staff missed the enjoyment of the shared workplace environment and *"informal colleague banter"* and shared an awareness that motivation levels were sometimes compromised: *"working remotely from home, I'm not as motivated."*

However, all staff reported an improvement in their wellbeing as learning ACT skills was like:

> *"A relief in the sense that there was something there that was actually helpful."*
> *"It was so helpful to put it down on a sheet of paper (ACT Matrix) and then, you know make your call on that. And you know you can go back to that sheet of paper and say yeah, that, that was the helpful move for me."*

Likewise, wellbeing was improved for some staff members as a result of Covid-19, due to the pace of life slowing down, fewer social demands, increased shared experiences for family and more time for self-care.

> *"I'm enjoying more time with my family. I'm getting out and exercising more, because I have that time as well, so I think it's actually improved my wellbeing."*

> *"New appreciation of each other, not the materialistic things."*

> *"I suppose my life has actually calmed down. I've no soccer training so I spend all my time here with my family. Yes, I miss these things, but do you know do I miss them that much? I don't know… cos I've gone into a quieter world really."*

ONLINE FLEXIBILITY ENHANCED LEARNING

Staff conveyed how they enjoyed learning online because of the flexibility of access, the freedom to engage when they felt motivated and the ability to replay content to process and consolidate their learning.

"It was lovely that... it wasn't scheduled... not every morning you wake up and... are kind of open minded and able... that was just one of the positives."

"Yeah, I'd agree there, with... Speaker 8 and Speaker 1. It was great to do it in my own time."

"You could do it at your own pace, you'd play the video again... if you missed out pieces in it... and it's done in chunks, that are very easily manageable."

"It was almost better online as well... so individual to you, do you know, you could use it how you wanted to."

Likewise, staff highlighted how traditional workshop formats subject the group to everyone's experiences, which is unhelpful to some.

"Then you'd be listening to somebody going on about their stuff, and you're thinking, jeez I don't know what they're going on about, because it doesn't relate to what I'm doing."

Moreover, although training time could be scheduled during work hours, some staff choose to complete it in the evenings or weekends as:

"Logging onto this almost felt like an act of self-care."

"I actually did it in the evenings, so I thought it was nice to look forward to in the evenings, you know after the day was done... I just thought it was really lovely that time."

Interestingly, all staff agreed that the timing of the training was optimal for their wellbeing, approaching the third lockdown, as they felt familiarised with technology and knew *'whilst we were in the thick of that, you were also getting a relief in the sense.'*

Positive online ACT experience

A 'Positive Online ACT Experience' emerged as one main theme from the focus group. All staff spoke of their participation in the ACT programme as being positive, describing it as *"fantastic,"* *"brilliant,"* *"powerful,"* *"great"* and *"enjoyable"* and an act of *"self-care."* They highlighted several features of the programme that they found beneficial. To a degree, staff were surprised at the ease of learning or applying the framework, or the strength of the impact of training on their wellbeing and psychological flexibility. All staff highlighted the multi-media design aiding engagement, as well as the helpfulness of the experiential practices, recaps and repetition of skills to deepen the learning online. Below, the subthemes 'helpful, user-friendly framework,' 'multi-media design enhanced learning' and 'variety of skills enjoyed and learned' are discussed in more detail.

HELPFUL, USER-FRIENDLY FRAMEWORK

Staff recognised how the 'Open,' 'Noticing' and 'Active' pillars used in the online ACT training framework were easy to learn and apply. Many staff discussed how the concepts *"resonated"* with them with *"a dimension of freshness and tangibility"* regardless of previous academic awareness or exposure to similar or different psychological theories or frameworks.

"The concepts I think that pulled, pulled me in."

"It's easy to grasp… it's experiential in the respect that you can ACT in the here and now."

"I felt like this (training) gave me a better understanding of it… I probably never really understood it… this kind of drilled down and gave you… that better framework to go from."

Staff identified reasons for their enjoyment, as it provided *"a fresh approach … to old ideas"* and conveyed a sense of *"a little bit of self-care time."* In contrast, one staff member relayed how their initial resistance before participation changed as a result of an awareness of how *"useful"* the framework and content were to their personal and professional wellbeing.

"The course certainly helped me to kind of stop racing, do you know, stop worrying about the stuff."
"And you hooked in a non-believer … a total non-believer and sceptic (laughter)."
"Yeah, I thoroughly enjoyed it anyway … I thought it was lovely, even personally you know."

As the training was online, staff also identified the unique nature of learning alone in a personally enjoyable way *"to look after yourself,"* as the skills and tools were *"so individual to you,"* yet also recognised how the skills addressed different perspectives.

"I think it opened, it stretches, you know when you think of inflexibility, it just stretches the mind to think of all the other different perspectives, you know that stretch man, whose been moulded and you stretch him, that's how I think of inflexibility … Stretch Armstrong."

MULTI-MEDIA DESIGN HELPED ENGAGEMENT

Staff reflected on the helpfulness of incorporating multi-media to facilitate engagement and learning as *"the presentation of it was actually fantastic"* and the content flow made sense. Staff reflected on the use of colour, incorporating verbal and visual media, supported by facilitator narration, as well as incorporating audio, video clips, experiential exercises, handouts (emailed), poems, quotes, resource links, images, diagrams, animations and videos.

> "*It was just so visual, so colourful ... that's what I really liked about it ... and there were videos in it as well, you were just learning in different ways all the time.*"
>
> "*Yeah, I thought the design of it was fantastic ... the way it flowed, so that you could do it on your own... so well designed and so it answered the questions as they were coming up for you.*"
>
> "*Sometimes it's like online training is so text heavy and it's black and white and you're kind of not taking it all in.*"

Some staff identified that their unique learning styles were supported because of the design incorporating various communication methods.

> "*The visual pictures of everything stuck with me.*"
>
> "*I suppose I'm not much of a visual learner ... I don't get the visuals ... so it's different for different people.*"

VARIETY OF TOOLS TO AID SKILLS

Staff reflected on how the ACT framework was supported by the consistent repetition and recap of skills using a variety of tools.

> "*I thought that was really good, really drilled it home for me, you know the continuous repetition of it throughout.*"

Each skill relating to an 'Open,' 'Noticing' or 'Active' pillar was taught in many ways. For example, the 'Open' pillar taught staff how to skilfully relate to the inner world by using tools such as the ACT Matrix for personal, client or team use; passengers on a bus metaphor; leaves on a stream, modes of mind, thanking your mind; cultivating a healthy 'distance' between thought and thinker and seeing the self as context. While staff differed in the tools they enjoyed that underpinned each concept, staff agreed that each helped once reminded.

> "*You'd forget the skills that you might already have learned, say The Passengers on the Bus now like, I just thought that's, that was a lightbulb moment for me. But what I was saying about recapping (ACT Matrix skills) ... brought it back to life.*"
>
> "*You're being introduced to unhooking from your thoughts, you're being introduced to values ... 'self as context,' that idea of watching the content of your mind ... I'm noticing the fact that or leaves on a stream or thanking your mind and then the idea was that you'd put it all together with the Matrix.*"

"There are very few trainings where you're able to actually concentrate for 40 or 50 minutes, but because of the variety it, it was quite engaging."

While some staff reflected on the significance of the 'Noticing' pillar with the mindfulness component, as *"it made a huge difference to me and to live in the now,"* other staff preferred the 'Open' pillar tools: *"I really liked thanking your mind as well. I, I liked that idea of kind of letting it go."* Most staff agreed that the value exercises and tools appeared to be vital to support the 'Active' pillar concept. It was conveyed as significant to their learning as it resonated with many to be able to be guided by their values in their response.

"I really liked the value piece, I suppose. You know like what are your professional values, what are your personal values."

"I thought was really valid you know was to be … guided by your values and beliefs that it kind of helps you aim towards what you do want to achieve."

"Follow your values … I have a mental visual image of it in my head, do you know, of where I am at and where I want to go… I think that's a fantastic tool."

The Compassion-Focused Therapy model was also very briefly introduced to complement the understanding of the evolution of the busy mind and how automatic our speedy thought process is, primed to survive. Some staff reflected on the helpfulness of learning to recognise compassion states in themselves and towards others: *"I really liked that compassionate bit do you know … I can be very critical of myself."*

Lifelong skills

Staff unearthed the importance of the application of skills learned in diverse personal and professional settings, and throughout life. Some staff reflected on the differences in previous *"wellbeing activities, but like this was a wellbeing skill,"* and they conveyed appreciation, as they *"got so much from it."* Staff reflected on the enduring nature of the skills, as the tools were dynamic, open to monitoring and change so they could *"refer back to and refresh as I go along."* Below, the subthemes 'personal and professional scope' and 'active and future use' are discussed in more detail.

PERSONAL AND PROFESSIONAL SCOPE

Staff reflected on their learning and application of skills, from their personal to their professional lives with clients, colleagues and people in general *"that struggle"* while recognising that *"your personal and professional life always intertwine."*

"I just think some of the skills that we were shown … like the Matrix or the Bull's Eye, like these are something we could even use personally yes, but also with

clients. Just if like they were kind of lacking motivation, goal setting or even trying something."

"I could just as easily see myself ... sitting down with a client in a keyworker session, talking to them about it and just as likely sitting myself down and talking myself through that exercise ... as well as a family member or a friend."

Staff illuminated their positive use of the skills professionally with clients since training, who may have been in a "*pattern of stuckness*" and how using the Matrix collaboratively with clients was beneficial.

"I start off like explaining it (Matrix) ... and it's amazing where they saw themselves and actually did the Matrix... it's given me a tool... to be able to 'unstuck' and work it in more effective ways with the clients."

"Definitely, I've learned an awful lot about the, the psychological flexibility."

Likewise, some staff highlighted how training has informed their personal relationships and understanding how their behavioural responses and values may impact them and others in the future.

"I was shouting at my teenage son and I just heard myself, is this the value that you want for you, you know? And what are the values you want to teach him?... And out of all the things that I've done in the past three years really, that's the one (values) that is still for me."

"I wasn't living a valued life in terms of self-care ... I was on autopilot ... I've been trying to ... use a little bit of the compassion, use a bit more flexibility."

ACTIVE AND FUTURE USE OF SKILLS

Staff highlighted that they are actively using the skills learned in interactions – "*I'm thinking okay, they have passengers on their bus now*" – and by becoming aware of this possibility, staff reported that their responses are more compassionate and flexible as "*it is so important to just understand where other people are coming from too.*"

"I did find the way of doing things ... if you're going to a meeting and you're bothered about it, or if you're doing you know, the bus thing ... just get those people to stay there. They'll always be there."

"I think it's the first training that I've taken that I could see myself using lifelong and that was really unusual for me, that I've never connected with the training like that where I thought these are actually skills that I could use throughout my lifetime."

Some staff reflected on actively using the skills in their personal lives to stay present in their physical wellbeing, or to recognise the skills they would like to incorporate in their future self.

> "*Since I did this course, I actually, I took off this watch (smart watch). I took it off… I actually, I don't use it to mark myself and I actually just walk … it made a huge difference to me.*"

> "*I've learned an awful lot about the, the psychological flexibility, do you know. And even going forwards it probably made me more aware now, in everyday actions.*"

Staff's reflections and hopes

Staff reflected on the organisational role in their wellbeing as they unearthed the difference between prior wellbeing events and this training and identified possible barriers. Staff also highlighted suggestions for their future training needs, collaborative learning and sharing ABI knowledge with the wider community and healthcare professions. Below, the subthemes 'organisational role in wellbeing' and 'future staff needs' are discussed in more detail.

Organisational role in staff's wellbeing

Staff reflected on the long-term implications of this training and their shared beliefs that wellbeing goes beyond the individual. Staff highlighted that the organisation's wellbeing group has provided shorter, welcome wellbeing activities previously, but questioned the length of impact of "*tokens*" compared to this much-valued "*longer-term investment.*"

> "*With this particular training, it (organisation) looked at investing in a staff member's long-term wellbeing … I suppose that's what I really liked about it, is the long-term investment versus the short term in yourself.*"

Staff also illuminated that resistance to training could be a barrier to learning helpful skills in an organisation. As one staff member highlighted, they took part "*to make up numbers*" initially, as they assumed training would be irrelevant and "*a load of rubbish.*" Having completed the training, all staff identified that if they "*could get people to use that Matrix as an, an organisational type thing,*" this tool could be very "*useful*" as it would offer a uniform way to address issues in a helpful manner if all staff completed training.

Staff unearthed a vital need for the role of external organisations, responsible for other healthcare professions, in their knowledge and wellbeing of clients with ABI. Staff highlighted that they were not surprised and expressed frustration that clients' experience of recovery with AHCPs lacked compassion, hope and respect and factors going beyond "*physical recovery,*" as "*what we assume to be the basics, don't seep* out to ... *other professions*" and "*aren't filtering out at all into the community,*" as the impact of ABI is "*complex*" and "*you're not going to get the pattern here.*"

> "*In all the different places I have worked in, there has always been people with acquired brain injury and have always been misunderstood, always. They have always been the ones that are seen as the 'trouble-makers.'*"
>
> "*Professions haven't been given the time to understand that information the way that's required.*"
>
> "*The sense of loss like (to ABI clients)... overnight their life as they know it is completely different.*"

All staff agreed that "*it's nothing like anything else, do you know*" and shared a strong desire for other professions to understand this.

Future staff needs

While all staff identified that the individual online training format suited them, they also shared a pattern of need for some future collaborative learning and "*inter-action in the middle of it somewhere.*" Staff highlighted that the webinar, which followed the training, helped to deepen their understanding of skills learned, as it provided a space for a summary of learning, clarification and discussion.

> "*Sometimes having the interactive element made me think differently about something, an assumption or something I was making.*"

Likewise, staff also identified their need for a platform for future peer-support space around skills learned. Staff conveyed this format provides a "*way of keeping it fresh in the mind*" and staff shared their hopes that the organisation would support this, given its benefits to wellbeing.

> "*would like to see it continued in a capacity in the workplace, in, as part of our wellbeing, and maybe the, the organisation's strategy in relation to staff wellbeing. How can we bring this in, you know? And continue it within the organisation?*"

Staff also reflected on their hopes for future ACT training as they found it "*was absolutely brilliant and really, really powerful.*"

> "*Even going forward, a separate one for ACT in relation to dealing with challenges ... with clients.*"

Discussion and reflections

The online ACT training programme, adapted for AHCPs in an ABI setting, was a novel, online programme in response to recommendations made in the literature concerning the development and implementation of wellbeing and PF programmes (Hayes et al., 2012; Lawn et al., 2017; Puolakanaho et al., 2020; Räsänen et al., 2016; Seligman & Csikszentmihalyi, 2014).

Previous research findings supported the use of ACT workshops in the workplace (Varra et al., 2008; Vilardaga et al., 2011; Waters et al., 2018) for AHCPs. However, the effectiveness and suitability of a virtual ACT programme with AHCPs, in an ABI setting, had not previously been studied. Moreover, research to date had not included PPI in an ABI setting, to support the concept of clients as 'co-producers' of health, something highlighted as fundamental to any data collection (Coulter et al., 2014; European Patients Forum, n.d.; Mulley et al., 2012).

In fact, there was a distinct lack of a mixed-methods approach in previous research. The efficacy of programmes had predominantly focused on the use of quantitative methods. Importantly, research did not seem to address a 'quadruple aim' of caring for AHCPs at the same time as caring for clients in order to improve the 'triple aim' of patient experiences, outcomes and cost efficiency (Bodenheimer & Sinsky, 2014; Sikka et al., 2015).

Therefore, this study sought to combine the strengths of both qualitative and quantitative research methods. In this way, the research was aiming to gain an in-depth understanding of the effects of the ACT programme and its associated processes of change. Building on these findings, the main aim of this chapter was to focus on the qualitative phase aimed to explore AHCPs' rich and personal experience of the ACT programme. In this way, the meaning of change, the processes responsible for any changes and any recommendations for AHCPs' care, their clients' care and any future programme development were explored in detail. Importantly, the qualitative phase of this study gave a voice to AHCPs and clients in an ABI setting, a feature that is lacking in this research area. Significantly, this study had been proposed and had initiated PPI in research, before the unforeseen impact of Covid-19. Subsequently, this study provided an opportunity both to gain an understanding of the impact of Covid-19 in this setting, as well as to explore the utility of an online, self-directed training programme.

Discussion of key qualitative findings

As outlined previously, the qualitative component of this research generated four themes: 'Covid-19 impact,' 'Positive Online ACT experience,' 'Lifelong Skills' and 'Staff's Reflections and Hopes.'

Covid-19 impact

AHCPs described their experience of the online ACT programme in the context of the enduring nature of the Covid-19 pandemic. This is not surprising, as the adjustment to this novel virus has resulted in challenges to the ability to function in daily life (World Health Organisation, 2020). In fact, there has been such an impact on wellbeing that the HSE delivered wellbeing programmes online to support the public's wellbeing (HSE, 2020, November 3). AHCPs conveyed their experiences of Covid-19 by highlighting the contributions of 'the role of technology,' the 'impact on wellbeing' and how 'online flexibility enhanced learning.' AHCPs have been working from home, 'remotely.' They explained how this 'new norm' has impacted their professional and personal lives. This corroborates with other research that suggests there have been benefits and risks to wellbeing, with the move to 'remote' working during Covid-19 (Bouziri et al., 2020). All AHCPs acknowledged the benefits of technology during Covid-19. They identified the benefits of having a different kind of access and connectedness with clients and colleagues professionally. In fact, there was a sense of gratefulness that they could still see and experience family and friends online in their personal lives also. They conveyed how technology prevented isolation in many cases. AHCPs also acknowledged the risks of Covid-19, mostly in relation to health and safety aspects of the virus itself. It was interesting to hear how AHCPs also missed the workspace for the informal chats with colleagues, and the energy that the space brings when working with colleagues and clients. In that sense, AHCPs relayed a feeling of sadness and loss of peer support that was possibly less noticed before it was enforced due to Covid-19. Unique to this online intervention, all AHCPs were encouraging about the use of online training formats, as a more flexible space to learn in. This is interesting, as this delivery method is cost-effective. It was pre-recorded and placed on a platform for access over lengthy periods. Moreover, it can maximise learning for AHCPs as it can be accessible to everyone, who might otherwise not be able to attend a training workshop in a physical location on a given day. It was very interesting to hear how some AHCPs had an assumption that this training would be irrelevant for them and "*a load of rubbish.*" As the training was online, they attempted it and reaped its benefits. One AHCP explained how they dismissed the intervention initially as unsuitable for them. However, after they took part, they described their enjoyment of it and how the skills were applicable to all AHCPs, regardless of their preconceptions of the intervention. In this sense, providing an online workshop may provide a safe space for AHCPs who may be reluctant otherwise to take part. The most important finding was how beneficial the training was in this person's life and how they have actively used the skills in their personal and professional life. For that reason, perhaps online delivery has a bigger reach capacity than a traditional format. However, AHCPs also acknowledged a need for a live face-to-face component, even online, as a way to consolidate their learning. Future research is warranted to investigate if and how these components impact the acquisition of knowledge for those who prefer to learn alone, online and those who prefer a live group format.

Positive online ACT experience

AHCPs described their experience of the online ACT programme as positive. Within this theme, AHCPs conveyed their experiences of the intervention as a 'helpful user-friendly framework.' They expressed their enjoyment of the 'multimedia enhanced learning' and acknowledged the 'variety of skills enjoyed and learned.' Since ACT workshops have been delivered in diverse formats and have been offered over varying durations, this was an encouraging finding for an intervention delivered online and is in line with previous research (Flaxman & Bond, 2010a; Waters et al., 2018). Indeed, during Covid-19, attending webinars has become the new normal, as a way of continuing professional development.

Interestingly, all AHCPs in this study highlighted the use of multi-media as a way of reaching both verbal and visual types of learners. In fact, by using multi-media, engagement with the material was enhanced. This finding, in an ACT online intervention for AHCPs in an ABI setting, had no previous research basis. It's an interesting finding, as AHCPs relayed their experiences of previous online webinars or workshops, and the impact on their engagement. Moving forward this is an important factor for organisations to be aware of. As there is commonly a cost implication, the goal is to maximise the delivery of training. It also has an impact on AHCPs continued professional development and they conveyed the impact of the presentation style on their ability to sustain their attention and motivation to learn.

Perhaps AHCPs can benefit from this knowledge. They identified their preferred ways of learning, presented in many visual and verbal formats to help their learning. In this way, AHCPs in this study became aware of how learners differ in the way that they acquire and consolidate knowledge. This is similar to concerns clients with ABI have stated (National Patient Experience Survey, n.d.). Therefore, AHCPs can learn from this, in order to work with clients in the future. Moreover, since communication between clients and healthcare providers has become a primary topic in healthcare internationally (Gremigni et al., 2008; Hemsley & Balandin, 2014), it seems that it would be in the best interest of AHCPs and clients to address this. Significantly, AHCPs enjoyed the variety of skills that they learned. Again, this is in accordance with the flexibility of an ACT framework to teach multiple ways of learning processes (Harris, 2006; Ruiz, 2010). In that respect, it was hopeful hearing that AHCPs were being actively innovative using skills with clients, following the intervention. In particular, it was powerful to hear how AHCPs were working collaboratively with clients who had been perceived as 'stuck' in their rehabilitative recovery. They conveyed how clients were becoming 'unstuck' by using the processes and tools that the ACT intervention provided (Bond & Bunce, 2000; Bond et al., 2016a; Flaxman & Bond, 2010a).

Lifelong skills

AHCPs described their experience of learning lifelong skills. Within this theme, AHCPs conveyed their experiences of the intervention as having a 'personal and professional scope' and their 'active and future use of skills.' This was a very encouraging finding, as the continuity of the use of skills can protect their and low levels of wellbeing have been associated with the prevalence and incidence of symptoms of mental distress (Keyes et al., 2005, 2010; Wood & Joseph, 2010). Importantly, AHCPs illustrated that they were aware that the skills could be used in any setting, as research has stated (Harris, 2006). AHCPs gave examples of their personal and professional use of skills. In fact, the scope of skills that AHCPs learned seemed surprising to them, and they especially conveyed surprise at the user-friendly nature of the model and their enjoyment in the experiential exercises and skills learned. For instance, the ACT Matrix provided an accessible way to understand the behaviour presenting itself. All AHCPs acknowledged the simplicity of the model, which added to its ease of use across personal and professional settings. Future research could explore how these skills, such as those depicted in the Matrix, evolved over time, as the tools are dynamic and open to goal setting and changes. Importantly, while this ACT intervention promoted wellbeing (Seligman & Csikszentmihalyi, 2014), it also aimed to teach a framework that was applicable in different scenarios. Consequently, AHCPs learned skills in how to be psychologically flexible, as well as learning how to become aware of self-care and wellbeing. This has significant implications in sustaining their wellbeing, especially as clients with ABI transition through stages and experience adjustment challenges in coping with their new reality (Klonoff, 2010).

Staff's reflections and hopes

AHCPs described their experience of their hopes as staff in a neurorehabilitation setting and reflected on the impact beyond an individual to an organisational level. Within this theme, AHCPs conveyed their experiences of the intervention, high-lighting an 'organisational role in staff's wellbeing' and their 'future staff needs.' Although all AHCPs have a vast knowledge of ABI as they work in this area, they identified that other healthcare professionals have a lack of knowledge in this area. This was addressed through the personal experience of AHCPs, who may have worked in other healthcare divisions and sectors previously. In that sense, AHCPs identified a role for the different healthcare sectors and external organisations to teach skills to their members. In that way, a client with ABI may feel more supported in their recovery, as they may feel more understood. Interestingly, AHCPs related their appreciation of this intervention as a long-term organisational invest-ment in their wellbeing, supported by findings that it takes a 'whole-system healthy workplace intervention' to improve health and wellbeing, while also promoting healthier behaviours in healthcare staff (Brand et al., 2017). AHCPs also discussed their desire for the skills learned to be used more widely in the organisation. They conveyed how they could use ACT skills appropriate to resolving conflict on many levels, supporting the use of *Acceptance and Commitment Training for Workplace Settings* by Flaxman et al. (2019). Importantly, AHCPs conveyed their need for peer support from colleagues to maintain their learning. In this regard, they relayed their need for organisational input to support them, as well as advocating for fur-ther training needs. Importantly, AHCPs enjoyed the protected time that the organ-isation allowed them to take part in the training during work hours. Feeling valued was important to all AHCPs in this setting. Perhaps future research could explore how organisational support can benefit the wellbeing of their staff, especially in a clinical ABI setting.

Strengths and limitations

It is important to note that the current findings are based on a small sample of AHCPs who consented to take part in this study. These findings denote the experiences of this unique group of participants. Subsequently, findings are tentative rather than conclusive and are not generalisable.

The greatest strength of the research was using a mixed-methods approach. This allowed a much deeper evaluation of the intervention by using qualitative and quantitative data. To date, there have been a limited number of qualitative studies that capture the voices of AHCPs in this setting. Importantly, there is a paucity of studies that explore an ACT intervention using quantitative and qualitative data to the extent of this study. This study has provided rich information in terms of how AHCPs experienced the current intervention. This has important implications for how an ACT intervention may be delivered going forward so that it continues to be engaging and informative for AHCPs and for client care.

It must also be noted that there was no control or comparison group, largely due to the restrictions of Covid-19 and access to other AHCPs. Therefore, this intervention was novel and delivered to a single group of AHCPs in different regions of the same organisation. While it followed a manualised protocol in delivery, it was also adjusted for the needs of AHCPs in this setting.

Despite the limitations stated, this study is original in terms of exploring a novel, online ACT intervention for AHCPs in this setting.

In the delivery of this online intervention, my value in creativity can be considered a strength in terms of designing and viewing an intervention from multiple psychologist and graphic design lenses, both, to communicate effectively.

The qualitative analysis process was tedious at times, as the focus group had eight voices to distinguish and viewpoints to report upon. However, this part of the research was both exciting and rewarding. As I previously stated, on a personal level, I thrive off people's energy, so I felt motivated to engage with the process to reach my goal of a story to be told when my sense of energy and humour was waning. The themes were felt to be an accurate representation of the data following an amount of uncertainty and self-doubt during the initial analysis.

Implications

Qualitatively, AHCPs described their positive experience of the intervention and active use of skills, and it would be interesting to gauge this over a longer period, to see if and how changes occur. As the AHCPs already stated, they want peer support to maintain these practices, and I am unsure if that space will be provided. Future research investigating the nature of the impact on clients going forward would be beneficial and consistent with the objectives of PPI.

Interestingly, although gender percentages were not recorded for this intervention, it is known that the majority of participants were female in this organisation. Therefore, it would be interesting to have a more even gender balance in research going forward. In this way, any gender differences that exist in PF and wellbeing following an ACT intervention could be investigated.

In conclusion, the findings in the current study supported the use of this ACT intervention; however, further research is warranted for more generalisable conclusions. That being said, by actively engaging with the participants, it was possible to capture their experiences of the ACT intervention and the positive impact of this on their personal and professional lives.

On a personal level, the research resonated deeply with my values of advocacy, empathy, compassion and empowering others to help themselves and others. It also taught me that my values of fun and creativity in the design continue to 'shine bright like a diamond,' as Rihanna would sing, and will continue to influence and complement my professional practice.

It seems that "if you want to teach people a new way of thinking, don't bother trying to teach them. Instead, give them a tool, the use of which will lead to new ways of thinking" (Richard Buckminster Fuller; American engineer, author, designer, inventor, and futurist; 1895–1983) (Buckminster Fuller Institute, n.d.).

References

Arciniegas, D. B., Held, K., & Wagner, P. (2002). Cognitive impairment following traumatic brain injury. *Current Treatment Options in Neurology, 4*(1), 43–57.

Arterburn, D., Wellman, R., Westbrook, E., Rutter, C., Ross, T., McCulloch, D., Handley M., & Jung, C. (2012). Introducing decision aids at Group Health was linked to sharply lower hip and knee surgery rates and costs. *Health Affairs, 31*(9), 2094–2104.

Bodenheimer, T., & Sinsky, C. (2014). From triple to quadruple aim: Care of the patient requires care of the provider. *Annals of Family Medicine, 12*(6), 573–576. https://doi.org /10.1370/afm.1713

Bond, F. W., & Bunce, D. (2000). Mediators of change in emotion-focused and problem-focused worksite stress management interventions. *Journal of Occupational Health Psychology, 5*(1), 156.

Bond, F. W., Flaxman, P. E., & Lloyd, J. (2016a). Mindfulness and meditation in the workplace: An acceptance and commitment therapy approach. In M. A. West (Ed.), *The psychology of meditation: Research and practice* (pp. 241–258). Oxford University Press.

Bond, F. W., Lloyd, J., Flaxman, P. E., & Archer, R. (2016b). Psychological flexibility and ACT at work. In R. D. Zettle, S. C. Hayes, D. Barnes-Holmes, & A. Biglan (Eds.), *The Wiley handbook of contextual behavioral science* (pp. 459–482). Wiley.

Bouziri, H., Smith, D. R., Descatha, A., Dab, W., & Jean, K. (2020). Working from home in the time of covid-19: How to best preserve occupational health?. *Occupational and Environmental Medicine, 77*(7), 509–510.

Brand, S. L., Thompson Coon, J., Fleming, L. E., Carroll, L., Bethel, A., & Wyatt, K. (2017). Whole-system approaches to improving the health and wellbeing of healthcare workers: A systematic review. *PLoS ONE, 12*(12), e0188418.

Braquehais, M. D., Vargas-Cáceres, S., Gómez-Durán, E., Nieva, G., Valero, S., Casas, M., & Bruguera, E. (2020). The impact of the COVID-19 pandemic on the mental health of healthcare professionals. *QJM: An International Journal of Medicine, 113*(9), 613–617.

Braun, V., & Clarke, V. (2006). Using thematic analysis in psychology. *Qualitative Research in Psychology, 3*(2), 77–101.

Brinkborg, H., Michanek, J., Hesser, H., & Berglund, G. (2011). Acceptance and commitment therapy for the treatment of stress among social workers: A randomized controlled trial. *Behaviour Research and Therapy, 49*(6–7), 389–398.

Buckminster Fuller Institute. (n.d.). *Bhungroo wins the 2017 Buckminster Fuller challenge.* https://www.bfi.org/dymaxion-forum/2017/10/bhungroowins-2017-buckminster-fuller-challenge

CDC. (2001). *Traumatic brain injury in the Unied States: A report to Congress.* Centers for Disease Control.

Clarke, J. (n.d.). *Stress in the workplace.* Irishhealthpro.com. http://www.irishhealth.com/article.html?id=1241

Coulter, A., Locock, L., Ziebland, S., & Calabrese, J. (2014). Collecting data on patient experience is not enough: They must be used to improve care. *BMJ,348*, g2225. https://doi.org/10.1136/bmj.g2225

Department of Health. (2020). *'Sharing the vision – Mental health policy for everyone'.* https://www.gov.ie/en/publication/2e46f-sharing-the-vision-amental-health-policy-for-everyone/

Diener, E., Scollon, C. N., & Lucas, R. E. (2009). The evolving concept of subjective well-being: The multifaceted nature of happiness. In E. Diener (Ed.), *Assessing well-being: The collected works of Ed Diener* (pp. 67–100). Springer Science + Business Media. https://doi.org/10.1007/978-90-481-2354-4_4

Diener, E., Suh, E. M., Lucas, R. E., & Smith, H. L. (1999). Subjective wellbeing: Three decades of progress. *Psychological Bulletin, 125*(2), 276.

Dikmen, S. S., Machamer, J. E., Winn, H. R., & Temkin, N. R. (1995). Neuropsychological outcome at 1-year post head injury. *Neuropsychology, 9*(1), 80.

EXPH (Expert Panel on effective ways of investing in Health). (2014). Definition of a frame of reference in relation to primary care with a special emphasis on financing systems and referral systems. European Commission Retrieved May 2016–June 2018 from https://ec.europa.eu/health/expert_panel/sites/expertpanel/files/004_definitionprimarycare_en.pdf

European Patients Forum. (2017, March 2). www.eu-patient.eu

European Patients Forum. (n.d.). *Patients' perceptions of quality in healthcare.* https://www.eu-patient.eu/globalassets/policy/quality-of-care/qualitysurvey-report.pdf

Figley, C. R. (2002a). Compassion fatigue: Psychotherapists' chronic lack of self care. *Journal of Clinical Psychology, 58*(11), 1433–1441.

Figley, C. R. (Ed.). (2002b). *Treating compassion fatigue.* Routledge.

Flaxman, P. E., & Bond, F. W. (2010a). A randomised worksite comparison of acceptance and commitment therapy and stress inoculation training. *Behaviour Research and Therapy, 48*(8), 816–820.

Flaxman, P. E., & Bond, F. W. (2010b). Worksite stress management training: Moderated effects and clinical significance. *Journal of Occupational Health Psychology, 15*(4), 347.

Flaxman, P. E., McIntosh, R., & Oliver, J. (2019). Acceptance and Commitment Training (ACT) for workplace settings: Trainer manual. City, University of London (February 2019).

Florin, D., & Dixon, J. (2004). Public involvement in health care. *BMJ, 328*(7432), 159–161.

Frögéli, E., Djordjevic, A., Rudman, A., Livheim, F., & Gustavsson, P. (2016). A randomized controlled pilot trial of acceptance and commitment training (ACT) for preventing stress-related ill health among future nurses. *Anxiety, Stress, & Coping, 29*(2), 202–218.

Godfrey, E., Wileman, V., Holmes, M. G., McCracken, L. M., Norton, S., Moss-Morris, R., Noonan S., Barcellona, M., & Critchley, D. (2020). Physical therapy informed by Acceptance and Commitment Therapy (PACT) versus usual care physical therapy for adults with chronic low back pain: A randomized controlled trial. *The Journal of Pain, 21*(1–2), 71–81.

Godfrey, E., Holmes, M. G., Wileman, V., McCracken, L., Norton, S., Moss-Morris, R., Noonan S., Barcellona, M., & Critchley, D. (2016). Physiotherapy informed by Acceptance and Commitment Therapy (PACT): Protocol for a randomised controlled trial of PACT versus usual physiotherapy care for adults with chronic low back pain. *BMJ Open, 6*(6), e011548.

Gremigni, P., Sommaruga, M., & Peltenburg, M. (2008). Validation of the Health Care Communication Questionnaire (HCCQ) to measure outpatients' experience of communication with hospital staff. *Patient Education and Counseling, 71*(1), 57–64.

Harris, R. (2006). Embracing your demons: An overview of acceptance and commitment therapy. *Psychotherapy in Australia, 12*(4), 2–8.

Hayes, S. C., Levin, M. E., Plumb-Vilardaga, J., Villatte, J. L., & Pistorello, J. (2013). Acceptance and commitment therapy and contextual behavioral science: Examining the progress of a distinctive model of behavioral and cognitive therapy. *Behavior Therapy, 44*(2), 180–198.

Hayes, S. C., Pistorello, J., & Levin, M. E. (2012). Acceptance and commitment therapy as a unified model of behavior change. *The Counseling Psychologist, 40*(7), 976–1002.

Health Service Executive. (2020, November 3). *Minding your wellbeing programme.* https://www2.hse.ie/healthy-you/minding-your-wellbeingprogramme.html

Health Service Executive (HSE) & Health Information and Quality Authority (HIQA). (2019, March 2). *Irish National Patient Experience Survey 2017 & 2018.* https://www.patientexperience.ie

Hemsley, B., & Balandin, S. (2014). A metasynthesis of patient-provider communication in hospital for patients with severe communication disabilities: Informing new translational research. *Augmentative and Alternative Communication, 30*(4), 329–343.

Institute for Patient- and Family-Centered Care. (2015, March 2). *Patient-and family-centered care: Core concepts.* http://www.ipfcc.org/pdf/CoreConcepts.pdf

Kashdan, T. B., & Rottenberg, J. (2010). Psychological flexibility as a fundamental aspect of health. *Clinical Psychology Review, 30*(7), 865–878.

Keyes, C. L. M. (2007). Promoting and protecting mental health as flourishing: A complementary strategy for improving national mental health. *American Psychologist, 62*(2), 95–108. https://doi.org/10.1037/0003-066X.62.2.95

Keyes, C. L. M. (2005). Mental illness and/or mental health? Investigating axioms of the complete state model of health. *Journal of Consulting and Clinical Psychology, 73*(3), 539.

Keyes, C. L., Dhingra, S. S., & Simoes, E. J. (2010). Change in level of positive mental health as a predictor of future risk of mental illness. *American Journal of Public Health, 100*(12), 2366–2371.

Klonoff, P. S. (2010). *Psychotherapy after brain injury: Principles and techniques.* Guilford Press.

Kret, D. D. (2011). The qualities of a compassionate nurse according to the perceptions of medical-surgical patients. *Medsurg Nursing: Official Journal of the Academy of Medical-Surgical Nurses, 20*(1), 29–36.

Kurz, A. S., Bethay, J. S., & Ladner-Graham, J. M. (2014). Mediating the relation between workplace stressors and distress in ID support staff: Comparison between the roles of psychological inflexibility and coping styles. *Research in Developmental Disabilities, 35*(10), 2359–2370.

Lappalainen, P., Granlund, A., Siltanen, S., Ahonen, S., Vitikainen, M., Tolvanen, A., & Lappalainen, R. (2014). ACT Internet-based vs face-to face? A randomized controlled trial of two ways to deliver Acceptance and Commitment Therapy for depressive symptoms: An 18-month follow-up. *Behaviour Research and Therapy, 61*, 43–54.

Lappalainen, P., Langrial, S., Oinas-Kukkonen, H., Tolvanen, A., & Lappalainen, R. (2015). Web-based acceptance and commitment therapy for depressive symptoms with minimal support: A randomized controlled trial. *Behavior Modification, 39*(6), 805–834.

Lawn, S., Zhi, X., & Morello, A. (2017). An integrative review of e-learning in the delivery of self-management support training for health professionals. *BMC Medical Education, 17*(1), 1–16.

Lutz, B. J., Ellen Young, M., Cox, K. J., Martz, C., & Rae Creasy, K. (2011). The crisis of stroke: Experiences of patients and their family caregivers. *Topics in Stroke Rehabilitation, 18*(6), 786–797.

Lyon, B. L. (2002). Psychological stress and coping: Framework for poststroke psychosocial care. *Topics in Stroke Rehabilitation, 9*(1), 1–15.

McIntosh, R., & Gascoyne, A. (2020, July). Contextual consulting. *Flexibility @ Work* [Online course]. https://contextualconsulting.co.uk/workshop/flexibilitywork-with-ross-mcintosh-and-annie-gascoyne

McCracken, L. M., & Yang, S. Y. (2008). A contextual cognitive-behavioral analysis of rehabilitation workers' health and well-being: Influences of acceptance, mindfulness, and values-based action. *Rehabilitation Psychology, 53*(4), 479.

Mikulic, M. (2020, September 1). *Number of employees in the health and social care industry in Ireland from 2000 to 2018.* https://www.statista.com/statistics/461957/health-and-social-careemployment in-ireland/

Miller, R. L., Griffin, M. A., & Hart, P. M. (1999). Personality and organizational health: The role of conscientiousness. *Work & Stress, 13*(1), 7–19.

Mischel, W. (1969). Continuity and change in personality. *American Psychologist, 24*(11), 1012.

Moore, K. A., & Cooper, C. L. (1996). Stress in mental health professionals: A theoretical overview. *International Journal of Social Psychiatry, 42*(2), 82–89.

Mulley, A. G., Trimble, C., & Elwyn, G. (2012). Stop the silent misdiagnosis: Patients' preferences matter. *BMJ, 5345*, e6572. https://doi.org/10.1136/bmj.e6572

National Patient Experience Survey. (n.d.). *Findings of the 2018 inpatient survey.* https://yourexperience.ie/wpcontent/uploads/2019/07/NPES_National_R eport_2018-1.pdf

Noone, S. J., & Hastings, R. P. (2010). Using acceptance and mindfulness-based workshops with support staff caring for adults with intellectual disabilities. *Mindfulness, 1*(2), 67–73.

Nyklíček, I., & Kuijpers, K. F. (2008). Effects of mindfulness-based stress reduction intervention on psychological well-being and quality of life: Is increased mindfulness indeed the mechanism? *Annals of Behavioral Medicine, 35*(3), 331–340.

Platania, S., Santisi, G., Magnano, P., & Ramaci, T. (2015). Job satisfaction and organizational well-being queried: A comparison between the two companies. *Procedia Social and Behavioral Sciences, 191*, 1436–1441.

Ponsford, J., Kelly, A., & Couchman, G. (2014). Self-concept and self-esteem after acquired brain injury: A control group comparison. *Brain Injury, 28*(2), 146–154.

Povlishock, J. T., & Katz, D. I. (2005). Update of neuropathology and neurological recovery after traumatic brain injury. *The Journal of Head Trauma Rehabilitation, 20*(1), 76–94.

Puolakanaho, A., Tolvanen, A., Kinnunen, S. M., & Lappalainen, R. (2020). A psychological flexibility-based intervention for burnout: A randomized controlled trial. *Journal of Contextual Behavioral Science, 15,* 52–67. https://doi.org/10.1016/j.jcbs.2019.11.007

Räsänen, P., Lappalainen, P., Muotka, J., Tolvanen, A., & Lappalainen, R. (2016). An online guided ACT intervention for enhancing the psychological wellbeing of university students: A randomized controlled clinical trial. *Behaviour Research and Therapy, 78*, 30–42.

Ruiz, F. J. (2010). A review of Acceptance and Commitment Therapy (ACT) empirical evidence: Correlational, experimental psychopathology, component and outcome studies. *International Journal of Psychology and Psychological Therapy, 10*(1), 125–162.

Runco, M. A. (2014). *Creativity: Theories and themes: Research, development, and practice.* Elsevier.

Ryff, C. D. (1989). Happiness is everything, or is it? Explorations on the meaning of psychological well-being. *Journal of Personality and Social Psychology, 57*(6), 1069.

Seligman, M. E., & Csikszentmihalyi, M. (2014). Positive psychology: An introduction. In M. Csikszentmihalyi (Ed.), *Flow and the foundations of positive psychology* (pp. 279–298). Springer.

Sharkey, S. B., & Sharples, A. (2003). The impact on work-related stress of mental health teams following team-based learning on clinical risk management. *Journal of Psychiatric and Mental Health Nursing, 10*(1), 73–81.

Sikka, R., Morath, J. M., & Leape, L. (2015). The Quadruple Aim: Care, health, cost and meaning in work. *BMJ Quality & Safety, 24*(10), 608–610. https://doi.org/10.1136/bmjqs-2015-004160

Soo, C., Tate, R., & Brookes, N. (2014). Psychosocial adjustment following acquired brain injury in childhood and adolescence: Executive, behavioural and emotional contributions. *Brain Injury, 28*(7), 906–914.

Torner, J. C., & Schootman, M. (1996). Epidemiology of closed head injury. In M. Rizzo & D. Tranel (Eds.), *Head injury and postconcussive syndrome.* Churchill Livingstone.

TTM Healthcare. (n.d.). Allied health professionals. https://www.ttmhealthcare.ie/disciplines/ahp

Varra, A. A., Hayes, S. C., Roget, N., & Fisher, G. (2008). A randomized control trial examining the effect of acceptance and commitment training on clinician willingness to use evidence-based pharmacotherapy. *Journal of Consulting and Clinical Psychology, 76*(3), 449.

Veroff, D., Marr, A., & Wennberg, D. E. (2013). Enhanced support for shared decision making reduced costs of care for patients with preference sensitive conditions. *Health Affairs, 32*(2), 285–293.

Vilardaga, R., Luoma, J. B., Hayes, S. C., Pistorello, J., Levin, M. E., Hildebrandt, M. J., Kohlenberg, B., Roget, N. A., & Bond, F. (2011). Burnout among the addiction counseling workforce: The differential roles of mindfulness and values-based processes and work-site factors. *Journal of Substance Abuse Treatment, 40*(4), 323–335.

Wall, T. D., Bolden, R. I., Borrill, C. S., Carter, A. J., Golya, D. A., Hardy, G. E., Haynes, C. E., Rick, J. E., Shapiro, D. A., & West, M. A. (1997). Minor psychiatric disorder in NHS trust staff: occupational and gender differences. *The British Journal of Psychiatry*, *171*(6), 519–523.

Wang, C., Pan, R., Wan, X., Tan, Y., Xu, L., Ho, C. S., & Ho, R. C. (2020). Immediate psychological responses and associated factors during the initial stage of the 2019 coronavirus disease (COVID-19) epidemic among the general population in China. *International Journal of Environmental Research and Public Health*, *17*(5), 1729.

Waters, C. S., Frude, N., Flaxman, P. E., & Boyd, J. (2018). Acceptance and Commitment Therapy (ACT) for clinically distressed health care workers: Waitlist-controlled evaluation of an ACT workshop in a routine practice setting. *British Journal of Clinical Psychology*, *57*(1), 82–98.

Wollenburg, K. G. (2004). Leadership with conscience, compassion, and commitment. *American Journal of Health System Pharmacy*, *61*(17), 1785–1791.

Wood, A. M., & Joseph, S. (2010). The absence of positive psychological (eudemonic) well-being as a risk factor for depression: A ten-year cohort study. *Journal of Affective Disorders*, *122*(3), 213–217.

World Health Organization. (2020). Novel Coronavirus (2019-nCoV): Situation report, 3.

Yadavaia, J. E., Hayes, S. C., & Vilardaga, R. (2014). Using acceptance and commitment therapy to increase self-compassion: A randomized controlled trial. *Journal of Contextual Behavioral Science*, *3*(4), 248–257.

Zhu, Y., Chen, L., Ji, H., Xi, M., Fang, Y., & Li, Y. (2020). The risk and prevention of novel coronavirus pneumonia infections among inpatients in psychiatric hospitals. *Neuroscience Bulletin*, *36*(3), 299–302.

Index

Printed in the United States
by Baker & Taylor Publisher Services